THE FALL OF BERLIN

The Fall of Berlin

Mendl Mann

Translated and with an Introduction by Maurice Wolfthal

https://www.openbookpublishers.com

English translation, Introduction and Notes © 2020 Maurice Wolfthal

This work is licensed under a Creative Commons Attribution 4.0 International license (CC BY 4.0). This license allows you to share, copy, distribute and transmit the text; to adapt the text and to make commercial use of the text providing attribution is made to the authors (but not in any way that suggests that they endorse you or your use of the work). Attribution should include the following information:

Mendl Mann, *The Fall of Berlin*. Translated and with an Introduction by Maurice Wolfthal. Cambridge, UK: Open Book Publishers, 2020, https://doi.org/10.11647/OBP.0233

In order to access detailed and updated information on the license, please visit, https://www.doi.org/10.11647/OBP.0233#copyright

Further details about CC BY licenses are available at, https://creativecommons.org/licenses/by/4.0/

All external links were active at the time of publication unless otherwise stated and have been archived via the Internet Archive Wayback Machine at https://archive.org/web

Updated digital material and resources associated with this volume are available at https://doi.org/10.11647/OBP.0233#resources

Every effort has been made to identify and contact copyright holders and any omission or error will be corrected if notification is made to the publisher.

ISBN Paperback: 9781800640771
ISBN Hardback: 9781800640788
ISBN Digital (PDF): 9781800640795
ISBN Digital ebook (epub): 9781800640801
ISBN Digital ebook (mobi): 9781800640818
ISBN XML: 9781800640825
DOI: 10.11647/OBP.0233

Cover image: Marc Chagall, *L'auteur Mendel Mann dans son village* (1969), reproduced at http://yiddish.haifa.ac.il/tmr/tmr12/tmr12021.htm. Courtesy of Zvi Mann.

Cover design: Anna Gatti.

For Diane, Judy, Leah, Adi, Raphael, and Elinora

With Love

Contents

Introduction	1
Summary of *At the Gates of Moscow*	9
Summary of *At the Vistula*	17
The Fall of Berlin	
Chapter One	25
Chapter Two	55
Chapter Three	88
Chapter Four	117
Chapter Five	147
Chapter Six	175
Chapter Seven	206
Chapter Eight	224
Index	233

Introduction

A million and a half Jews fought in the armed forces of the Allies during the Second World War. They served in the armies, navies, and air forces of their native lands. Many who were forced to flee the Nazis then joined the war effort in the countries that had given them refuge. Between 490,000 and 520,000 Jewish soldiers fought in the Red Army.[1] Most of them were native-born Soviet citizens; others were refugees from Poland and other lands occupied by the German Army. More than 120,000 Jews in the Red Army died in combat, and another 75—80,000 were murdered by the Germans as prisoners of war.[2]

Mendl Mann's series of Yiddish Second World War novels—*Bay di Toyern fun Moskve* [At the Gates of Moscow], *Bay der Vaysl* [At the Vistula], and *Dos Faln fun Berlin* [The Fall of Berlin]—recount the war against Hitler from the unique perspective of Menakhem Isaacovitch, a Polish Jew who flees the Germans and finds refuge in the Soviet Union. Although the trilogy is a long saga that reflects Mann's experiences as a frontline soldier, each book can stand on its own. Although Mann was fluent in Polish and Russian, he chose to write in Yiddish, both out of his devotion to the language, and because he aimed to reach what was left of the Yiddish-speaking world. In 1939 there had been an estimated eleven million Yiddish speakers, but the Nazis and their collaborators murdered more than half of them. Only *At the Gates of Moscow* was translated into English.

Menakhem, the protagonist of the saga, is now called Mikhail. He fights in the Red Army, both to defend the country that welcomed him and to seek revenge on the Germans who are destroying Poland and exterminating the Jews. By introducing us to ethnic Russians,

---

1 Yitzhak Arad, *In the Shadow of the Red Banner: Soviet Jews in the War Against Nazi Germany* (Jerusalem: Gefen, 2010), p. 5.
2 Ibid., p. 126.

Belarussians, Ukrainians, Kazakhs, Tatars, Kalmyks, Georgians, Caucasians, Mordvins, and Siberians, Mann emphasizes the multiethnic character of the Red Army's war against Hitler. But Mann makes clear that in their defense of the Soviet Union, the Jewish soldiers, like the other "nationalities," were struggling to fight a war in the shadow of Stalin, a dictator whose paranoia and whose murderous secret police, the NKVD, poisoned the war effort.[3] In addition, as the trilogy reveals, the Jews were fighting to defend a country where antisemitism still persisted at all levels—including the armed forces—despite more than twenty years of official Soviet ideology.

While the three books reflect Mann's grueling years as a frontline soldier, his life before that had been vastly different. Born in 1916 in Plonsk, Poland, he spent his childhood in the nearby village of Sochocin, which had been settled by Jewish farmers in the nineteenth century. His memoir, *Mayne zikhroynes fun plonsk* [My Memories of Plonsk][4] lovingly evokes this rural life: the open skies, the meadows, rivers, lakes, farms, orchards, water mills, horses, cattle, shaggy dogs, and country folk. His friends were the children of farmers, Jewish and Christian. Mann's trilogy is suffused with affection for village life.

The family moved to Plonsk when he was eight, and lived on the *Shulgas* [Synagogue Street]. His parents sent him to a *kheyder* (traditional Jewish religious school), a *khinukh yeladim* (modern Hebrew-language Zionist school), and a Polish public school. The politics of the Second Polish republic were frequently discussed at home, and Mann witnessed a Socialist demonstration when he was ten. At age twelve he studied Polish with a private teacher, who instilled a love of Polish poetry in him, but he was becoming increasingly aware of the precarious status of Polish Jews.

His neighbor, a tailor who sang as he worked, invited him to a meeting where he saw a portrait of Ber Borochov, with the inscription:

---

3 NKVD The People's Commissariat for Internal Affairs, abbreviated NKVD, was the interior ministry of the Soviet Union. Established in 1917 as NKVD of the Russian Soviet Federative Socialist Republic, the agency was originally tasked with conducting regular police work and overseeing the country's prisons and labor camps (Wikipedia entry, https://en.wikipedia.org/wiki/NKVD).

4 Mendl Mann, 'Mayne zikhroynes fun plonsk' [My Memories of Plonsk], in *Sefer Plonsk ve-ha-Sevivah* [The Book of Plonsk and its Surroundings], ed. by Shlomo Zemach, Mordekhai Ḥalamish, and Mendl Mann (Tel Aviv: Irgun Yotsey Plonsk be-Yisrael, 1963), pp. 570–90.

"Long Live the Jewish Working Class in Palestine." But that meeting of the *Poalei Zion* [Workers of Zion] was disrupted by "Reds" who saw Zionism as nationalistic betrayal of Marxist ideals. But the movement appealed to Mann by holding out the hope for Jews to have a land of their own, where they would cease being an oppressed minority, and he became a leader of a Poalei youth group. He began to write poems, most in Polish, some in Yiddish, and the dream arose of becoming a writer.

Mann's older brother Wolf (Velvl) was an established painter who did landscapes in oils and watercolors and drew portraits in charcoal. Mendl, too, was drawn to art from an early age, and his teachers recognized his talent. He later followed him to Warsaw, where he studied at the Academy of Fine Arts and exhibited his work. He began publishing Yiddish poems in *Literarishe bleter* [Literary Pages], the *Folks-tsaytung* [People's Newspaper], and the *Arbeter-tsaytung* [Workers' Newspaper].

When the Germans invaded in 1939, Mann escaped to Tuczyn, where he met Sonia, his future wife, and then to Kharkov. He attended a teachers' institute and was sent to teach in Tengushay, Mordovia. Their son Zvi was born there. Mann was mobilized by the Red Army to drive out the Germans, and he fought from Moscow to Warsaw to Berlin. His wife was also mobilized, and she sang for the troops. Mann's knowledge of German was an asset in interrogating captured soldiers both in the USSR and in Germany.[5] His fluency in Polish was useful when the Red Army advanced towards Germany. Mann's artistic talent contributed to war posters and newspaper propaganda. Once, on the occasion of Stalin's birthday, he was told to produce a lifesize portrait and to hang it prominently outside. But a fierce wind was blowing, and as he tried to fasten the portrait he accidentally drove a nail through Stalin's forehead. For this perceived insult to the leader, he was sentenced to the mines in the Urals, but he managed to survive and rejoin the army at the front.

In the meantime, the Germans had forced the Jews of Plonsk into a ghetto. They had systematically murdered about 12,000 Jews from the city and its environs.[6] After Mann's discharge from the Red Army, he returned

---

5   The Union of Soviet Socialist Republics or Soviet Union, abbreviated USSR, was a federal socialist state in Northern Eurasia that existed from 1922 to 1991. It was a one-party state governed by the Communist Party, with Moscow as its capital in its largest republic, the Russian SFSR.

6   Geoffrey P. Megargee, *The United States Holocaust Museum Encyclopedia of Camps and Ghettos, 1933–1945* (Bloomington: Indiana University Press, 2009), p. 26.

from Berlin to Poland, hoping to start a new life and to help rebuild the Jewish community. He went to Plonsk and learned that his entire family had been murdered, as had his wife's in Ukraine. She was overwhelmed with survivor's guilt for the rest of her life, particularly because she had not taken her baby sister with her to the USSR. Mann went to Lodz and devoted himself to work on behalf of Jewish children who had survived and were now orphans. He headed the department of culture and education of the Central Committee of Jews in Poland. There he wrote an anthology of poems, *Di shtilkeyt mont* [The Silence Demands its Due], the first book published in Yiddish in Poland after the war.

In 1946 Mann attended a meeting of survivors in Warsaw held to commemorate the Ghetto Uprising of 1943, at which the importance of finding the Ringelblum archives was discussed.[7] Increasing Communist repression and outbreaks of antisemitic violence culminating in the Kielce pogrom of 1946 drove him to leave Poland.[8] He settled in Regensburg, where he continued to be active in the Jewish community. There, in 1947, he co-edited with Yekheskel Keytlmann[9] an illustrated Yiddish newspaper, *Der nayer moment* [The New Moment], named after the Warsaw paper that he had written for before the war, *Der moment*. They also produced a literary journal, *Heftn far literatur, kultur, un kritik* [Volumes for Literature, Culture, and Criticism]. Mann contributed to the journal *Fun letstn khurbn* [From the Last Extermination], whose purpose was to document the Holocaust. Published in Munich by the Central Historical Commission of the Central Committee of Liberated Jews in the U.S. Zone, it was distributed to all the DP camps and abroad.[10]

---

7 Samuel D. Kassow, *Who Will Write Our History? Emanuel Ringelblum, the Warsaw Ghetto, and the Oyneg Shabes Archive* (Bloomington: Indiana University Press, 2007), p. 205.

8 Between 1945 and 1947, an estimated 150,000 Jewish survivors left Poland for the DP camps in Germany. See Laura Jockusch, "Paradise Lost? Postwar Memory of Polish Jewish Survival in the Soviet Union," in *Holocaust and Genocide Studies*, 24 (2010), 373–99.

9 Jechezkel Keitelman was one of a cadre of survivors devoted to maintaining Yiddish literature after the Holocaust. Among his works were: *Oysterlishe geshikhtn un andere dertseylungn* [Strange Stories and Other Tales] (Regensburg: Yidishe zetser, 1947), *Oysgehakte velder* [Cut Down Forests] (New York/Philadelphia, 1952), and *Oyfn veg keyn Uman: un andere dertseylungen* [On the Road to Uman: and Other Stories] (New York: Tsiko, 1967).

10 See, for example, Mendl Mann, "*Der oyfshtand in tutshiner geto*" [The Uprising in the Tuczyn Ghetto], *Fun letstn khurbn*, 9 (September 1948): pp. 59–66.

Mann never felt at ease in Germany, and he wrote of his ambivalence about living in the country that had nearly exterminated the Jews.[11] He attempted to go illegally to British Palestine with his wife and son on the steamship Exodus in 1947 alongside 4,500 other Holocaust survivors, but the British sent them back to Hamburg. Mann managed to get to Israel in 1948 and served in the army for eight months. He then lived in the former Arab village of Yazur and continued to write. He wrote intensely and prolifically, primarily at night.

Though some of his work now reflected his life after the war, his devotion to Yiddish continued unabated, and he corresponded with Yiddish writers abroad. He moved to Tel Aviv in 1954, and worked with Avrom Sutzkever on the editorial board of the premier Yiddish literary journal in Israel, *Di goldene keyt* [The Golden Chain], to which he contributed poems and literary criticism until the end of his life, as well as to a dozen other periodicals. He continued to draw and paint, particularly scenes of nature, as a way to relax. Mann visited the United States and Paris.

Though Mann took pride in the new Jewish state, he grew increasingly bitter at the vilification of Yiddish as the despised language of a weak people without a homeland.[12] The fact that Prime Minister David Ben-Gurion led this campaign was particularly galling to him, in that Ben-Gurion was himself from Plonsk. Mann left Israel in 1961 and settled in Paris, where he edited *Undzer vort* [Our Word]. When survivors from his hometown published the memorial book *Sefer Plonsk ve-ha-Sevivah* [The Book of Plonsk and its Surroundings], he was one of its editors, contributing extensive sections in Yiddish. Mann's son, Zvi Mann, recounts that when his father presented Ben-Gurion with the *Sefer Plonsk*, Ben-Gurion disparaged the book because Mann had written his essays in *"zhargon,"* a term denying Yiddish its rightful status as a real language. Mann took the book back and slammed the door.[13]

---

11 Michael Brenner,'Impressionen jüdischen Lebens in der Oberpfalz nach 1945', in *Die Juden in den Oberpfalz*, ed. by Michael Brenner and Renate Höpfinger (Munich: Oldenbourg Wissenschaftsverlag, 2009), p. 241.

12 Tamar Lewinsky,'Dangling Roots? Yiddish Language and Culture in the German Diaspora' in *We are Here: New Approaches to Jewish Displaced Persons in Postwar Germany*, ed. by Avinoam J. Patt and Michael Berkowitz (Detroit: Wayne State University Press, 2010), pp. 308–34.

13 See National Yiddish Book Center, Wexler Oral History Project, interview with Zvi Mann, son of Mendl Mann, June 18, 2014, https://archive.org/details/ZviMann18Jun2014YiddishBookCenter

Mandl Mann in 1966 by unknown photographer. Courtesy of Zvi Mann.

Mann exhibited his paintings in Paris in 1967. He collected art, and Marc Chagall became a close friend. When Mann published an anthology of short stories, *Der shvartser demb* [The Black Oak] in 1969, Chagall provided an aquarelle for the frontispiece. It depicts Mann going back to his hometown and taking notes, with the souls of the murdered Jews floating in the sky.[14]

Marc Chagall, 'L'auteur Mendel Mann dans son village'(Author Mendel Mann in his hometown). Aquarelle with Chagall's handwritten dedication[15] to Mendel Mann. Reproduced in Mandel Mann's *Der shvartser demb* [The Black Oak], Paris: Undzer kiem, 1970, and at http://yiddish.haifa.ac.il/tmr/tmr12/tmr12021.htm. Courtesy of Zvi Mann.

---

14 See "Signed Marc Chagall Aquarelle" by Zvi Mann and David Mazower, in *The Mendele Review: Yiddish Literature and Language*, http://yiddish.haifa.ac.il/tmr/tmr12/tmr12021.htm

15 The note reads:
Dear M. Mann, I am sending you a few of the features I promised you. In them I wanted to express—as far as I was able—the fate of the Yiddish writer in his "former" land –
With best wishes
Mark Chagall

Many of Mann's works were translated into English, German, Hebrew, French, Danish, Spanish, and Italian. Mendl Mann died in Paris in 1975 at the age of 59 as a result of old war wounds, and his son brought him back to be buried in Israel in Kibbutz Kfar Giladi.

Book covers of French editions of Mann's trilogy: *Aux Portes de Moscou* (Paris: Calmann-Lévy, 1960); *Sur la Vistule* (Paris: Calmann-Lévy, 1962); *La Chute de Berlin* (Paris: Calmann-Lévy, 1963). Courtesy of Zvi Mann.

Bibliography

Arad, Yitzhak, *In the Shadow of the Red Banner: Soviet Jews in the War Against Nazi Germany* (Jerusalem: Gefen, 2010).

Brenner, M. and Höpfinger, R., eds, *Die Juden in den Oberpfalz* (Munich: Oldenbourg Wissenschaftsverlag, 2009).

Jockusch, Laura,'Paradise Lost? Postwar Memory of Polish Jewish Survival in the Soviet Union', *Holocaust and Genocide Studies*, 24 (2010), pp. 373–99.

Kassow, Samuel D., *Who Will Write Our History? Emanuel Ringelblum, the Warsaw Ghetto, and the Oyneg Shabes Archive* (Bloomington: Indiana University Press, 2007).

Kostyrchenko, Gennady, *Out of the Red Shadows: Anti-Semitism in Stalin's Russia* (Amherst: Prometheus, 1995).

Lewinsky, Tamar, 'Dangling Roots? Yiddish Language and Culture in the German Diaspora', in *We are Here: New Approaches to Jewish Displaced Persons in Postwar Germany*, ed. by Avinoam J. Patt and Michael Berkowitz (Detroit: Wayne State University Press, 2010), pp. 308–34.

Mann, Mendl, *Mayne zikhroynes fun plonsk* [My Memories of Plonsk], in *Sefer Plonsk ve-ha-Sevivah* [The Book of Plonsk and its Surroundings], ed. by Shlomo Zemach, Mordekhai Ḥalamish, and Mendl Mann (Tel Aviv: Irgun Yotsey Plonsk be-Yisrael, 1963), pp. 570–90.

Mann, Mendl, 'Der oyfshtand in tutshiner geto' [The Uprising in the Tuczyn Ghetto], *Fun letstn khurbn*, 9 (September 1948), pp. 59–66.

Mann, Zvi and David Mazower, 'Signed Marc Chagall Aquarelle', *The Mendele Review: Yiddish Literature and Language*, http://yiddish.haifa.ac.il/tmr/tmr12/tmr12021.htm

Megargee, Geoffrey P., *The United States Holocaust Museum Encyclopedia of Camps and Ghettos, 1933–1945* (Bloomington: Indiana University Press, 2009).

National Yiddish Book Center, Wexler Oral History Project, 'Interview with Zvi Mann, son of Mendl Mann', June 18, 2014, https://archive.org/details/ZviMann18Jun2014YiddishBookCenter

Yoffe, Mordkhe, 'Mendl Mann', in *Leksikon fun der nayer yidisher literatur'* [Biographical Dictionary of Modern Yiddish Literature], ed. by Ephraim Auerbach, Yitskhak Kharlash and Moshe Starkman (New York: Alveltlekhn Yidishn Kultur-Kongres, 1956–1981), pp. 431–34.

At the Gates of Moscow

Cover of *Bay di toyern fun Moskve* [At the Gates of Moscow], New York: Alveltlekhn YidishnKultur-Kongres, 1956.

October 1941. The Germans have occupied Poland and invaded the USSR. Menakhem Isaacovitch, a Polish Jew who fled the Nazis in 1940, is warmly welcomed by the villagers of Tengushay and is now called Mikhail. As the German onslaught threatens Moscow, he is called up by the Red Army, along with local ethnic Russians, Mordvins, Bashkirs, and Tartars. The young artist, twenty-two, longs for his hometown. The destruction of Poland and its Jews, and now the devastation of the USSR, drive him to seek revenge on the Germans.

When the recruits arrive at the reserve camp, Commanding Officer NKVD man Akim Suzayev learns that Menakhem is Jewish and offers insidiously to do him special favors. But Menakhem insists that his only wish is to fight on the front with the men of Tengushay. They are sent by train towards Moscow where the remaining population freezes, starves, and struggles to prepare its defenses. Antisemitism rears its head in the city with the slanders that Jews are draft-dodgers and war profiteers and are living lives of luxury in the eastern republics.

The men of Tengushay are assigned to the 316th Infantry, commanded by a Jewish general, Pliskin. Menakhem meets him just outside Moscow, the first Jew he has seen in a long time. Near a field hospital he meets a wounded Jewish soldier who informs Menakhem that the Germans are exterminating the Jews in Smolensk. Exhaustion and fever land Menakhem in the hospital, where he meets Anna Samuelovna Korina, a Jewish nurse from Moscow. Romance grows between them. Menakhem asks for paper and a pencil to do some drawings, which are admired by some officers. As he leaves the hospital, Anna tells him that she has just earned her medical degree. She asks him to visit her mother in Moscow when he catches up with the 316th. The troops are poorly fed and armed, already demoralized by the collectivization of the farms and by Stalinist repression.

Mid-November. When he reaches his unit, news comes that the Germans have broken through Moscow's outer defenses. The men welcome him warmly, and they push on towards Moscow. As the roar of battle comes closer, *Politkommissar* NKVD Nikolai Zhillin orders the men to stop the Germans at all costs. To their shock, a line of Siberian troops with machine guns stand right behind them. Zhillin orders them to shoot any infantrymen who desert or retreat.

The German Willy Ropp is taken prisoner in the battle, carrying a letter for Division headquarters. Menakhem, Adrian, and Zakhar are told to take him to Vladikino, but the camp has moved on, along with the field hospital and Anna. Famine and chaos rule in Moscow as civilians evacuate and thousands of recruits keep arriving. Rioting erupts in resentment against the well-stocked shops reserved for Party members. Police and NKVD try to maintain order. Menakhem searches for headquarters and runs into Gen. Pliskin, who orders him to take Ropp to headquarters in the Kaluga underground station. Menakhem repeatedly suppresses the urge to kill the arrogant Nazi.

Anna's elderly Jewish mother cares for her five grandchildren in an apartment shared with another family, while her sons are at the front and their wives are at work. She has recently been disrespected and insulted, both by Zinin—her building superintendent—and in public by strangers in the shops. Rumors abound that the Germans have already won. A pro-German mob carries crosses and swastikas, roars "Death to the Jews," and sings the Tsarist anthem. Zinin welcomes this Nazi sentiment, which he hopes will soon deliver her apartment into his hands.

Menakhem and his men confront the crowd. Seeing the swastikas, the prisoner Ropp runs towards them, gives the Nazi salute, and shouts "*Heil!*" Menakhem shoots him dead. A battle ensues. Zinin and others are killed. The men find the headquarters. They are warned not to tell anyone about the Russian Nazis they had met. *Politkommissar* Zhillin greets them, reads the German letter, and sends the men to await new orders. Menakhem seeks out Gen. Pliskin, who is delighted that Jews are fighting at the front and tells him in Yiddish that his job is to kill German soldiers. The men have a free day until they are reassigned. Menakhem searches for Anna's house. He sees leaflets that German planes have dropped to incite hatred of the Jews. A foreigner, Menakhem misses his hometown and the company of Jews, but is glad to be alive in Moscow.

Memories haunt him of the Polish countryside, of his father forced to wear the yellow star, and of Tengushay, especially of the village girl, Lioska. Anna's mother greets him affectionately, first in Russian then in Yiddish. He then finds Anna's hospital, where she is now operating on wounded soldiers. Their bond is still strong, and she kisses him as he leaves. Menakhem returns to headquarters, finding that the 316th has been sent to the front. Capt. Suzayev again talks to him in innuendoes with phony camaraderie. Col. Petrov reassigns Menakhem to stay at regimental headquarters; his knowledge of German will be useful. He takes tearful leave of his two companions.

Menakhem is assigned to interpret and to interrogate prisoners, and is given instructions how to treat them. The first German questioned is Johann Stimmelmeir. Menakhem asks him if Munich is beautiful, then if Warsaw is. Then the prisoner is driven around to appeal on a loudspeaker to German soldiers to surrender. Menakhem's close friend Frolitch, a peasant from Tengushay, brings a warm letter from Anna at the hospital. Menakhem begins drawing again.

As the battle rages around Moscow, a tank unit arrives. Two of the officers are Jews who want their names changed on their identification, because they fear that their comrades will betray them if they're captured by the Germans. But Menakhem refuses to change his name. Zhillin sees Menakhem's drawings at headquarters and thinks they may be useful to the war effort.

Two reconnaissance men—one of them Jewish—are found guilty of failing to have cleared a minefield, leading to the death of soldiers. Both are shot. Menakhem overhears Suzayev and others blaming the Jew. He then asks to go on a dangerous patrol in Navilkovo. Suzayev scowls, but Petrov agrees. The mission goes well, but Menakhem returns wounded; Anna treats him. Zhillin shows them newspapers with Menakhem's drawings.

Lt. Col. Tcherkass, a Jew, leads the battalion. When the fighting ends, it turns out that the two men had indeed cleared the minefield, but the Germans had mined it again. Suzayev had wrongly blamed and executed the men. Menakhem returns to the command post. Anna has his drawings in her room. Soviet bombers and tanks are routing the Germans, with partisans playing a vital role. Menakhem heals and returns to the front. On one mission, Petrov reflects on the situation of Jews as a minority. Petrov cites their heroism among the troops; Menakhem recalls antisemitism.

Tcherkass is wounded in a fierce counterattack. Petrov sympathizes with his zeal to kill Germans, but says it is reckless. During a lull in the fighting in Zabori, Menakhem declares tremendous pride in defending Moscow and his wish to remain in Russia after the war. The memory returns of his parents forced to wear the yellow star. Called on to interpret, he goes into shock when he learns of the massacre of 25,000 Jews in Minsk. Petrov is sympathetic; Suzayev is not.

Menakhem again interrogates German prisoners, and one of them, Hugo Rudoss, admits having been in the Jewish ghetto in Minsk. Menakhem flies into a rage, smashes his revolver twice into Rudoss' face, and then orders the guards to take him away. When Suzayev finds out, first he mocks Menakhem for not having killed Rudoss, then he rants incoherently against the Jews. Tcherkass is brought in mortally wounded when he attacks a tank unarmed.

Anna's mother's life in Moscow is a struggle, made even more unpleasant by the Tartar and Ukrainian daughters-in-law whom she has taken in. But she remembers Menakhem's visit affectionately and sees his war drawings everywhere in newspapers and magazines. In the hospital, *Politkommissar* Zhillin praises the drawings' usefulness to the war effort, but belittles Menakhem's ability to portray Russian faces because, Zhillin says, he's not a Russian himself. Anna bristles at this slighting of Jews.

Then she is summoned to treat Tcherkass in a dugout. But it's too late; Frolitch is overcome with grief. After Tcherkass is buried in the frozen ground, *Politkommissar* Zhillin makes a speech in which he belittles Tcherkass's heroism, calling his action suicidal and reprehensible. Menakhem leaves in disgust. As the winter freeze arrives, Soviet morale soars while that of the Germans plummets. Division Headquarters snatches up Menakhem's drawings as soon as he makes them, and Frolitch begs him to make one of himself, which he does gladly.

At Suzayev's instigation, the NKVD Special Section charges Menakhem with dereliction of duty for having sent the prisoner Hugo Rudoss away without completing his interrogation and without making sure that he reached detention. In the midst of the hearing, Col. Galinkov suddenly asks Menakhem why he didn't join the Polish army that was forming in the USSR, and whether he plans to return to Poland after the war. Menakhem explains that he was not able to complete the interrogation because of his fury that Rudoss had massacred Jews in Minsk. Galinkov sympathizes, but rebukes Menakhem for breach of military discipline and suggests that the Germans may even have secret agents among the Jews. But he drops the charges.

Menakhem is promoted to lieutenant for a series of military actions and is also given a medal; Frolitch celebrates. Anna comes to the dugout to congratulate him. Their affection is great, and she kisses him as she leaves. Menakhem reads the morning announcements from Moscow to the men and goes out on patrols at night. The soldiers in one dugout insult him with antisemitic taunts, and he sends one of them sprawling.

The Vladikino dugouts expand into a military base with a hospital and nurses. Menakhem sees official reports of the German slaughter of Jews in Minsk, Grodno, Vilna, and Rovno—reports that merely call the victims "Soviet citizens." As the Red Army advances, troops who were from west of the front line are deserting. Paranoia in Moscow leads to the pre-emptive deportation of such troops to the mines in the Urals. Menakhem receives a warm letter from Lioska in Tengushay and writes back that he is deeply disturbed by reports of the massacres.

Another German prisoner is brought in for interrogation. He is insolent and says, "I do not talk to Jews." Enraged, Menakhem sends him away on the pretext that he had simply refused to talk. Col. Petrov rebukes Menakhem for not doing his job, thereby possibly endangering the troops. The next day his weapons are taken from him, and he is led under guard to Division headquarters. Col. Galinkov makes disparaging remarks about Jews, accuses him of treason, and insinuates that Menakhem did not join the Polish Army in the USSR for some sinister reason. He then orders a court-martial.

Menakhem hears more antisemitic slurs while awaiting trial. He is interrogated at length, then charged with breach of military discipline. Because of his earlier infraction in the case of Hugo Rudoss—but in light of his heroism in battle—his sentence is to be demoted in rank and to be sent to a disciplinary unit. Capt. Suzayev, called as a witness, says Menakhem is unreliable because of his "foreign" ways and his hypersensitivity as a Jew. *Politkommissar* Zhillin echoes these views, adding that Menakhem favors the company of Jewish soldiers over that of ethnic Russians, and that his drawings indicate a pro-Jewish bias that plays into Nazi propaganda. Col. Petrov merely agrees that Menakhem committed a serious breach of discipline. Frolitch testifies that Menakhem was well-liked by the villagers of Tengushay. The defense argues that Menakhem has the same right to hate the Germans as ethnic Russians do; that the German prisoner's refusal to answer Menakhem had been a provocation; that a court-martial was unnecessary, and normal discipline would have sufficed. Menakhem requests that he be sent to fight at the front line. Instead, he is demoted and ordered to report to the Special Unit in Gorki.

He wanders around Moscow while waiting for the train, comes across Kalmuk soldiers, Tartars, Ukrainians, Cossacks, and sees his war posters on display. He tries to find Anna without any luck. On the train, Nina, a railway guard, invites him to her compartment, offers him a drink, and tries to seduce him without success. Furious, she gets the police to haul him to the Barashovo police station. The train to Gorki leaves while they peruse his papers. A sled takes him past the Temlag labor camps through Alexandrovo and Krasni-Yar towards Tengushay. He is warmly embraced by the villagers Maria Periferovna and Ivan Ivanovitch, with whom he had lived before the Germans invaded. Lioska runs to their cottage to greet him. He is moved to tears by the affection she shows him. The pain from his battle wound surges up. The next day he visits Lioska and her mother at home and spends the night with her. They go to the train in the morning, accompanied by Maria and Ivan.

Chaos reigns at the Gorki headquarters. The food is atrocious. The prisoners are Caucasians, Tartars, Chechens... every Soviet nationality except ethnic Russians. Menakhem says there's been some mistake, but to no avail. His deportation to the Urals fits into the NKVD plan to keep suspect soldiers far from the front line. The men in the train from Gorki freeze and starve to death. With the help of others, Menakhem barely survives until they reach the mines. The German Army is bogged down as it retreats from Moscow under constant harassment. Dr. Anna Samuelovna Korina is sent by plane to work with partisans near Smolensk.

At the Vistula

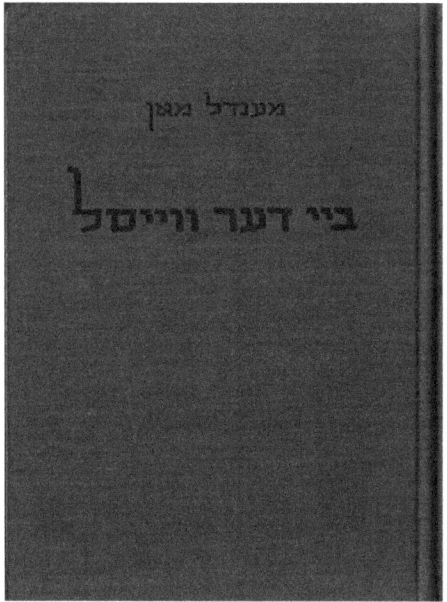

Cover of *Bay der vaysl* [At the Vistula], Tel-Aviv: I. L. Peretz Bibliotek, 1958.

Menakhem toils in the Urals for months, working in the grueling, nauseating coal mines, along Cossacks, Tatars, Kazakhs, Georgians, Ukrainians, and other Jews. The food is both meager and revolting. Dreams of Poland, Tengushay, and Moscow haunt him. He longs to be back at the front. A military commission arrives to recruit prisoners, and Menakhem volunteers. Khatshapuridza, an antisemitic Party member, ridicules him, but Menakhem is mobilized, sent by train to Gorki, and assigned to a barracks.

He does not divulge his rank or how he ended up in the mines. A First World War veteran hums a song about Warsaw and the Vistula River. Menakhem hears that the Germans are still holding Smolensk. The miners assemble for inspection. Menakhem confesses that his scar is a battle wound, but he doesn't mention his service in defense of Moscow. He sings proudly with the men as they return to the barracks.

January 1942. The Red Army and Soviet partisans have been repelling the Germans, liberating sixty cities. Anna Samuelovna has been working with a partisan unit outside Smolensk under Capt. Mikhailov. *Politkommissar* Zhillin is sent to join them. She wonders whether it's a coincidence. She remembers their last meeting outside Moscow. She suspects that he and Suzayev had something to do with Menakhem's disappearance. She tries to avoid him. She is sure that he arranged for her to be posted there after being assigned there himself.

Extremely upset when she returns to the field hospital, she steels herself for the arrival of planes to transport the seriously wounded, and for the partisans' imminent advance into German territory. Unable to sleep, she returns to the hospital and runs into Zhillin. She asks if he knows what happened to Menakhem. First he stays silent, then he nonchalantly mentions a trial, a German prisoner, and being sentenced to the mines.

Capt. Mikhailov has refused to accept Belarussians or Jews into his partisan unit, except for Shimen Moiseyevich Gross, a Polish Jew who leads the reconnaissance men. He had fought the Germans in the streets when they occupied Warsaw in 1939 and had taken refuge in Justina's apartment. Then he fled to Russia while Justina stayed behind. Zhillin now takes command, and he leads the unit towards Nadezhdino, where the Germans are quartered.

Menakhem, Zhillin, and her mother dominate Anna's nightmares. At dawn, Gross tells her that two Jews were found in the village. Interrogated by Zhillin and Mikhailov, they say they're soldiers who were ambushed but got away, one of them wounded. Zhillin calls them cowards and deserters. The wounded man is outragted and shows his scar. Anna asks to attend the interrogation but is not permitted to. Zhillin says he will let the men join the partisans only if they first hand over their machine gun—leaving them only a single revolver and some grenades—and then go blow up a German freight yard bridge.

Gross intercepts a German radio transmission that indicates their whereabouts. The partisans advance, the Germans retreat. German leaflets mock the partisans as being full of Jews who are fighting not for Russia, but only for themselves. The two Jews request a third man for their mission. Zhillin and Mikhailov refuse, expecting them to fail and thereby justify their rejection of Jews in the unit. Gross asks for a mission to liberate Jewish refugees being held captive by Germans in the forest. Mikhailov again refuses but encourages him to stay in Russia after the war.

The partisans move into hamlets near Nadezhdino. Awaiting the coming battle, some partisans accuse the two Jews of having betrayed them. Zadurkin blames the Jews—"anti-Christs"—for the war itself. Gross warns him to shut up. When the fighting ends, the partisans find one of the Jewish soldiers hanging from a tree, the word "Jew" affixed to his back. Radio instructions from Moscow emphasize strict discipline and the political importance of stressing the Russian nationality of the partisan fighters. Gross tells Anna that he feels more Jewish now than ever before. Anna learns of the hanging and blames Zhillin for having driven the Jews away.

A Russian peasant named Mikhaliuk had betrayed the dead man to the Germans. The other, Mark Khinoy, fights his way out, and along with Jews from the woods, blows up the train bridge to the freight yard and lays mines that derail a German troop train. On his way back to the partisans, he recognizes Mikhaliuk and shoots him. Anna is loved by the peasants whose families she treats, but they often blame the Jews—"anti-Christs"—for Bolshevik rule and for the war.

One night, Zhillin, reeking of brandy, visits Anna's hut. He declares his love, tries to embrace her and pushes her onto her bed. She resists and screams. He seethes because she loves Menakhem, a Jew, whom he had betrayed. He is summoned by Mikhailov and returns to find that the three Jews have returned and carried out his orders.

Zhillin doesn't even recognize the men. Mikhailov predicts that the Germans will retaliate for their daring exploit, and preparations are made. A delegation of peasants comes from Nadezhdino, accusing the partisans of murdering one of their men. They identify the three Jews. Furious, Zhillin rants that the Jews' obsession with being persecuted blinded them to commit murder, which reflects badly on the Soviets. He calls a meeting of the general staff, at which he announces a dawn attack, condemns the actions of the Jews, and sentences Khinoy to death.

Anna says Zhillin will have blood on his hands. Already drunk, he argues with her incoherently, throws her down, and lands on her. It is as if she were lying in a field of nettles. She struggles and manages to leave, with Zhillin's aide Zadurkin laughing behind her. The attack on

Yermakovo is launched at dawn, with Shimen Gross in the vanguard. Anna races to join the forward detachment. As they move out, Zhillin retracts his order to execute Khinoy, in light of the ongoing extermination of the Jews. As the battle rages, Anna is taken prisoner, gives her name as Morozova Claudia Ivanovna, and is sent to a German labor camp in East Prussia. Mikhailov's group occupies Yermakovo, but Zhillin and his unit are forced to retreat, to his shame. Gross decides to fight his way back to Poland on his own. Zhillin refuses to work with Jews from Smolensk who have been living in the nearby forest. But antisemitic peasants trick them into believing that he wants them to join his partisans. The peasants massacre them when they try to do so.

June 1944. The Germans are in retreat. Menakhem and others from the mines are battling on the Belarussian Front. He is summoned by Col. Yefimov, who knows that Menakhem has already fought at the front, was arrested, and was sent to the mines. Khatshap warns Menakhem that it's dangerous for him to fraternize with Jewish civilian refugees. Menakhem eagerly fights the Germans in the woods to avenge the Jews murdered there by the peasants. His unit advances into East Prussia, and Menakhem is again assigned as an interpreter. He meets an antisemitic Polish aristocrat and accuses him of hating Jews and welcoming the Germans. Menakhem relishes the thought that Poland will now be occupied by the Soviets instead, and the Jews will return to the cities they had helped to build. He discovers that the aristocrat doesn't know that his wife, Sabina, is Jewish. Menakhem urges her to flee when his unit pulls out.

Yefimov's division heads for Warsaw by way of Mlawa, Ciechanow, Sochocin, and Plonsk, Menakhem's childhood home. Yefimov assigns him to guide the troops and to help the men cross the Ukra River. Many cannot swim, and Menakhem saves one of them from drowning. A bullet shatters a bone in his hand, sending him to the hospital. He learns that Poles murdered Sabina, and that the Red Army is now approaching the banks of the Vistula outside Warsaw. Soviet bombers make daily raids, and the Germans are evacuating the city. A year after the Jews in the Ghetto launched their uprising, Soviet radio calls on the Poles to rise up against the Germans. The Red Army begins to move towards the Praga suburb, but sudden reinforcements of Panzer tanks strengthen German determination to hold the city.

As the Red Army nears the Vistula, the Polish insurrection breaks out in the city, wearing red and white armbands. Shimen Gross has made the long trek back to Warsaw after fighting to drive the Germans out of Vilna. He is greatly moved to be back in his hometown. He joins a group of Polish fighters who are not antisemitic as they battle the German Army in the streets. Behind the scenes, Soviet forces begin to disarm and deport Polish partisans. Gross and his men meet Jewish fighters who had survived the 1943 Ghetto uprising, as well as others who had fled from Hungary and Greece. Then they liberate the concentration camp on Gesia Street in the former Jewish Ghetto. Gross is horrified by the living skeletons he finds there. And he is pained that there are still Christian Poles murdering Jews while the Germans continue their atrocities. As incendiary bombs fall on the ruins of the Ghetto, he hopes against hope that Justina is still alive.

Politkommissar Zhillin infiltrates Warsaw, comes to resistance headquarters, and leads the Poles to believe that the Red Army is about to enter the city. Emilia, who had already fought in the Ghetto uprising, is sent with a message from the resistance to Marshal Rokossovksy at Soviet headquarters, and vows to return. Menakhem recuperates in a nearby village, triggering childhood memories, but the Jews are gone. The painful realization grows that Poland is no longer his homeland.

He rejoins his unit. Warsaw is in flames as they near the Vistula. He is again assigned to interpret. Menakhem and Shimen Gross struggle with deep despair. A battalion of Vlasov's[1] fascist army of Russians and Ukrainians terrorizes and massacres civilians. While the Germans continue their bombing raids, the Red Army fails to cross the Vistula. Menakhem cannot bear it any longer and asks to be sent into Warsaw on a mission. Yefimov denies his request, because, he says, he must put the interests of the USSR ahead of those of Menakhem's homeland. In August 1944 Emilia parachutes into Warsaw from a Soviet U-2 plane, which also drops Lt. Zirkov behind enemy lines. She brings a letter making it clear that the Red Army is waiting for the Germans to crush the uprising, and that the insurgents should flee cross the Vistula. She

---

1 Andrey A. Vlasov was a Red Army general who, when captured, defected to the Germans and organized a regiment that fought with the Germans against the Soviet Union and murdered Jews.

is sent to Monter;[2] head of the *Armia Krajowa*[3] in the Old Town, and can reach him only through the sewer system, through which she had fled the year before. Days later the Polish general staff begin to escape through the sewers.

Emilia is wounded and captured and taken to a field in Zielonki held by Vlasov's men led by Antip, a Don Cossack. The Germans are using these Slavic auxiliaries to massacre civilians and attack the remaining insurgents in the Old Town. Lt. Zirkov has joined them and won their trust with antisemitic and anti-Soviet propaganda. His mission is to wean them away from German control. Groups break away, often drunk, wreaking havoc in the countryside. Women prisoners are brutalized and raped en masse in Zielonki. Emilia, protected and disguised as a Carmelite nun, leads a delegation to Antip to complain of the atrocities and accuses Shaliugin of murder. Zirkov is there, and he assures them that they will stop. Antip takes Shaliugin outside and executes him. Zirkov realizes that Emilia is not a nun, and that he has seen her before, in the airplane. He is terrified that she will betray his real identity to Antip. Her dead body is found the next day.

Antip's men, joined by Hungarian fascists, Lithuanians, and Latvians, continue to massacre civilians and hunt for Jews. The Germans aim to totally obliterate Warsaw, which they had started to do in 1939. Food and water shortages weaken the insurgents. The uprising lasts sixty-three days, with little help from the Red Army. On October 2, 1944, a delegation of Poles surrenders to Gen. Von dem Bach. Jews remain in hiding in bunkers, cellars, and sewers, and they are still being betrayed to the Germans and murdered. The Germans send Antip's battalion to guard along the Vistula, facing the Soviets, calculating that they are expendable. Zirkov goes with them, but he assassinates Antip as they approach the river, and takes command.

Soviet troops seize the German train taking Anna Samuelovna to slave labor. While exhilarated to be free, she still fears that Zhillin will find her. A riot erupts when some Soviet troops try to break into the

---

2 This was the code name of Polish Col. Antoni Chrusciel, a leader of the Armia Krajowa resistance to the Germans, who was promoted to General when he led the 1944 uprising in Warsaw.

3 Polish: Home Army, the principal armed Polish resistance to the Germans during the Second World War.

women's wagons to rape them. But they are stopped, and the train continues towards Poland. Yefimov's division, including Menakhem's unit, waits on the eastern bank of the Vistula. They can see that Warsaw is being reduced to rubble. Isolated civilians manage to escape. They read in their newspaper that Antip's men shot him as they were crossing. By mid September, the Red Army has full control of the Praga suburb. The men relax, play cards, and sing to accordeons. The streets are teeming with refugees, collaborators, deserters, and Vlasov's men.

Anna Samuelovna is assigned to treat the wounded. She is tempted to join with Jewish survivors in the streets and evade Zhillin. One of her patients, Zakharchenko, is near death. Another, Capt. Isaac Farber, has a chest full of shrapnel. Just before Anna operates, she is horrified to learn that Zhillin is in Praga, and that he was promoted to colonel and decorated. Nurse Yekaterina Yurievna and old Dr. Leszniak see that she is overwrought and sympathize with her. Menakhem watches from Praga in despair, powerless, as his beloved Warsaw is being destroyed. Warsaw's Jews have been exterminated. When the Red Army finally crosses the Vistula in January 1945, he walks through the ruins in a daze.

The Fall of Berlin

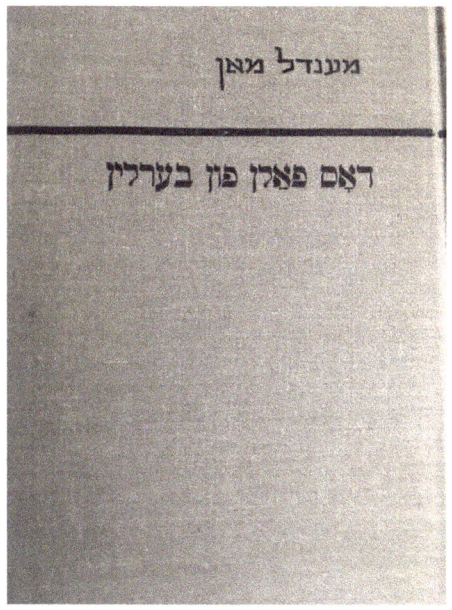

Cover of *Dos faln un Berlin* [The Fall of Berlin], New York: Tsiko Bikher Farlag, 1960.

Chapter One

Towards the end of January 1945, two personal events deeply shook Dr. Anna Samuelovna Korina of the Red Army's military hospital in the Praga district of Warsaw on the Vistula. They were sudden and so unexpected that they unnerved her, making her afraid to perform even the simplest operation. Under the pretext of fatigue, she entrusted the fate of the wounded soldiers to Dr. Leszniak. The snowstorm that had been raging for three days seemed to be pounding in her temples. She stood for hours on the top floor of the building, staring, immobile, through the little window at the snow-clad world.

Nearby a rusty brown sheet of metal broke off from a shattered roof, ripping clouds of snow in a fierce blast of wind. She could not tear herself away from the window. She stubbornly refused to leave the desolate landscape. The clouds of snow that blasted against the windowpane swirled back into her memory that terrible experience with Zhillin in the swampy woods of the partisans, in the village hut, on the night they had lost the battle. Anna sensed the wind and felt the cold, and she felt better. The very whiteness, its wildness, the sharp snow cooled the fever in her eyes. She turned as white and translucent as the clouds of snow.

No, the fatigue was not an excuse. She could overcome that. But she *was* terrified of her hands, of the trembling in her fingers. She held them up towards the gloomy evening light in the window and leaned her large, round forehead on the half-frozen pane. Now she again felt the fever pounding from her eyes.

Anna's agitation had begun as soon as she learned that Nikolai Zhillin was in Praga, and that he could show up at any moment. Would Zhillin dare to appear at her door? How would she react to his smile, the smile of NKVD Col. Zhillin, who had been awarded the Order of Suvarov First Class, and who had been honored "for distinction in the occupation of Praga and operations on the Vistula." She ran over to the little white night table and threw down the newspaper. When she closed her eyes she once again smelled his sweaty, liquor stench all over her. She again felt his steel pistol against her with his weight. Once again it was if she were sinking down into a field of nettles. She again heard Zhillin's orderly Zadurkin outside, laughing his snide little laugh.

Now Zhillin had resurfaced on the banks of the Vistula. He had reached her through fire, through blood, swamps, nights of debauchery, and snowstorms. The next day, after a sleepless night, they brought Menakhem to the hospital in Praga.

Anna was in the midst of night rounds in the surgical ward. Here was the bed of Isaac Farber lying next to Zakharchenko, and then, suddenly, a familiar face: thick eyebrows, a chiseled jaw, finely formed lips, and two small creases between his brows. She looked at the dark eyelashes, and an ancient memory surged from a time years ago, outside Moscow. Her gaze grew blurry and she couldn't see anything. Was it from tears or from the clouds of dry snow?

She brushed his jaw with her fingers shaking, as lightly as if it were in a dream. It felt good to run her long fingers over the face of the young injured soldier, a face battered by snow gusts, pounded by storms, yet still so gentle.

The wounded man narrowly opened his eyes, moist, black, deep. Anna recognized him. She bent over and read the chart near his bed, and her lips whispered, "Menakhem, Mikhail." The two creases between his eyebrows smoothed out, and a real smile radiated from the corners of his mouth. He sank into a soft white haze, luminous, and silvery, and his hands felt the warmth of a sunny meadow.

Menakhem's sudden appearance made the image of Zhillin's face all the more repugnant to her. The few sentences in *Pravda* brought to life the pale-hued Russian from deepest Russia, the *Politkommissar* with the colorless, watery eyes that turned from clear to cloudy. His thin, sharp lips played with words insolently, words with the power to reduce to dust anyone he came into contact with. But Zhillin was not hated. More than once he had shown courage, even bravery. He was like a fox which, with its fur ablaze, can run through wheat fields, burning them down without being harmed himself. Instead of walking behind a traditional plow or driving a swing plow over the fields back home, he had been uprooted from his native village and dragged off to the barracks in a Moscow suburb, where he was trained to be in the Special Section, a *Politkommissar* in the Red Army. Mistrust, suspicion, and hatred were instilled in him. They riled up his latent peasant slyness and cultivated it with scientific methods.

They twisted around every word that was uttered by suspects and transformed them into acts. Their own words were like sweet, enticing seeds for birds that have been poisoned. Zhillin's instructors were half-baked Russian intellectuals, "professors" from the *Rabfacs*,[1] experts in Leninism, smooth Party theoreticians, and dull journalists who were tired of endlessly writing the same editorials.

By the time war broke out with the Germans, Nikolai Feodorovich was already a full *Politkommissar* attached to a military unit. He was well versed in the sayings of the "Father of the Nations"[2] and the reports

---
1   Workers' Faculty: schools started in 1919, to prepare workers for university.
2   In the 1930s, Stalin was routinely honored with hyperbolic titles, among them, The Standard-bearer of Peace, The Great Helmsman of the Revolution, and The Leader of the International Proletariat. This one referred to his leadership of all the "nationalities" of the USSR.

of the *Informburo*.[3] He searched for suspects, for traitors to the Soviet homeland, and he would often be taken with an overwhelming need to root them out. And yet he was apt to speak humanely. Life around him was like a barbed wire fence that entangles people in the dark of night.

The war was a relief to him. But by then his heart had hardened. The consciousness that he wielded power with his words was intoxicating. He was called on to prove his diligence, and in his intoxication with power he weighed the lives of people on the scales of his twisted morality. But whom should he choose? He had to denounce someone. Moloch was waiting. Who should it be? Through ice-cold eyes he considered a long series of people—everyone he had met. Whom should he denounce? He drank too much and laughed a cold little laugh with those nearest to him, even slapped their backs in camaraderie. But he imagined each of them in the snow-laden fields of Siberia or going down stone steps to a black cellar. Sometimes he would feel swept up by the flood of the people who had been sentenced, and a great sympathy—for his poor old self—would overtake him. But he believed that there was an enemy from within. Who was it?

Anna had witnessed it, that first winter outside Moscow—how Zhillin had denounced Menakhem to the military court. And now, four years later, the wounded Menakhem had been brought to a hospital near Warsaw, and at the very same time there came the news that Zhillin was alive, and that he had risen to the rank of colonel.

It was indeed a bizarre knot of coincidence, and she held the tangled threads in her hands: the Russian from a faraway village, the Jew from Poland, and Anna Korina from Moscow. Zhillin was somewhere near, very near. She could sense it. Something was bound to happen. It was a wintry night at the end of January, bluish snow against the dark windowpanes. The sudden reappearance of Menakhem frightened her. He had not seen her. The whiteness, the evening quiet had prompted his exhausted smile. His half-closed eyes had been seeing something far away from there, beyond his reach. He had been gazing at a dream.

It was dark in Anna's little room, with dry snow banging against her window. The beams from the searchlights could not penetrate the storm to the frozen skies. They fell along with the snow on the wreckage of the

---

3   Soviet Information Bureau, organized in 1941.

Kierbedz Bridge. Only a thin ray of light hung to the side, rocking on the black waters of the Vistula.

Yekaterina Yurievna, the nurse, was speaking softly. Anna lay with her eyes closed. It was good to hear the gentle voice of this daughter of the Don steppes. Her voice was like a foothold in the dark for Anna. It was all heat and light, like the endless wheat fields ringing with the sound of scythes and the far-off singing of women tying up the sheaves. It reminded Anna of cradlesongs in a farmhouse among alder trees, with roosters crowing and wings fluttering.

If not for Yekaterina Yurievna's talking, Anna would now be watching herself wandering over the snow-covered fields near Moscow in the winter of 1941. She would again see the snowy Mokhovaya Street, the ugly birdlike face of Zinnin the house watchman, her sad old mother, the shadow-people swarming in the hungry streets, little Oleg, Fatima, Sasha, and Nina—the children in her apartment of wartime Moscow.

Yekaterina's voice lulled her but it could not drown out the roar of the trains speeding away to distant places... the siege of Moscow... imprisonment... the German camps... the liberation... the horrible nightmare with the drunken Red Army soldiers... Zhillin... Everything was swirling together in an awful tangle. She could never rid herself of the night-time laughter of the orderly... The faces came at her, crude, with scars, pimply noses, huge ears, greasy, sweaty... the clawing hands... the stink of liquor... the glint of steel... the vile words... hands grabbing, forcing themselves, like thorny weeds... the night-time screams of women being raped on the sidetracks... the shattering howl of Zakharchenko when she had amputated his feet... the stream of blood running from the mouth of the Jew who had been hanged in Smolensk... the Germans shrieking... her mother's prayers in their Moscow apartment.

Yekaterina's hand was warm, and it guided her through her nightmare. The string of lights that had hung on the wrecked column of the bridge fell into the abyss below. A single shot rang out nearby, then all was quiet. This was a different kind of quiet, satisfied, sated with human blood. The shot did Anna some good, easing the tension from her heightened expectation that something was going to happen. No, it was not a death shot, but the innocent bang of a single solitary rifle, a shot aimed at the cloud of a shadow.

Anna prepared herself for her talk with Menakhem. She knew that his wound was superficial. The earlier wound in his shoulder had reopened. He was in a weakened state. She saw huge drops of sweat on his forehead whenever she stopped at his bed. He had been in a sleep of exhaustion for two days. He had woken up only once, and the nurse had forced him to drink something. Then he fell back half asleep.

Anna was afraid that their unexpected reunion would be dangerous for Menakhem, though she wanted to see how he would take seeing her again. She remembered the infirmary in the village near Moscow. She could see Menakhem with his narrow shoulders, bent over white paper. His drawings were somewhere in her apartment. Four years had passed. A shock of gray hair now fell over his forehead. His face had grown even more bony, and the wrinkles deeper, more furrowed. There were creases radiating from the corners of his eyes. Anna remembered the clearing in the woods on the night before he disappeared. They had been walking to the nurses' station. He had stopped suddenly. She could see the snowflakes dissolving on his trembling lips. She could still taste the melting snow.

Yekaterina Yurievna watched Anna wipe the sweat from Menakhem's brow. She stood to the side and looked on with affection. She knew all about Anna and Menakhem, and her tenderness overflowed. She choked up. That Yekaterina was going to weep; she could not stop her tears.

Someone was talking about sleeping—short, choppy sounds as if from a well. Sobbing was coming from another room. Heavy, raspy breathing, like dull saws suddenly getting stuck in an old tree trunk.

Anna knew all the patients. She knew every wound, and she knew the succession of all the battles of the war from the succession of wounded troops. Here was Gavronov from a village near Murom, who had been wounded in Warsaw. There was Karakin, and near him lay Sapogov and Zeitlin from Minsk, and Farber—seriously wounded—from Shpola. The hospital was flooded with wounded from the latest battles. Two weeks later many of them were sent deep into the far reaches of Russia. They were not kept near the front. Only those too sick to be moved and those who were lightly wounded would stay there until they were sent back to their regiments. A massive attack was being prepared. It was going to be the last assault on Germany. It would bring the long-awaited victory.

Chabayan the Tatar woke with a start and peered through folded eyes.

"Why don't you sleep, Chabayan? Does something hurt?"

He laughed and gave the doctor the grateful smile of a wounded man. "Pain and suffering purify the soul", Anna thought. His coarse face looked like it was veiled in a heavenly glow. Only the pockmarks on his nose and cheeks kept him looking real and mortal, rooted in the good, patient earth.

"Do you get letters from home?"

Now his whole face really laughed, his teeth big and dazzling white. His hand lay on his blanket, and he looked sadly at his fingers. Menakhem was awake, peering wide-eyed into the half-darkness. Anna's hand was still hovering over his brow. In her hand trembled a little silk cloth, a white reminder of long ago.

"Anna," he said.

That single simple word brought tears of thanks to her eyes. He had said it so naturally, so matter-of-factly, as if his lips had prepared to say it. That was the way to greet the dawn of a new day. That was the way to greet the stars after a cloudy night. She was kneeling, whispering quietly. Then it occurred to her that she was talking to herself and Menakhem would not understand her. But he did understand, for his whole being sensed what she was saying.

"Anna. Anna Samuelovna. It's been such a long road. From Moscow to Warsaw. Such a long road."

She touched his forehead with the palm of her hand. She was near him now, as near as sleep, as near as the quiet night.

Soon Anna was standing at her little window. The sky was turning gray somewhere far away, on the other side of the Vistula. The snow had stopped falling. The window was covered with frozen tracery. It was cold in the room. She wrapped herself in her coat and fell asleep right away. The head nurse Yekaterina Yurievna did not sleep. You could hear her footsteps on the stairs.

A week later Menakhem took his first steps. His wound was healing well. Anna knew that he was no longer in danger. He had been a wreck when they brought him to the hospital, and he could not get a hold of himself for quite a while. A mine had blown up right near his feet, and the force of the explosion had hurled him onto a snowy ruin. It had happened on the first day that his unit had reached Poland's capital. The front line was rolling towards the west. Bombardment could be heard every night in the distance and gunfire in the streets of Praga. When he first opened his eyes, he saw a mountain of snow. It seemed like he had been ripped off the snowy Earth. His fingers clutched at mounds of soil, grasped at clumps of frozen snow. His fingers turned to wood until he touched the debris of a cornice. He could still remember how his fingers felt the gypsum leaf stems, then the Earth rocked, and he turned into a cloud lying at the bottom of the snow mountain. When he regained consciousness in the hospital, Anna was already near him.

The grimmest hours in the hospital were in the evening, between day and night. That was when the seriously wounded died. The nurses went around like shadows. Someone leaned closer to hear a patient and listened to the whispered ravings of delirium. Would it be his last whisper?

Menakhem took his head in both hands. His shadow was translucent. Chabayan was singing a mournful song about an injured soldier: "The little green blade of grass cannot sway in the field. A soldier staggers, falling dead in the steppe…" He sang it quietly and his lips quivered. His voice broke into a sob. Chabayan was now somewhere far away, very far from there. He himself was the soldier staggering on his way home from the battlefield, and his mother greets him: "Why do you drink hard liquor, my son? That's why you're drunk and can't find the way back to your hut." And the wounded son, lying in the grass, answers: "Bitter Fate has made me drunk with three drinks: the first, a bullet of lead; the second, a naked sword; the third, a long spear."

Anna was worn-out by evening. Menakhem was sitting in her little room, silent. The nights were cold. Anna got a little iron cookstove, and the only light came from its red-hot coals. She came over to Menakhem, wrapped him more tightly in the hospital gown, and brushed the lock of hair away from his left eye. She told him about her mother's letters and added, "I'll write to her about your coming."

"Then she remembers my visit in Moscow?"

"She has mentioned it many times in her letters."

Menakhem was happy to hear it. "I'm glad, Anna. It's the only greeting I've had in my loneliness."

"You're not alone."

Her upper lip half smiled and the corners of her eyes lit up. She didn't want him to speak. Silence was better. Words would only take them back to the world of war, which would plunge them into darkness and sorrow.

On her day off she took Menakhem for a short drive. It was a sunny Sunday. Volodka Sayanov, the hospital's driver, drove them over the Vistula on the temporary wooden bridge, and they reached the former Jewish quarter. This was the first time that Menakhem saw the obliteration.

Snow still lay on the ruins. Only the unshelled roads were usable, covered with yellow clay mud. Menakhem stared stonily at his old neighborhood, now a wasteland as far as the eye could see: bare concrete columns with deformed ironwork; stones; bricks; facades; gates blown off their houses—gates leading only to ruins.

Volodya pushed his cap to the back of his head and stopped at a church. It was the only thing still intact in a vast sea of devastation. A man stood on a little hill, as if frozen. Was it a statue or a person?

"Wait, Volodya!" said Menakhem. "Let's have a smoke."

Volodya took out his little pouch of tobacco. Menakhem stepped over the stones, and he wanted to stride over a boulder. Anna held his arm to guide him. She walked silently, stepping onto a mound of bricks.

"This is my house. This was where I began my journey out into the world." He bent down and sifted the earth through his fingers. A sharp splinter of brick lay in his hand. He put it in his bag. Anna did not see tears in his eyes. But he had turned to stone.

The stranger was still standing on the same spot, his head turned up. He was elderly, gray, and his face deathly. Menakhem held out his hand as he approached him and said, "We've come back home."

Anna felt the profound grief in Menakhem's Yiddish words, and her heart was grief-stricken. The man was silent. Anna took Menakhem's hand and said, "Come. I can't take it anymore."

The stranger's stony gaze frightened her, and she pulled Menakhem closer to her. The man finished saying his evening prayers. Then they talked at length, trying to recognize their home from the half walls and the streetcar poles. The bells were ringing when they passed the church on Leszno Street. Half the roof had been torn off, and the shattered stained-glass windows looked like unraveled spider webs.

Menakhem learned from the man that there was a Jewish Committee not far from the hospital in Praga, where Jews who had survived got together and were compiling a list of names. Anna promised Menakhem that she would go there and inquire about his family. She would also give them his name, in case any of his family were searching for him.

Volodka came back despondent. "This was your home? Well, Mikhail, you'll find your family... See how the lady doctor worries about you?" When Anna turned towards the window Volodka took a flask of liquor out of his pants pocket: "Let's go! Drink up! It'll do you good! Fast, before the doctor sees!"

Night fell again. Someone was dying. Chabayan was sitting on his bed, his empty sleeve swinging. He sang his song about the lonely soldier, the wounded one who staggered across the fields. Yekaterina Yurievna ran by again, disappearing into the dark corridor.

Anna's workload became much heavier. She did not leave the surgical ward for hours on end. The doors kept on opening. An eery quiet unsettled the patients in nearby wards. All you could hear was the cold creaking of white hospital gurneys covered with sheets and the footsteps of the nurses.

Menakhem was alert to the slightest rustle. Past the threshold of the white doors was a world where words carried no weight. Peace and tranquility ruled: white bandages and Anna's hands and the cold gleam of surgical instruments. It was all suffused in a silky whiteness, laden with the smell of chloroform. And once when he saw Anna on the threshold when the doors opened to wheel out a patient, she seemed distant and strange: cold, steely eyes, creases around her temples, and her hands in rubber gloves looked like raw, cut-off branches. Her white apron was stained with blood in one spot. Menakhem felt his head get dizzy, and his eyes bulged with an unusual fear.

She came to his bed in the evening, but now she was different. "You're depressed today," she said. But he could not smile. The other Anna—the one at the threshold—had been alien to him.

He took her hand and brushed his fingers along her arm. The day before she had gone through the streets of Praga looking for the Jewish Committee. Through a dark gate, up black wooden steps, she encountered shadows through long, eery corridors, and open doors. Deathly faces, circles of people sitting around bare tables. They invited her into a room. An elderly woman was leafing through papers with names. They spoke to her in Russian, surprised at this Soviet woman officer wearing the medical insignia. She told them she was searching for Menakhem's parents, for his brothers.

What should she say to Menakhem? Tell him about these last surviving Jews in dark staircases, in a dark, narrow room? He understood her silence.

He was sitting in her little room a few days later. It was the evening; the snow had a bluish cast. Anna watched the branches from the chestnut tree banging against her window from time to time. It made a moaning sound as if the gloomy evening were calling her to the doomed and the dying. Now they were lying with open wounds under God's heavens. A week later a military commission arrived, and Menakhem was sent back to his unit.

The men in his regiment were already gone. Some of the Soviet units had already reached the Oder River at several points. The Germans were putting up desperate resistance. Would that be his last meeting with Anna? He had so much to tell her. Would she stay alive, and the farmers in Tengushay? Maybe the peasant girl Lioska, and her mother, Molkina?

That snowy night Menakhem talked to Anna for a long time, unfolding the roads of his long odyssey, and she travelled along with him.

As he spoke, she could see the house of Menakhem's parents emerge from the ruins. She could see his father, the idealistic dreamer with the short, trimmed beard, who had manned the barricades in 1905. She met his mother, the village girl from Kukhar, the daughter of generations of Jewish farmers. She saw Menakhem as a child in a little town on the high banks of a stream, a barefoot kid standing on the bank with a fishing rod. She could see his school years, his first painting, the stirrings of love, then suddenly the German invasion... the Polish army... manning a machine gun on the roof of a house on Leszno Street... wandering through the German hinterland to Belarus... then to Tengushay on the Moksha River deep inside Russia... demobilization... Anna... the front... his trial... back to Tengushay... his last night in a peasant hut... Lioska... the prayers of her mother, Molkina... working in the mines... the Georgian Khatshap... Zhillin... the Vistula... Warsaw... meeting Anna again....

He needed her to know everything. Everything. He wanted to share with her all that was nearest and dearest to him. He needed nothing more.

He drew a lot during his last days there. He was restless, and he channeled that restlessness onto drawing paper. He drew people and landscapes, and Anna recognized them from their long nighttime conversations. The closer the day of his leaving approached, the sharper Zhillin's face became in Anna's mind. He would show up again. She was doomed to see him even after the war in Moscow, her hometown. He would wait for her in the dark gateway on Mokhovaya Street. She could see him standing and plotting with the dead watchman Zinnin. He was the victor, the conqueror, the all-powerful in this war. His was the evil weed that was blossoming across our fields that could not be eradicated unless the Earth swallowed it up. She appreciated the long hours she spent with Menakhem. He had opened up a new world for her; a world that she had long-suspected must exist.

Now she could see it, the world of the soul. She had grown up in an era of secrecy and fear, in the years of terror and suspicion. At night she had listened for steps on the staircase. She knew them, the Zhillins of the world. The country was full of them. She had recognized their dark souls when the Germans were laying siege to Moscow. She had seen them when they stormed the trains transporting women prisoners. Now they would be the victors, thanks to the blood shed by the Farbers, the Mikhails, and millions of farm boys. They would parade around in clumsy, rigid, ridiculously shiny epaulets and all kinds of medals and bombastic, outlandish, military honorifics.

She hated them, mocked them, sneered at them, on that night in devastated wartime Poland. The workload had changed her. She was no longer the Anna whom Menakhem had first met in a village infirmary. Her fingers no longer trembled. Her voice had lost its thin, soft, girlish magic. She was now tough as metal, and sometimes her voice was dry. Her eyes were sharp, no longer clear and translucent. He missed that Anna, who had left the little village Tshulan, a brown fur jacket on her back. He caressed her forehead, feeling the web of barely visible wrinkles at her temples. Her long fingers scared him, and the thought of Lioska came to him, that night on top of the oven, covered with straw mats and sheepskins, the scent of fresh-cut hay wafting from Lioska's body. But it only lasted a second. His desire for Anna's warmth came over him, and it seemed to Menakhem that the ice in her eyes had melted. They sat hugging and listening to the snow falling quietly. It was his last day in the hospital.

He left the next morning. Volodya drove him to the train station. Anna had just been called to the operating room. He waited for her to show up again. It was a long time until the door opened. The driver honked downstairs. Several other soldiers were waiting to get to the train. He was standing with his satchel, his face turned towards the door. Yekaterina Yurievna came out first, then Dr. Anna Samuelovna Korina. She stopped in the open door, her hands raised, looking at Menakhem. He saw the corners of her eyes welling up with tears. She nodded to him and quickly turned towards the window.

Warsaw. The beginning of February 1945. The deep freeze was beginning to thaw. The puddles of snow froze only in the early morning. The banks of the Vistula were covered with a yellow-gray mess of snow. Passers-by were rarely seen. Somewhere between the ruins a ribbon of smoke spiraled up. Laundry was hanging on a pole. An elderly man wrapped in a brown shawl. A woman carrying two pails of water. A pale girl in a tattered man's jacket was collecting kindling. In the middle of the desolate street lay an overturned German Panther tank. The turret was covered with soot, the wheel chains were drooping. The cogs, covered with snow, looked like steps. Nearby, on both sides of the street, near the sidewalk, lay yellow-flecked Panzer tanks, wrecked cannons, and overturned diesel trucks. A company of troops went past, through the narrow passageway between the ruins. You could see the devastation of the old city through an opening.

Menakhem's truck stopped often to let marching troops pass. The air was clear and crisp. He could see his old home from the lower part of the truck. His head was bare, and every bounce of the wheels resounded in it, and it hurt. He wished to close his eyes but could not. Dizziness lulled him, and it felt as though the truck had become light and was floating through a fog. Someone was speaking loudly, the tank driver, Platon Voronka:

"Ferdinand,[4] Katyusha[5] greets you!"

---

4   Jagdpanzer Elefant tank destroyer designed by Ferdinand Porsche.
5   Multiple rocket launcher used by the Soviets.

He was pointing to a destroyed German tank, a "Ferdinand" that was half buried under brick rubble and snow.

"Boys, this kind of a machine almost killed me in Lublin! But you can count on Katyushas! This was their doing! I can recognize it by Ferdinand's torn-up backside."

The silver wings of a Messerschmitt were glinting in the morning sun near a ditch in a snow-covered city square. Six soldiers rode in the truck. Traveling to the assignment point, besides Menakhem and Platon, were Sgt. Sergei Orlov, Papavkin from a *kolkhoz*, Zipunov, recently drafted, and Lt. Lev Oshanin. Zipunov had been working on a German estate in Posen. He had wandered on Poland's desolated roads after the Germans retreated. A patrol had found him in a ruin, frozen and drunk, and drafted him into the army. Platon told him, "You're lucky that they didn't hold you under disciplinary guard. All those who were in German forced labor are under suspicion."

Papavkin had never really yet been under fire. He had rambled aimlessly from one town to another. Before the war he had been a manager in a *kolkhoz* not far from Gomel. He was always on the sidelines, and something always seemed to happen just before he was called to be sent on the offensive. Once it was that he had twisted his hand. The second time he had fever. The third time he just could not be found, and they even informed his wife that he must have been killed when they attacked across the Vistula.

His sleepy eyes were watery, his shoulders hunched if he had forced his way through a narrow door. The brittle yellow fuzz on his face made him seem old and weary. But he was thirty years old at most. He peered at everyone with dog-like humility.

"Where are you from, sonny boy? Hey, you, bad luck, huh? Seen some tough times, huh?"

Sgt. Orlov told him, "Hold on tight, little man! You're gonna fall off the truck!"

"Where could you fall? The Earth is always right here. Sooner or later... What's the difference?"

"You're gonna end up in the infirmary again," said Platon.

Zipunov and Vanyushka Papavkin, the two farmers, understood each other. Those two had clicked as soon as they first met in Volodya's truck. They immediately sensed a peasant kinship, and they felt as close as two peas in a pod.

Lt. Lev Oshanin was quiet. To Menakhem he whispered, "*We* have to be the first to get to Berlin." He squeezed his hand as he emphasized "we." Now it was clear to Menakhem that Oshanin was Jewish. Why hadn't he realized it before? Dark, thick eyebrows, an aquiline nose, black curls, a long olive face, with big brown almond eyes.

The truck was leaving Warsaw. They passed bare fields, blown-up train tracks, destroyed train cars, tangled iron fences, bombed-out water towers, knocked down telephone poles, boxes of weapons sunk in the snow, guardhouses, farmers' wagons, carts, the carcasses of horses, flocks of crows, piles of black soil ripped out of the ground. Smoke spiraled nearby from chimneys in mounds of earth. Those were the earthen bunkers of the infantry and trenches that had just recently reached all the way to the first front lines. Farmers were rummaging through them with shovels. They all looked very old, their faces unshaven, with sacks on their backs, tattered boots, fur caps pulled down to their eyes. They avoided the military vehicles that were passing by. When a patrol stopped at their hedges, the men hid behind the curtains or hid on top of the ovens. Only the women went out to the troops, wringing their hands, their faces mournful, lamenting their bitter fate, their possessions that had been looted, the man of the house who was totally worthless and could barely stand on two legs. They related far-fetched stories about children whom the German bastards had taken away.

But at night, behind closed shutters, the farmers would straighten up their backs, comb their matted beards, and have a good time. Oh, how well Papavkin knew those Polish *muzhiks*! He thought, "The German bastards must have left behind what they had plundered. The barns are crammed with rye. And there are piles of gold hidden in the ground. And you, poor guys, have to run across the front lines, and you can't even stop to catch your breath!"

He said: "Sonny boy, what times we live in! Little brother, I know where to look. I can tell just by looking at their eyes. I'll find exactly where that Jewish gold is! By now the Poles have gotten all their gold. It'll be too late by the time we get back from Berlin. They'll take everything. It'll be no use to even try to find it."

Menakhem and Oshanin looked at each other. Voronka announced, "The road is now open. You can see Warsaw in the distance."

The truck hurtled towards the west. They soon reached a large estate. Headquarters was in a brick building. Half a viorst away stretched long, low structures, barracks fenced in all around with rolls of barbed wire. Units of the German 17th Army had been quartered there, as well as a tank unit from the 4th Army. A large airport lay not far away. Dozens of German planes had been destroyed there, still in their hangars, before they could even take off. Now Soviet planes were based there. The highway was full of tanks. The military administration was paving the side roads. They assembled hundreds of farmers to clean up the roads leading to the airfield. Warning signs were posted everywhere: "Mines!" Guards were stationed at empty crossroads, near granaries. Airplanes thundered. Diesel truck engines that couldn't start roared. Tank wheels dragged in a thick stew of mud. Horses shrieked wildly.

Menakhem stood on the steps of a brick house. He could see Warsaw. He recognized the misty blue, familiar contours of his hometown. It was from there that the Focke-Wulf bombers, the Heinkels, and the Messerschmitts, had flown to incinerate his city. It was from there that the tanks had launched their attacks on Warsaw. Warsaw, which had staged an uprising half a year later. He had stood on the other side of the river then, powerless as the city lay dying. His home was now ashes. Where was he going? West! He was going to destroy Berlin. He had to be there! In Warsaw he had realized the evil did not reside in Berlin alone. It was all around. It lurked from the huts of greedy farmers. It hid in all the Zhillins of the world. It sprouted like poisonous mushrooms on the ravaged and desolated fields of war.

In early February the Soviet army's First Ukrainian Front completed the liberation of central Poland. They had marched more than 480 kilometers from the Sandomierz bridgehead and fought their way across the Oder River. The Germans struggled bitterly to hold the eastern bank of the Oder. Much of the German force on the eastern side was wiped out that first week of February, and many bridgeheads were captured on the road to the west.

Marshal Zhukov and his army crossed the border into central Germany and launched offensives on German soil. But the Germans were holding fast to Küstrin, their stronghold on the Oder, a fortress already known in the sixteenth century. It was the gateway guarding the roads to Berlin. Menakhem's unit was rushed northeast to Küstrin. Their mission was to take the fortress. Lev Oshanin and Sergei Orlov were also assigned to that unit. A few days later he ran into Papavkin and Zipunov in a liaison unit.

The Küstrin region is swampy, especially the northeast. Two rivers join there, the Warta and the Oder. Though it was still the first half of February, the marshes were no longer frozen, and the defensive trenches were filled with mud. The soldiers slogged between the bushes and masses of reeds. The German plains spread out before them. It was easy to see that the new structures on the land—farms and estates—had been erected along the border according to the plan and specifications of military headquarters. The walls facing eastward were concrete, and the cattle stalls and granaries had narrow openings for cannons instead of windows.

Lev Oshanin was assigned to command a reconnaissance team, which also included Menakhem, and which carried out all kinds of nighttime missions through the forests and swamps in the area. Oshanin spoke German fluently, and the information that he gleaned from German farmers and from liberated Soviet citizens who had been dragged off to forced labor was very useful. There followed an endless advance of motorized infantry, cars, baggage trains, and tanks. The siege of Küstrin was being prepared. Whole sections of forest were mowed down, as if with a scythe. No civilians walked on the roads.

On one of their reconnaissance missions in a German village, Menakhem and two others entered the cellar of a magnificent house. The cellar was concrete and filled with a vast quantity of war materiel: stockrooms with bullets, fuel oil, and Avio bombs. They also found cases of French wine, barrels of Danish butter, Polish sausages, and Dutch cheese. The estate seemed to have been abandoned. One of the troops brought down an old woman from the attic room. She was the lady of the house, a young boy who spoke Polish told them. She was dressed in black with a black tulle veil across her face. The Russian asked, "You're a German woman?" She uncovered her veil. He perused her face for a long time. Menakhem brushed off her cold stare and walked away without a word. But she cast a foul shadow that stayed with him.

Then he stood in the huge rooms of the mansion and waited for the trucks that were coming to haul off the weaponry. It was his first time in a German house. He saw big nickel beds bedecked with piles of comforters; paintings of hunting scenes in gilded frames; wall hangings embroidered in red Gothic lettering with rhymes of proverbial sayings; credenzas; black wooden armchairs upholstered in leather; brocaded sofas. He walked on parquet floors. Nauseating opulence oozed from every corner. Clocks rang out, big and clumsy; the hours marked in Roman numerals, with a clutter of naked angels with golden laurel leaves and copper wings. A glass-enclosed cabinet held books. He took out a volume and leafed through it. It was Heinreich von Kleist. He put it back in its place and took out another, of Schiller's works.

The soldiers assembled Germans in the courtyard. They were kept under guard, waiting for orders from Lev Oshanin. He walked through the lines and peered carefully into each German face. They found only one of military age and sent him to headquarters in a wagon. The rest were released. On the way there, he reported that he was Martin Pannwitz, age forty-five, born in Crossen an der Oder. His posture clearly revealed an experienced military man. They could see it in his bearing, his stride, and his answers.

Oshanin said, "He's going to sing like a bird… I can see it…He's a high officer." The first interrogation was fruitful. Martin Pannwitz commanded a German tank unit, and he was a major. His wife and children were in one of the captured villages. When Menakhem returned to headquarters from a reconnaissance mission, Pannwitz was sitting at a table, marking with a pen the German fortified positions on a map of Küstrin. He knew every house in the city. Lieutenant Oshanin sat nearby, rolling a cigarette. The captured war materiel was sent to division headquarters that night.

Maj. Martin Pannwitz answered with precision the questions that were put to him. His division had recently been transferred from France: "But it was too late, gentlemen! Our armaments industry is shattered. Our synthetic oil factories in Stettin and Braunschweig were destroyed… on January 14th, our refineries in Magdeburg, Derben, and Bohemia. The situation compels Hitler to send reinforcements to Austria and Hungary to hold on to the gas and oil refineries, because they're critical for Panzers and the air force." The next day came the order to send him to the head of the division.

The Germans bowed obsequiously to every Soviet soldier, whispering fearfully, "Comrade Soldier!" These were Gestapo men, SS men, and *Volkssturmer*.[6] The "master race" was groveling in the dirt. Menakhem had seen it the very first time he set foot on German soil. Menakhem accompanied Martin Pannwitz to division headquarters, keeping quiet the whole way. He ignored every effort of the German to make conversation. The Soviets were preparing their artillery. It was clear that the final onslaught was soon to begin.

Menakhem went out on reconnaissance again that night. On a rampart half covered with snow, the body of a communications specialist lay near a trench, holding a telegraph wire in his hand. He had managed to use his bloody fingers to write in the snow: "Extend the wire further." Menakhem took the wire and dragged it into the enemy's territory. That night the Germans began to bomb relentlessly, hoping to blow up the "Berlin Bridge" that the Soviet engineers had erected across the Oder River. Pontoon bridges were floated on both sides. Menakhem went through the communications trenches. Fire swept the sky, raging between the clouds, and falling to the bluish snow on the ground. Every step was fraught with danger. Mines were blowing up in the fields. Machine guns kept firing again and again.

German deserters prowled around at night, SS men, and all sorts of suspicious characters and paramilitaries who were now surrounded by Soviet troops and were desperately trying to get back to the *Vaterland* that was shrinking day by day. The nights were windy and rainy. Sometimes a wet, yellow snow would fall and melt before it hit the ground. The fields were shrouded in fog. These were mists that drifted between the trees on the roads and the stretches of forest. Islands of snow still clung in places.

Menakhem was on guard duty, his eyes searching far and wide. He knew that he was in enemy territory. His binoculars pointed to the west. The cold copper field glasses framed a village in fog… wet fields… bare poplar trees… the shadows of low-lying clouds… plumes of smoke from village chimneys… cows standing near a stable… He could hear their mournful whining… Peering very carefully, he could see only the stone walls of the barn still standing. Fire had destroyed the roof, and you

---

6   Members of a national militia organized by the Nazi Party when the German army was in full retreat.

could look at the black sky from inside. A farmer was walking from the fields, leaning on a cane.

So this was the land of the enemy? He searched through the short bushes and peered at the field wagons. His eyes came to rest on the bare poplars, high up where dry leaves were fluttering. They had held on through the winter, and spring was coming soon. The hidden buds would blossom. Maybe it wasn't leaves after all, but little birds, common barn birds whose nest had been burned. They would soon fly up to the evening sky and disappear into the forest. He was tired. The cold damp always stirred up piercing pain in his old wound. The farmer appeared again. He was going to the village, taking the same field road. Old willow trees stood on one side of the road, recognizable by their tousled branches twigs and their hollow trunks.

Searchlights scanned the skies when dark fell. They would crisscross the night, slice through the woods and the sky, and slash through the wandering mists, shining a harsh light on the dead, naked corpse of God's creation, a corpse like the blue-gray remains of dead, skinned animals left on the roads in wartime. He knew that here was the lair of the beast. It was here that "the Führer" was ranting and raving. Menakhem scanned the rainy vista for traces of that insane evil but couldn't find it. Evil was widespread all around him, from the Urals, from the Moksha River, all the way to the Oder River. And everywhere it was the same fluttering of birds, the same nighttime shadows, the same whining of cows, the same desolate fields, the same shady paths through the forests, the same sunlit roads through the fields.

Where was the borderline between good and evil, between the predator and the prey? It was a blur; there was no borderline. Take Zipunov, for example, the little farmer from Belarus. He had looked forward to the Germans coming to his hometown. He had thought: "Now things will be different!" He would no longer have to stand in the courtyard of the *kolkhoz* and wait for the *brigadier* to give him orders. The markers of the land he had inherited were still—barely—visible. The stone was still there; the one that he had secretly placed after they had confiscated all the land and plowed over the boundaries, leaving only a flat border that you could hardly see. He had often gone to the field with his son and wiped off the soil that covered it. "This was mine!" A narrow strip of land along the Sozh River where it flows into the Dnieper, barely enough to sustain a peasant family. But it had been his own. The Germans were good to the farmers at first. They let them go into town to loot the homes of the Jews. Then Zipunov was recruited into Vlasov's regiment, which was terrorizing Poland. And when it was destroyed, he hid on a German estate. He changed into civilian dress just before the Russians arrived. And now he was again a Russian soldier. He was manning a machine gun on the front line. The next day he would either march into Berlin or die from a bullet.

Sergei Orlov came to relieve Menakhem. They sat down on blocks of wood and smoked. Menakhem took his embroidered pouch and rolled a cigarette. It was hard to get a light. The sparks kept going out. It was raining aslant, and heavy drops rolled off the earthen rampart. The flame was tiny, and the wind blew it out. He leaned towards Sergei and breathed in his warmth. Looking up, Menakhem saw his welcome, gentle face and big hands, lit up. The nearness of his breath renewed his spirit. The nearness of his warm hands calmed him in that war-torn blackness of night, in that desolate alien land, in that tense stillness. Was Sergei, then, different from Zipunov? In that instant they were the same to Menakhem. The night, the rain, the death that stalked them beyond the rampart, the skies slashed by searchlights—all of it brought them nearer to each other. The tiny flickering flame and a good smoke that remind them of their houses, their homes—those, too, brought them closer. It made them brothers.

What made people better than the indifferent Earth, the fields, and the skies? Why was there no boundary in the sky to distinguish the torturers from the tortured? How gently did the Earth give in to everyone who walks on it! How patient it was! Why did he expect any more from people than from the skies? Or from the Earth? After all, they are insignificant by comparison! After all, they are made of the Earth's dust!

Menakhem returned to the earthen hut. He trudged among the bushes, slogging through the mud. The sky was getting light in the east. Now you could see the Oder clearly. Its western bank was high and dark, resembling a steel bridge connecting sky and water. He listened to whispering nearby. The wind carried the quiet words to his ears. The wind brought a taste of spring: the smell of earth, pine tar, roots, and peat. Russian soldiers were manning the machine gun and puffing on cigarettes. You could see the smoke. They were talking about their homes far away, where the fields lay buried in snow and the rivers were frozen until May, and spring arrived suddenly, so powerful, so unexpected, that the Earth erupted in pain and joy. You could watch the grasses sprouting, the buds blossoming, the seeds springing up before your very eyes, that winter had sown. The air was suffused with the scent of blooming meadows and reborn forests. The ice broke on the rivers, sending streams radiating through the valleys. The cattle were impatient to get out of their stalls, to rush through the gates out to the fields. The udders were full, and the call of the oxen spurred them on. Nowhere is spring so abrupt and short, two weeks long at most, than along the rivers of deepest Russia.

Sergei Orlov was talking: "I was at home this time last year. But only for a week. I was in charge of a regiment from the Urals. They gave me a week's leave to go home. Well, the women flocked to greet me. There were no young men left in the village, only the elderly and one invalid with a limp. The women from my street gathered on my porch in the evening. You could hear the sheep bellowing in their stalls. The eyes of the women were limpid, their bosoms drawn. They looked at me with longing. It was, after all, the time when the plows worked the soil, when the sheep ran bellowing in the fields, and the cows roared, looking for bulls. And here there were no young men, only women and more women. But my wife Pelageya was as pleased as could be.

"Suddenly my neighbor Katya gets up and screams like a madwoman, 'Ha! Pelageya! Aren't you lucky! You get to sleep with your *muzhik*! You're the lucky one! But what about us? Are we made of clay? Doesn't blood run in our veins? Who even knows if our men are still alive?! It's been three years, and not one letter!'

"She stopped short, choking on her saliva, and wiped her mouth. Her lips were burning, swollen. 'We're flesh and blood, not clay! You've got it all with your *muzhik*! Let me have him for one night. What would it cost you? What is it to you?' His wife looked down, and Katya left. Said Orlov, "I could hear her yelling sharply at her cow at home: 'You're disgusting! Shameless! Lascivious!' She hit her neck with her fists and kicked her with her knee. Then she calmed down. I could hear Katya crying. The next morning, she went for water with her yoke. She passed our hut. I could tell she was angry from the way she banged her empty pails."

A soldier laughed hoarsely, "You stuck with your wife?"

Another added, "Oh, Sergei, if I had been in your shoes all the women in your village would have been happy."

"I couldn't go out once all week. My wife was watching. How greedy is the female sex! Not to let the women neighbors have some fun!"

Papavkin had already picked out a German woman with big hips and a triple chin. Dimples broke out on her cheeks whenever she spoke. "Brother, is she soft! Like dough."

Zipunov shuffled his feet and rubbed his palms together. He looked sideways at Menakhem. Something mean and mocking was stirring in his small, pointy-head. How long ago was it that he had flung hand grenades into cellars crammed with Poles? He had been in Warsaw, with the Kaminski Brigade.[7] Now he was as insignificant as the dead trunk of the bare willow trees.

He said to Menakhem, "Hey, Mikhail! Why are you quiet? Why so sullen? You're from Poland? Zipunov groaned, wiped his face, and scratched his head with his hand. Menakhem answered, "Yes, I'm from Poland, from Warsaw."

"From Warsaw? You poor bastard! Boy, did your people suffer!" Zipunov whispered the words "your people" softly, as if it were a forbidden word. He did not want the others to hear it. Menakhem gave him a long, hard look. Zipunov turned away, turned up his collar, then bent towards the ground as if he were looking for something:

"We slaughtered your people... Mikhailo, you're going to have a hard time after the war... Everyone hates your people, by God!... Even God! Even our side, the Soviets... But I'm a fair *muzkhik*! Why shouldn't we let the Antichrists live on God's little world? Everyone's an Antichrist now... New times are coming... The Orthodox churches are open again... My wife wrote me about it from home... It's a bad world for you... I'm sorry for you... Poor guy, just got out of the hospital..."

---

7   Military force formed by the Russian engineer Andrey Kaminski with Russian and Ukrainian collaborators who fought with the German Army. It was absorbed by the Waffen-SS as Sturmbrigade-SS R.O.N.A. and spearheaded the annihilation of the last remaining Jews in the Warsaw Ghetto Uprising in 1943.

Vanyushka Papvkin interjected, "What's that Zipunov babbling about? They must have found themselves a German whore. That Zipunov is gonna drag our Mikhail into it. He's a *muzhik*'s *muzhik* like the nettles that sprout everywhere!"

Zipunov answered, "Mikhail is a Jew. Jews are different. They won't go near a German girl. My wife writes that Orthodox churches are ringing their bells again in Russia. I remember when they took down the copper bells from the churches. People said the Antichrists had ordered it."

Zipunov added, "There was a church in the Kremlin in Moscow that had a roof made of pure gold. A Jew, a Red *kommissar*, sold it to Jewish bankers in England and America, and with that money he bought weapons so that the Russians would murder each other. He was a top *kommissar*; Judas Trotsky was his name. He brought disaster to our people. Then our Little Father, Stalin, came and drove him out... by God!... drove him out... After all, Stalin's Orthodox... Russia's catastrophe began when they took down the golden roof... But our people have come to their senses... When this little war is over we'll bring back the golden church roof, and the bells of St. Basil will shine again, by God!... Stalin promised this to Patriarch Sergius, the new head of the Soviet Orthodox of all of Russia... The picture of the Patriarch was in *Pravda*, with a big cross over his heart, in ecclesiastical robes..."

Menakhem turned his back to the soldiers. Dawn would soon break. You could tell from the rims of the clouds. Sgt. Orlov was in a quandary. Zipunov's words were straightforward, and he had not spoken against the Soviet regime. Patriarch Sergius had indeed been photographed for *Pravda* wearing his cross, and Stalin had welcomed him in the Kremlin. Orlov was a Party member, and that made him responsible for this kind of talk in the trenches. What if someone were an informer for the Special Section? Then there'd be trouble, with interrogations. He looked around. Who could be the informer? The Jew Mikhail? The way he stands aside, his ears perked up, listening, being careful with his words? Once, when they had sent Orlov from his village to attend a course for Party activists, there were two Jews there. They were smooth talkers, and they had such strange eyes. Those two were always the first to volunteer. When they started talking about Marxism, oh, brother, it was as if they formed a troika. Devils!...What a strange nation... good people... like our own... they speak our language, and yet they're foreign. It's fine to drink with them, to have a good time, but then you feel odd. You think less of yourself, you lose your self-worth. You're no longer Orlov. You have to pay attention, do what they say, they're always right. Such demonic power! You can't argue with their smooth tongues. You have to follow their orders and repeat their words, their clever sayings. And when you drink with them you see that Satan has you in his power. Is what that shrimpy muzhik

Zipunov says true? Is it true that a Jew named Judas ordered the golden roof taken down from the church? Things were becoming clearer to Orlov the farmer's son, things that he hadn't grasped before. Now he knew why Jews were hated.

Menakhem left unnoticed. He didn't head for the communications ditches, but rather right across the early morning swampy fields. His machine gun was slung on his strong back, the field glasses hung around his neck. His face was marked by shadows, and he himself was like a night cloud that crept along the ground. He didn't mind slogging through the ditches and the bombed-out fields of fire. He walked through a plowed field with deep rows of furrows. The bombing grew closer. The steel wings of a Messerschmitt swooped down across the dawn clouds and the shimmering light. Menakhem avoided the sunken wreck of a tank. The burned corpses of Germans lay scattered nearby. Crows scavenged around.

And when he closed his eyes for a second, familiar faces came before him. Only one of them shone with a wonderful glow that drove all the shadows away from him, from the fields and woods, from the rivers and the skies—Anna's face. And however surprising it may have been, her face was always followed by that of Lioska, barefoot, quiet, embarrassed, wearing her flowered kerchief on the streets of Tengushay. He sensed an aura around him. Was it the snow or the sun? It sometimes happened that you woke up and God's light blinded you and you couldn't tell whether the light came from the sky or from the Earth. Everything was translucent, clear, radiant... trees, grasses, houses, people. These were rare moments, and not everyone was so lucky. Menakhem experienced just such a rare moment of happiness on that foggy dawn in a desolate, swampy area near the Oder River, among all the tributaries of the Warta River. He prayed, "Oh, God, protect my dangerous path through this alien, evil soil, and take me to the city that lies on the other side of the river. Lead me to Berlin. Give me strength. I will etch with fire the symbol of your people on its walls. I want to proclaim that the forsaken Jews who lost this war have won the great battle against their oppressor. He's now cringing in terror down in some deep stone cellars somewhere."

It was dawn, and the last of the snow lay on the grass, dissolving like salt. A farmer was standing near his red brick hut, peering into the distance. The village street was full of Russian soldiers. They were washing up in the courtyards, pouring water from copper vessels, shining their boots, brushing the caked, black mud off their clothes. A cannon, its muzzle facing westward, stood near the small village monument: a bust of Bismarck in black iron, set on a marble stone, with letters under brown oak leaves made of tin, listing the names of those who had fallen in the First World War. Wilted wreaths drooped from iron fences.

You could hear the Russian language coming from barns and courtyards. German women in colorful aprons wore white kerchiefs on their heads. Oshanin rode down the wide street. His horse threw back his head and neighed. Menakhem's unit had been stationed in that village for three days. The reinforcements had arrived the night before. The war prisoners and suspect civilians had been assembled in the long stone barn near the church waiting for orders. The troops were lined up in a courtyard to get soap rations. Soldiers sat on stone thresholds eating breakfast from tin bowls. They had caroused at night with German girls in their houses.

At first they had stood quietly, in front of the doors and touched the brass doorknobs with respect, and tried ringing the doorbells. As he shaved, a Tatar soldier with huge, sharp teeth recounted: "Featherbeds piled all the way up to the ceiling! The German girl kept mumbling, 'Das, Was, Was'... Couldn't understand her! If only Oshanin or Mikhail had been there... I made a sign to show I was thirsty. So she cooked up some bitter, black, muddy coffee, 'Kaffee, Kaffee'... So I said to her, 'Frau, drink this shit yourself!" And she says, 'Was? Was?' So I took out a flask of liquor and said, "Have some, bitch!" And she laughed, 'Danke schön!' I saw a crucifix around her neck. Her mouth was like silk. I looked over the house, opened the closets, and searched the corners. She flirted with me and laughed very close up to my mouth. It got me all excited..."

The German houses were unrecognizable the next morning. The beds were filthy, windows broken, doors ripped down. German girls with downcast eyes stammered obsequiously to "the Russian gentlemen." The soldiers returned from their first night in the village of Altlinden with trophies: square watches, cigarette lighters, razors, and gilded trinkets.

"Brother! These German girls aren't like the Polish girls, who you can't touch—except for the prostitutes on the street corners. The German girls are pitiful. They'll do anything. She wiped my boots, cleaned my clothes. What a loser! She was afraid I'd muddy her rugs and pillows.

"I can't stand it! If only they'd put up a fight or scream! They just wait for you. They hide their men in the cellars. You look into their eyes, but you can't tell what they're thinking. If only we could get some leave here in Altlinden!"

Zipunov came into the yard to wash up. He was wearing silk underwear and smelled of perfume. His boots were gleaming. A pocketwatch hung from a silver chain.

"Mikhail, you fool! Are you angry with me?" He stared at him with his pointy eyes, laughed, and rubbed his palms. His tiny head, his shrunken face, his drawn lips, and the mocking smile at the corners of his mouth were particularly irritating that morning. He laughed: "Why are you staring at me like a sheep at an unfamiliar gate, Mikhail?

"Get lost, devil!" Menakhem wanted to add something else, but he bit his tongue, left, and went down the street. It was soon his turn to stand guard. He walked down the communications ditches till he reached the edge of the forest. They were waiting for him. On the way he encountered a gray-haired man in a general's military coat, accompanied by an adjutant. He watched the general shorten his steps to look at him. His temples and eyebrows were gray, his eyes dark and deep-set, his eyelashes gray—a face worn with worry, his broad shoulders slightly stooped, as if they carried a burden. He looked like a middle-aged Jew, possibly from Minsk or Kiev. Menakhem was sure that he discerned in the general's look a secret joy of having run into each other on German soil, as if it said, "See, we're meeting here on the road that will take us to Berlin!" And Menakhem's eyes answered: "The evil predictions of the Nazis have not come to pass. This will be *our* victory!"

Menakhem stepped inside the headquarters, which had formerly been the pastor's house near the church. He met Oshanin there.

"What's the general's name, who just got here?"

"That's Lieut. General Shamshin."

"Shamshin?" repeated Menakhem.

A station wagon drove up with the soldiers' mail. The troops were waiting for it at headquarters. Who could possibly write to Menakhem? Anna's face came to him again. She's always in that same open doorway coming out of surgery, wearing a white surgical gown. She's floating among the white beds. How strange her face was then!

The sounds of an organ were pealing from the church. It was a soldier from Leningrad who was playing Tchaikovksy. He was sitting in a corner of the church, bathed in the colorful light coming from the stained-glass windows. The music evoked expansive Russian meadows, long rows of birch trees, familiar village nights. The German Jesus was awkward, with a plump chest... dark Crucifixions... black iron candelabras... tin wreaths.... tin silvery angels... rows of stone and iron pews... steel railings around the altar... Even the doors of the church were iron. A tin and iron rooster perched atop the church tower.

Menakhem received a letter from Anna. His hands shook. He couldn't open the envelope. How silly! His own weakness pained him. He always grew uneasy whenever his name was called out. The slightest attention paid to him made his heart pound. But this time it was a different kind of unease. Anna. Anna. But it wasn't simply Anna, but rather a world of calm that beckoned to him. She had written: "Mikhail... Misha... My eyes gaze towards the west. I am with you on alien soil, with my love and my prayers." He could read no more. A tide of warmth embraced him. His breath grew short. The words stuck in his throat. He was filled with light. It was as if he had been redeemed and returned to Creation, like the day, the pure air, the Earth. The very thought that Anna existed re-created the world for him. He himself felt he was a changed man. He was soaring to heights that he had never imagined. The hateful Earth had changed.

Anna had written: "I often stood over your bed in the hospital peering into your face. I don't know if it's true that hereditary traits re-appear after generations. But it seemed that I could see ancient traces of them that had almost died out. You're Jewish, and I first sensed it when we were outside Moscow. Your face reminded me of my own heritage. I knew my grandparents only from photos. My relatives live somewhere on the other side of the border. Your eyes, your eyelashes, your full lips, your black hair, your forehead with deep wrinkles at the temples. And I heard you speaking Yiddish when you were on the operating table. I know that language only from my mother's whispers. Suddenly an awareness of something I hadn't known swept over me, something that lay hidden from me. My Jewishness welled up in me. In these times, all decent people should feel Jewish, even if they're not of Jewish descent. If not, then there's something lacking in their humanity. I'll always be grateful that you came into my life because it changed me. And it's good that you never spoke of it. Your simple existence was enough to do it. We've found each other and lost each other, but now we're growing closer and closer. Every step that you take further west brings us nearer and nearer together."

Menakhem read the letter over and over, but he could not believe it. Zipunov's words, the trenches in the swamps, his grief and loneliness seemed to melt away like the fog of the night. Late that night his reconnaissance unit closed in on the banks of the Oder. They went right to the water's edge, and under the cover of dark they were able to take up positions among the willows and hurriedly dug ditches in the sandy soil.

Col. Gusyev had addressed them before they left: "Have you ever watched how cattle-drivers round up their herds? I'll tell you, because I'm a Kalmyk and I drove horses when I was young, all the way to the Caspian Sea. You do it by waving your whip and flailing it in the air. You have to constantly flail it over their backs and heads. It's not the pain but the fear of the whip that drives them on. If you beat them, then they'll just come to a stop anyway. You gotta flail the air! Threaten them with the flailing whip and they'll run!"

Col. Gusyev looked at the troops and continued: "You reconnaissance men are the flailing whips over the backs of the stampeding German herd! Don't give them a minute's rest! It's up to you tonight! We'll shoot a red rocket tonight. That's the signal to open fire."

Lev Oshanin went from man to man, urging them on with tough, angry words, "Make them keep their heads down. Way down!" He scooped up mounds of moist earth in his hands. Shadows skittered, bushes swayed. The other riverbank was high up, shrouded in a dense black-brown thicket. The river was gray-silver, dark garnet in places. Something floated in mid-stream, rocked by the waves, and disappeared. There was shooting on the left flank, but shooting was so normal that it was just a part of the night. If it had stopped, the troops would have been uneasy. It would have meant that the enemy right then was running right at them with his rifle outstretched. The constant shooting put them at ease. It meant that the enemy was far away. A cease in the firing would have made them nervous, and every shadow a suspect.

Oshanin used his flashlight to check his watch. Suddenly fireworks lit up the black sky like a fountain spray with a million sparks. Lieut. Oshanin laughed, "The fire peacock has lost its feathers! You can set your watches. It's eleven o'clock. Good buddies, we're starting! Open fire!"

A clatter rang out like a hailstorm falling on tin. A hand grenade exploded. The earth shook from the blast, and the night sky tore open as the clouds vanished.

"75 milimeter artillery... Katyusha rockets... But the enemy fire is feeble. Looks like the Germans don't want to reveal their artillery positions. That's the purpose of our attack tonight, to force them to show us."

The night sky was shattered to bits over the other riverbank, so Oshanin could easily see where the enemy artillery was, and he could tell the caliber of their guns by their fire and by the sound of their explosions. He called on the field telephone: "This is Night Owl... Can you hear me?... Night Owl... Three meters to the right... Another two meters... Heavy artillery fire... Fantastic!"

Menakhem felt the weight of his machine gun. His old wound was hurting. Someone handed him more rounds. He remembered: "My eyes gaze towards the west... Every step that you take further west brings us nearer and nearer together." Now he felt just like the other troops. He had his country behind him. He was part of God's world. He was just like Sergei Orlov, like Platon Voronka, like Col. Gusyev.

Every step, every breath brought him closer to Anna. Everything was connected to her: the nights far, far away from her; the shallow soldiers' ditches; the white and red rockets exploding in the skies; the mines and grenades; the scattering shadows on the other river bank; the exhaustion of plodding through enemy territory just as spring was about to bloom.

Chapter Two

The Third Belorussian Front launched its offensive under the command of Marshal Vasilevsky in the first half of March. The purpose of the attack was to wipe out German positions in eastern Prussia and push to the Baltic Sea, to Pilau and to the Bay of Danzig. Twenty German divisions were stationed there, important military units for special missions. In addition, there were significant remnants of shattered divisions that had made their way back from regions in Belarus and Lithuania.

The Geman units were each locked in a separate vise, a separate stranglehold. They tried in vain to break through and reach the Vistula by attacking the Second Belorussian Front led by Marshal Rokosovsky, in an effort to join up with German units at the Warta River and the Oder. At the beginning of the war, East Prussia had been the most secure, the quietest place in Germany. The air forces of the Allies had not been able to reach it. The German generals, the SS officers, the high Nazi party officials, had come to East Prussia on holiday to be with their families.[1] They had sent their wives and children away from central Germany to peaceful regions in the east. The families of big industrialists lived there in serene villas and castles. This was where they took refuge from the Flying Fortress bombers: Bartow, Neustettin, Schimmerwitz, Gross Tuchen, Neuhot. The Germans put up a vigorous defense. Prussia was turned into a mighty fortress.

NKVD Col. Nikolai Feodorovich Zhillin was assigned to the headquarters of the Third Belorussian Front. He headed the Special Section in charge of political activities in Marshal Vasilevsky's army and was in the inner circle of the Marshal's advisors. Zhillin had risen to the top overnight, right after the death of Gen. Chernyakhovsky—under unexplained circumstances—in a little village in Prussia. He had arrived the evening before the death of the commander of the Third Front, carrying secret orders. It was a quiet night in the Prussian village Mehlsack when Zhillin assumed his post. The next day it was reported that a wayward bullet had killed the commander of the Front. Moscow

---

1 The *Schutzstaffel*, abbreviated SS, was a major paramilitary organization under Adolf Hitler and the Nazi Party in Nazi Germany, and later throughout German-occupied Europe during the Second World War.

sent two orders: First, that Marshal Vasilevsky was named to replace Gen. Chernyakhovsky; second, that Nikolai Feodorovich Zhillin was to report immediately to central headquarters.

He climbed onto a U-2 airplane that had been prepared especially for him. It was a foggy dawn. Only a U-2 could quickly get through the thick fog and the black clouds. Freezing rain mixed with snow burned his face. But he was not alone on the plane. A plump man wearing a loose military coat of English cloth looked at him through watery eyes, a fellow with no eyebrows, no eyelashes. His puffy cheeks and the bags under his eyes bounced to the rhythm of the roar of the airplane. He must surely be a Kazakh, thought Zhillin, someone from the military buraucracy. But he had no idea where he was flying. The order had simply been: report to headquarters. Maybe his unknown silent fellow traveler was assigned to watch him? No, that could not be. No one was assigned to him. The Kazakh could not be connected in any way to his unexpected trip. But Zhillin was had been nervous for quite some time now.

A few weeks earlier he had been interrogated about his time in General Bohr's headquarters during the Warsaw uprising. He had been the intermediary between Rokosovsky's army and the Poles. They questioned him about the role of various Poles that he had supposedly encountered at the headquarters. Then they again brought up that mess about the liquidation of the partisan units in Belarus. They were insistent questions, and they disturbed him. At first he thought it was all a misunderstanding. "They can't do anything to me," he whispered to himself. He was like an agitated child standing at the edge of a stormy sea. This light-eyed young Russian who had climbed from a rural village in the north to the highest ranks could not feel fear. But he had become troubled. An unseen web was being woven around him, which darkened the light from the little airplane window.

He looked long at the mug of his neighbor and suddenly the desire welled up in him to get rid of that heavy, plump mass with cold fish eyes. The icy stare of the Kazakh's eyes made him shudder. He wanted to strangle that fat neck with both hands and throw him out into the clouds. But when he closed his eyes he could feel the stranger moving. Zhillin was angry with himself for that moment of fear and he transferred his hate to the stranger. The plane flew low over darkened fields. As he dozed he saw himself again in Belarus... Mikhailov's forest partisans... The night of defeat and drunkenness... Dr. Anna Samuelovna... His orderly Zadurkin was laughing. Now the general was dead. This was all connected to him. He was trapped in a dark web, and a bright silvery spider sat weaving at its center. He threw himself at it, trying to stomp on it, but the big blood diamond on its blue body terrified him. It moved on hundreds of spider legs. He had never seen such a large blood diamond.

His dreams exhausted him. The airplane had already landed when he woke up. The Kazakh was laughing at him. Zhillin could not see his face clearly, only a pinkish blob.

"Had a good sleep, Nikolai Feodorovich?"

How did he know my name? Should I ask? No! Had he talked to the stranger the night before? But Zhillin could not remember any such conversation. That put him at a disadvantage. There was something haughty about this strange person. As experienced as he was, he knew that he could not stand up to this Kazakh. It was only when Zhillin saw the spacious snow-covered fields and the soil of the airfield that he could rouse himself awake and throw off the dark spiderwebs of the night.

An officer stopped him at the exit from the airport and asked, "Documents?" He handed them to him with a barely visible smile. He was smiling to himself, the smile of fear.

"Nikolai Feodorovich, why are you running away from me? We didn't even say goodbye." He felt a heavy hand on his back, the Kazakh's.

"I'm not in a hurry... I'm just used to walking fast..."

But Zhillin immediately regretted his words. It might look as if he were defending himself, so he added, "You didn't even introduce yourself!"

"Babadjanin... My name is Babadjanin... Now we can have a drink. You can't refuse?" They walked next to each other. Zhillin wanted to tell him clearly and defiantly: "Stop your games! We're equals, after all! I can see you through and through! Show your cards! Are you guarding me? Are you taking me there...? Tell me! Speak plainly! I know your tricks! I'm a frontline soldier, and I like the plain truth!"

They were in the airport restaurant. They drank a full glass of vodka and remained silent. Who would speak first?

"Barabadjanin? The name reminds me of Kazakhstan."

"Drink up, Zhillin! Another glass! Let us drink to the bright memory of General Chernyakhovsky!! What's wrong, Col. Zhillin? Your hands are shaking. Eh, sonny boy? Don't get riled up when his name is mentioned.... It's a bad sign... Ha, ha, ha!" And after they had downed their second glass, the Kazakh stood up: "All right, you can go now. Now we can say goodbye... I hope we meet again somewhere..." Zhillin found this insinuation insulting, yet he was also thankful to the Kazakh. His feelings were mixed: resentment and gratitude.

He walked through the evening streets of Moscow alone. It took a long time for him to shake off his encounter on the plane and the conversation over full glasses of vodka. He felt as though he were clawing his way out of the spider's web, but the spider kept jumping into his face every time, with its blood diamond and its hundreds of black legs.

A thick crystal layer of snow covered the squares of Moscow. Zhillin was wearing a new military outfit. The overcoat fitted him perfectly, and his epaulets shimmered in the streetlights. There were so many people on the streets. So many lights, buses, black Zis limousines. The lights! So much light! His eyes opened wide from joy, the joy of being alive, of being young, of walking on the streets of Moscow!

He was on Red Square that night. Fireworks exploded in the garnet sky. A rainbow of rockets burst over the towers of the Kremlin. They lit up the cupolas of Uspensky Sobor. Purplish-red light flooded part of the crenelated Kremlin wall. Twenty-four cannons resounded near the old Kremlin ramparts. It was a celebration of the 300th order to salute given to the armed forces. The first such salute had been ordered in August of 1943, in honor of the liberation of Oriol. The 300th was to honor the victory over the famous fortress, Küstrin, the most forward defense of Berlin.

It was a mild, snowy evening. Muscovites packed the streets around Red Square, men in dark coats and fur caps, officers in fitted overcoats, women with white woolen shawls, policemen at every turn. They stopped a young man at a gate and asked for his papers. Dozens of people walked past without even turning their heads. Moscow had become a magnet for all kinds of suspicious characters. The former Russian borders had been broken open. Trains now ran from Vladivostok to Warsaw. Moscow was the central rail hub.

The guard changed at the Kremlin. You could hear the sounds of a military march. One of the Kremlin gates was guarded. The church of Vasily Blazhenny shimmered in the light of the fireworks. The mausoleum was dark. Few visitors stopped by. The guards called out, "Keep moving! Don't stop!" Another rocket exploded, sending fountains of phosphorous sparks that died out. It was as if green and red waterfalls were cascading in the sky.

Murmuring erupted in the crowd. A huge car slid by on the damp, gleaming asphalt, surrounded by military on motorcycles. It was a Soviet dignitary. The heavy Kremlin gates opened.

Eyes were dancing. People were celebrating. But some walked with serious, somber faces. It was the middle of March; the start of spring, but you couldn't feel it yet in Moscow. When the fireworks died down a moist mist descended, shrouding the Kremlin tower.

The train stations were crammed to overflowing. Refugees were coming back from Tashkent, Alma-Ata, and the wilds of central Asia. Poles freed from Komi came through Moscow, western Ukrainians from villages deep in Siberia, and Jews from everywhere. Entire families slept there for weeks, waiting for trains to Lemberg, to Kiev, to Minsk. They had nothing left of the meager things they had taken with them when they fled. They wore raggedy cotton jackets, tattered caps stitched together from threadbare goatskin, clumsy shoes of woven hemp, frayed boots. The women wore useless galoshes. The children were wrapped in worn-out blankets. Whole families sat on wooden crates. Men ran with tin plates to fetch hot water.

They all spoke various Slavic dialects. They felt strange on the marble steps, among the stone mosaic walls of the Moscow train stations and metros. They wandered the streets nearby, desperate to buy something at the stores, which were empty. The Muscovites were already used to seeing them.

The stations and subways were also teeming with Moscow residents who had evacuated and had returned. But they could not get their old apartments back. Other tenants had moved in. People were pushing towards an entrance gate on Sadovsky Lane. A man in a military coat was surrounded by police. A woman sat weeping with her children: "This is my house!"

Someone wearing a round fur hat with red trim grumbled to himself, "They're just taking too much... Hooligans in the street...!"

A man of about fifty years old wearing glasses shoved his way through the crowd. He was the house custodian. The woman said to him: "Citizen! We used to live here! The whole street knows it!"

"You shouldn't be complaining! And you, citizen Greenstein, should still be at the front!"

Fights were breaking out every day. "Those Jews are everywhere. They're the first to leave Tashkent and the first to abandon the front... That's for sure...They sure enjoyed the warmth of the sun in Tashkent!"

"Hundreds of thousands of them are coming to Moscow. They're coming from far away, Jews who never even lived here! They're carrying gold, and they buy up what's left of the bread in the stores. There'll be a famine in Moscow, starvation!"

A policeman watched the crowd in front of the big dark house, but he didn't know what to do. "Why are they giving them permission to come into the city? We stayed here during the tough times, and now they come here from their country homes..." "There was a shooting in the Arbat neighborhood. A Jew killed a war invalid."

"How do you know that, citizen?"

"I heard about it."

"It's a lie."

"A lie?! I can tell you're not a real Russian!"

The people who had moved into the apartments of the evacuees were nervous. The former occupants of their apartment might show up at any moment. The policemen did not get involved in these arguments. They were powerless to act. They only stopped mobs from rioting, and they listened to all the quarrels.

"And how do you come to be in Moscow?"

"How?! I was born here!"

"Your passport?!"

"Here it is!"

"And your official release from your job in Samarkand?"

"I had to turn it over to get my papers."

"Well, now I see that I'm dealing with someone who deserted the Soviet labor front!"

Every train coming into Moscow had a special compartment for the police. Even people who had permission might not be allowed into the city. But they kept coming. They pretended to be headed for Gomel or Kiev, but they stayed in Moscow. Hatred of those who returned from far-off Soviet Asia grew by the hour among those who had stayed. They were mostly Jews, as well as some Party members and scientists.

"They won the war. Our men died on their account… Now they're coming back and driving us out of our homes!" They were scorned in the bread shops. There wasn't enough bread for those who had stayed.

An old man, a Jew, knocked on a door on New Pyeshchan Street with trembling hands. Would they let him back into his apartment? He had returned from Soviet Asia. His son had died in the battle of Stalingrad.

A quiet Jewish woman in dark, ragged clothes presented her papers to the regional Party secretary in Moscow: "Look, my son is Yosef Yaffe. He's twenty-seven years old, the head of a military unit, the mortar cannons. He's fighting in Berlin. Surely I can get my apartment back." The Russian lowered his eyes.

A brawl broke out at the Kazanskaya Train Station. Invalids from the Fatherland Front in the First World War beat up Jewish refugees who had returned. They went from train wagon to train wagon searching for "dirty Jews."

"Leave the invalids alone, they're just a little drunk… They've suffered enough…Let them have a little fun…" And the police stood by. "Don't even try to interfere, you bastards! See these medals? They're drenched in our blood! Jews and policemen are parasites!"

A Party official pleads with a group of Jewish arrivals in a concerned, fatherly tone, "Go to Vinnytsia." And he adds with a hint of irony, "Vinnytsia is a good place for you. Or else Berditchev." But he can't order them to leave. No law has yet been passed… "The Father of the Nations is preoccupied now with the conduct of the war. He has to bear such heavy burdens! A solution will surely be found."

"These Jews are a real pain!"

"See how they're coming from Tashkent? They made huge fortunes over there! They've got all the gold of Asia on them!"

Long troop trains were arriving daily in Moscow. Cooperative workshops were running again. Ruined factories were being rebuilt.

Trained specialists were needed. The NKVD did not rest. The Kremlin had never been so closely guarded as now.

The same night that spectacular fireworks were lighting up Red Square and everyone was staring up at the magical sky, the cellars of Lubyanka Prison were crammed with prisoners. This was the time to clean out the enemy from within. That was what had happened when the Germans were at the gates of Moscow, and it was the same now when our army was standing at the gates of Berlin. Then the order had come from on high. The almighty ruler had feared that the Germans would find collaborators among our traitors. And now it was time to wipe out those enemies from within, because the iron curtain around the USSR was shattered, and Moscow was being overrun by strangers. The border markers had been torn down. Only Soviet tanks stood in their stead. Huge areas in the western territories were left without Soviet control.

A Soviet Jewish journalist was having a talk with a Ukrainian official, an uncomfortable man with a shiny fat face, a smudged nose, and quick, tiny eyes.

"You're of Jewish origin, right? So you know that your people are riling up Moscow? It's quite an invasion. Ha, ha, ha! When they went to Tashkent they pushed the local people out of the prettiest streets. Now they've left Tashkent empty, desolate... They're like a swarm of locust. Every Soviet citizen who lives in Moscow has sons at the front... When have we in the Soviet Union ever had inheritance of private property? Russia is big enough. What right do they have to settle in Moscow specifically?"

This man from the *Politburo* smiled a barely visible sly smile. The Jew looked down and said nothing.

"Why so downhearted? Think about it. There are now so many desolate towns and villages, so many ruined *kolkhoz*. Why don't your people go there? Moscow is overcrowded. The food supply is in chaos. People have to stand on line in the shops. Foreigners can see it. What sacrifice are your people making for our Cause? You all have suffered, I know that. But the Jews of Moscow have the least to complain about... We protected you."

He spoke a lot. Sometimes his cheerfulness erupted into wild laughing. The Ukrainian poked him good-naturedly in the chest, "Let me be frank with you. After all, you're one of us. I'm talking to you like a brother. I run things in Ukraine. Do you know why I'm not letting Jews into Kiev? It's for their own good. Let them go south. To Kremenchug. No, further south, to Simferopol. We're sending all the trains with Jews to the south. D'you understand? I know that HE esteems you."

The man from the *Politburo* raised his hand with a threatening finger, and his tone grew serious: "It's your job to convince the Jews. You have a newspaper. You have the reputation of an experienced journalist. I read your articles in *Pravda*. We have Jewish writers…There are two options: let the evacuees stay where they are now, in central Asia, or settle in the villages south of Kiev, in the Vinnytsia district, let's say. Wouldn't that do? Or even more to the south, where there once were Jewish villages, but I don't remember exactly…"

"You mean Kherson?"

"Well, that's not bad either. There's an area near Kherson with lots of empty land."

The Jew could not understand why the man from the *Politburo* was refusing to say "the Crimean peninsula." Why could he not bring himself to say "Crimea?"

So he asked him directly, "Do you think that Crimea would be a good place for new Jewish settlement?"

The Ukrainian jumped up and placed his hand on the Jew's shoulder. His fat little eyes shimmered like tiny fish swimming on top of turbid water: "A brilliant idea! Crimea is empty! The Tatars were traitors! Having a loyal nation like yours there would be a valuable guarantee! You'll be able to build a new republic there! And they, the Tatars, can stay in the *taiga*! A wonderful suggestion! But the proposal has to come from you. You have to do it… The Jewish Committee… Jewish celebrities who care about the fate of the Jews… You haven't done enough for your people, that's my reproach… Now you have the opportunity to make up for it. We can't force you to do it. It has to come from you alone. And you'll have support. Do you know why I'm talking to you? The problem of what to do with Jews in the liberated areas sticks right here." He pointed with his small hand to his chubby throat. "Yes, Crimea is the ideal place for the Jewish nation. You're right! Your suggestion must be considered seriously. I promise you my support."

"But it's not *my* idea! It's yours!"

"Stop it! I don't like your parliamentary tricks, ha, ha, ha! It comes from *you*! Don't you understand?" The man from the *Politubro* grew uneasy when he saw the challenging look in the man's eyes. It was the nervousness of a farmer when his exhausted horse refuses to move in the middle of a meadow at night. He slapped the Jew again on the back and said: "It's the only way. The sooner your people do it, the better for all of you."

An orchestra was playing nearby. Waiters carried trays of wine. Women were wearing long evening gowns. A younger woman accompanied a general. The Ukrainian's eyes grew moist: "Greetings, Semenkov! Don't you recognize me?" The general put out his hand.

"Is she your war trophy?" asked the man from the *Politburo*.

"This is my daughter."

He laughed, his lips gleaming, his teeth sparse, his brow knitted. The Ukrainian turned bright red. But the journalist was preoccupied. He leaned against the table, unable to decide whether to leave or to stay with the empty vodka glasses.

Zhillin waited in front of the closed door for over an hour. Not so much as a rustle could be heard, not even steps in the corridor. People passed by like shadows walking on dark carpets. The doors were upholstered with leather padding. He was tired, having dragged himself through the streets of Moscow the night before. The wandering had exhausted him. He had gone to the addresses of all his old acquaintances but found no one. A prostitute had led him through narrow alleys, and when they approached the steps to her house, a war invalid with no legs was laughing out loud. She begged him, "Don't wake up the kids. They're sleeping!"

After that, Zhillin stood on Red Square watching the fireworks and counting the 300 cannon salutes. If he had the time, he would visit the military hospital where Anna had once worked. Perhaps she was still in Moscow?

Doors opened. You could tell which doors they were when the rays of light shone through when they opened. He saw large writing desks, upholstered armchairs and sofas. The Father of the Nations stood in a gold-framed painting, leaning on a plush red table, his body bent forward. His bluish, watery eyes looked bored. He passed more doors. The innermost guards wore well-pressed military outfits, thin, shiny boots, and revolvers hanging at their sides. A telephone was ringing somewhere. Zhillin saw another portrait of Stalin, this one full-size and walking, with the Spasskaya tower in the background, with its spires and clocks. He was walking on the bridge, wearing a military overcoat whose folds flew in the wind from the river. His left hand was buried in his bosom, and his round cap was pulled down to his eyes. The artist had gone to great trouble to paint the smallest creases in his boots, the slightest shimmer of wool in his coat. His face was delineated tenderly in the most delicate colors reserved for religious icons.

Zhillin had an escort. They left one building and entered another. The floor was paved with square, chiseled stones. His steps could now be heard. He passed more doors. Someone spoke to him, but he did not hear what was said. Zhillin waited near empty tables. His eyes focused on a huge map of central Europe with hundreds of little red and black flags. A door opened suddenly.

The Great Man himself was no longer in a gilded frame. He was standing in the open door. A greenish light shone through. The walls were covered with bright fabrics. The windows were narrow and long, from floor to ceiling. Red carpets covered the floor. Military personnel were whispering, as if to themselves. You could not hear what they were saying, just a rhythmic hum. Zhillin bowed. He knew no one there. Only one person came near, the Great Man, who watched him from the front wall.

No one seemed to know why he had been summoned. Every movement of the bodyguards caused him to shudder. Their faces betrayed nothing, as if a great secret had been sealed inside them. The clock struck, breaking the quiet. It was ten. Every ring was echoed by dozens of other clocks, resulting in a cacophony of bells... one... two... and suddenly a tremor swept through the hall.

The clocks suddenly stopped ringing, as if the tongues had been ripped out of the copper bells. The room was empty at the end, where the door was upholstered with silk. The guards spread out and pressed their palms against their bodies. The Father of the Nations stood in the open door. Zhillin felt his knees buckling under. His hands shook as a sudden fear befell him: terror that he would not be able to stand where he was, that some unknown force would propel him forward.

But his fear dissipated as soon as the Great Man took a few steps, and Zhillin could see him from head to foot. It was a short man with short legs who approached Zhillin, swaying forward on the long narrow carpet. He held one of his hands stiffly at his side, while the other rocked like that of a mannequin. His entire body was reminiscent of a stuffed torso. Perhaps it was because of his clothes, which were sewn and padded by tailors who wished to enhance his appearance just as painters had done with his portraits?

Zhillin noticed that the Great Man of the Kremlin had a coarse face, his jaws and nose peppered with pockmarks, and ears a bit too big for his face. Zhillin's nervousness was gone. His lips stopped quaking, and his temples ceased throbbing. His worldview had been shattered, and he was sorry. He had never expected such a disappointment. He had been better off when he was still waiting. Zhillin was like someone who looks at things or people but does not see them anymore. It was all a blur: parquet floors, turquoise walls, tapestries, rugs, cupolas, doors covered with leather, brocade, epaulets, pleated boots, leather straps, the talking, the laughing. The swirl irritated him. He wanted to observe it all calmly, but his disenchantment grew even worse when he heard the Father of Nations speak in hushed tones, words unfurled like strings of pearls, bathed in an aura of tranquility, and he heard his heavy alien accent—not Russian. A toast was offered to him, and a second later the toast echoed from all those assembled. Zhillin, too, joined in, raising his goblet high.

How had he reached the long, covered table? How had he gotten there with his broken knee? He drank standing up. The mannequin body swam past him. Zhillin stiffened up like a yardstick and the blood drained from his face. The Man from the Kremlin said only a single word to him, offered him his small, cold, slippery hand, then turned right around. It seemed that he did not want to stand too close to the tall, healthy, young, blond Russian, who was a head taller than he. From the side he watched the young officer through inquisitive eyes.

Aftern Zhillin left the Kremlin escorted by a group of military men; he found the highest Medal of Honor pinned to his lapel under his military coat, Hero of the Soviet Union. Nikolai Feodorovich stayed in Moscow for three days. He flew back to Warsaw on the last day, carrying an order for the commander of the Third Belorussian Front. He had new instructions from central headquarters. He had some time before the flight. It had been snowing. He did not find Anna at the hospital on Kaluszskaya Square. The staff had changed several times, and no one remembered that a young woman doctor had worked there a few years earlier. He could easily find the house on Mokhovaya Street where her mother had lived, but something kept him from going there. He was afraid of meeting her.

Zhillin was still feeling the impact of his reception at the Kremlin and the medal that had been bestowed on him. On the one hand, he had seen him, a common man made of flesh and blood, with a coarse face and a stammer, who walked like a cripple. On the other hand, there were all those paintings and statues of the Great Man throughout the land. The sharp contrast was painful to him.

In his youth, in his home village, he had once seen a silvery snake with a brown zigzag marking not far from the granary. A white sat rabbit sat nearby, its red eyes watching the snake raise its head. The rabbit's fur did not even tremble; its glassy eyes did not blink. Only the snake's poison tongue moved. The rabbit was stony, hypnotized by the snake's breathing. Little Zhillin stood to the side, and he could not understand why the rabbit watched the snake's head with such calm. Now, in the Kremlin, standing in the turquoise hall, he remembered the rabbit and the snake.

On the way to the airport he ran into a childhood friend, Aleksei Karasov, whom he had not seen since the start of the war. Zhillin hardly recognized him. Aleksei looked much older. He wore his fur cap to the side, a lock of black hair over part of his forehead. Webs of little wrinkles radiated from the corners of his eyes and mouth.

He said, "Such a meeting! We have to have a drink!"

Zhillin answered, "Drinks are on me! I'm treating for vodka! Good to see you..."

Karasov cut him off: "There's a restaurant near here. Valya works there... Let's go, Nikolai! You've been a success... If only my Nadya could see you now!"

"Nadya? Who's that?"

"What's wrong with you? You used to run after her. You gave me a lot of grief, brother! You bastard! Ha, ha, ha."

He pressed Zhillin's hand, laughing freely. A young waitress hung around Karasov, stopping every so often to lean over and laugh into his black curls.

They drank full glasses and snacked on a beet and cucumber vinaigrette.

"I have to go to the publisher."

"Aleksei, you're still writing poems?" Zhillin laughed and looked at Valya the waitress. Now he remembered his affair with Nadya. That had been in Kazan, two little iron beds in a tiny room. There was a stool in the little space between them. A mandolin hung from a blue strap on the wall. Aleksei had been late. You could hear Nadya's laughing voice in the corridor. Then the little light over his bed stayed on all night. He didn't go to school the next morning. Nadya came home, and all three sat on the beds. Karasov read the poems that he had written the day before. Zhillin left for the military academy. Journals published Karasov's poems. Zhillin had once bought his little book, *Bright Skies*, in a bookshop. Its first poem was dedicated to the Father of the Nations.

"You're wasting your time in Moscow, brother, you and all your medals. This is your time, Zhillin! Reap the corn while it's ripe!" He was a bit tipsy, and his speech was garbled. It wasn't his first drink of the day. Soon I've got to go see that editor with his glasses and his big nose, his nose hairs drooping like those of a horse who sticks his head in a trough and the chaff comesflying out of his mouth.

He went on: "Nikolai, you don't know what it means to lay this stack of poems on the desk of Yakov Moiseyevich. You're doing well. You're a free man. You give orders, while I'm being judged all the time, with every sentence I write. They read meanings into your poems! They dissect them! Their tongues are like a snake's, they're quick and they bite. That Yakov Moiseyevich Gurman! You should see how he handles your notebook in his pudgy fingers as if it contained dynamite! Your fate rests in that big nose of his. First it squirms, then the hair on his dark mole quivers. Drink up! Have another! And boy, are they smooth talkers, like Gypsies! Pretty soon you believe what they say. Russia! Homeland! Soviet Union! Damn it, d'you know how those words sound, coming from citizen Gurman?! He's gonna teach Karasov how to be a Russian?! D'you understand, Nikolai?"

Zhillin listened quietly for a long time. He remembered the Father of the Nations. The words that he had heard in the Kremlin came back to him. An unfortunate country, he thought. Karasov went on: "Foreigners rule the country: Georgians, Jews, Armenians, Ukrainians. They think *they're* the heirs of Kutuzov, of Suvorov, of Pushkin!" He stood up, but it was not clear to him whether he had said those words aloud or had only thought them secretly.

Zhillin sensed panic in Karasov. He seemed to fear Zhillin's silence. How could Karasov know whether he had spoken those words aloud or not? *No, I didn't say anything! It was only in my head.* He had not gone too far. The blond waitress returned: "What's your name, honey?" Valya laughed close to his face. That calmed him down. It meant that nothing had happened.

They walked a bit, not speaking. A car was waiting for Zhillin at Lermontovskaya Square. It would take him to the airport. The weather was good, sunny. The fresh air had a very fine dusting of snow. Karasov had drunk too much. His eyes had opened wide, and his eyelashes darkened. His mother lived in a village not far from Kazan and worked in a *kolkhoz* with empty cattle pens, hungry horses, and pitiful sheep. Nadyezhda, his young wife, lived there now. She was a teacher. They had sent his two sisters to work in the peat fields north of Moscow. In his poem he had addressed the Father of the Nations: "Your word brightens our skies."

Karasov laughed bitterly: "You're flying away and I'm going to Gurman the editor." It was a laugh of self-mockery and grief. They had reached the car, with only a few minutes left. "Why are you silent? Can't you speak to me like a brother?" He held Zhillin's arm. "You're afraid of me, Zhillin?! I'm going to give it all up and go back to the village. In me runs the blood of Russian *muzhiks* and Tatar *khans*. It's bound up with the soil. You think I avoided the war? Well, take a look!" He unbuttoned his jacket and showed him a zigzag scar like lightning. "Got it at Stalingrad. There's still shrapnel, but they can't take it out. Too near the heart. I'm not supposed to drink whiskey. Starting today... I won't last much longer anyway. Some day you'll see my name in a newspaper. It'll be in a black frame. Don't be surprised that I'm talking so frankly. I might as well. They can send me to the white fields... It's all the same to me."

"Aleksei, what are you blabbering? You're drunk! Good times are coming! Berlin will fall soon. Then there'll be big changes here."

Karasov whispered up close: "Nothing's going to change. It'll only get worse. D'you know why?" He looked around. It was noisy on Lermontovskaya Square, with buses, passers-by, and military trucks. Karasov's words burned Zhillin. They hurt, but Zhillin couldn't get away from him.

"D'you know who's at the foundation of our economy? Who makes the uniforms? Who makes our iron, our coal, our timber? Who builds our industries? Who cuts down our forests? Who provides the cannons and ammunition? You don't know?! You're silent?! Well, then I'll tell you. Fifty million prisoners in the labor camps! Those are our slaves who work for nothing, for a bit of watery soup, for a crumb of bread. It's thanks to them that I can write my poems. Ha! Why so pale? Don't get scared! Don't pull away! You don't want to hear it? Don't be afraid, you Hero of the Soviet Union! D'you think they're going to free those millions? You fool! They're going to send millions more! The labor supply in the camps has to be replenished. If they free them all and disperse the camps, that'll be the end of our *Beloved Homeland* and our *Bright Skies!*"

Zhillin felt Karasov's warm hands. The car was full. No one could hear what the two young people were saying in the middle of Lermontovskaya Square. They were both glad that this would be their only meeting. Their roads would part now. Zhillin pitied him, as if he were some contaminated sick person who would bring disaster to all his friends. In his mind he already imagined him lying on a stone floor in a cellar, unshaven, among *kolkhozniks* and criminals. His one little published book would disappear, and his name would be erased from everyone's memory. No one would remember him. Only his old mother would kneel in front of icons and whisper his name.

When the airplane soared, all that remained below were quadrilaterals and triangles.

Moscow was a crisscross of streets, squares, and canals. Clouds hung over Moscow, soft and puffy. Zhillin was tired. He could still smell the whiskey breath of poor Karasov, who was already just a shadow of himself. His brain swirled—Yakov Moiseyevich Gurman, Aleksei, the partisans in Minsk, the Moscow train terminals, the Jews, the face of Anna again, the officers at central headquarters, the silent soldiers, that night in a Prussian village, General Chernyakhovsky, the fog over Moscow, the quadrilaterals. It was a tangle without beginning and without end.

Zhillin wished to get to the headquarters of the Third Belorussian Front as soon as possible. The offensive was proceeding with unusual speed. On March 19th the enemy's units were forced to the edge of the Baltic Sea. The German divisions were squeezed into an area twenty-five-kilometers long and ten-kilometers wide. The weather cleared up, permitting the Soviet air force to begin its onslaught. More than 80,000 German troops and officers were wiped out, and more than 50,000 were taken prisoner. Thousands drowned when Soviet airplanes oparrePolishened fire as they tried to swim across the Frisches Haff Lagoon.

He read the military communiqués very carefully. His army was on the march, and he was up in the clouds. He just had to be there. The Hero medal on his chest called to him. How would the front-line officers react to it? What would the mud-drenched, exhausted soldiers think, they who carried the burden of the war? They who lay in the trenches under a hailstorm of bullets?

It had happened in Prussia. Zhillin had himself seen a Soviet tank throw its weight against a six-wheeled German Panzer Rena. The Panzer Rena burst into flames. A column of German armored cars came to a halt and the Germans jumped out into the ditches. The tank opened fire. The tank commander was called in to headquarters that evening. He was exhausted and black with filth. His name was Aaron Levitin. Why had Zhillin suddenly remembered him?

The new orders from central headquarters would be read out to the regiment. Zhillin would be honored, but he himself wanted it to be over, to be left in peace. He would announce: "650 tanks, 3500 cannons, and a huge quantity of loot have come into our hands." That operation had been planned by the general who was killed by an unknown bullet after he had prepared the whole attack.

Zhillin looked out the little airplane window. It was night, but the clouds below were still bright.

Back then, that night had been foggy. They had drank from crystal goblets. Another drink to victory, to our women and children, to the powerful Party. The commander of the Front had downed four goblets. Just one more... Then Zhillin had raised the sparkling goblet high, his hand shaking. The whiskey might spill. Even now in the airplane he again felt that strange trembling. He had known that it would be the commander's last drink. His last! Zhillin had announced: "A toast to the man who planned this victory over the German army," then he stopped short and took a deep breath. "To the Father of the Nations!" And the officers shouted "Hurrah!" The general had smiled a little scornful smile. But it had calmed Zhillin. It had eased his conscience.

Now, high above the Earth, he could distance himself from that night. He was afraid of no one now. He did not have to account for his actions to anyone. There was a reason for everything that had happened. He knew what was good for the homeland and what was bad. He had needed to weave through a labyrinth with hidden paths. Those paths would lead to the light of day. A crimson, red day! He could not rest. A force impelled him. He would push on, not like Aleksei Karasov, who would be crushed under roaring wheels.

Russia was the scene of the mass migration of its peoples. Just as the waters of a river that has overrun its banks—flooding the fields, the meadows, the roads, and the walking paths—begins to return to its original river bed, so, too did people begin to return to their former homes, which they had abandoned with the invasion of the Germans. Hundreds of trains were sent westward every day from all over Russia. They were being sent to bring back war booty from the occupied territories before the local people dragged it off or marauding looters tried to take it. Freight trains rushed westwards empty. They were sent from junctions everywhere in Russia, and refugees trying to go home were massing at those train stations.

The government treated those homeless people decently for a variety of reasons. First of all, the western regions were bereft of a labor supply, and they were needed in the desolated villages and ruined cities. In parts of western Ukraine and Belarus, there were not even enough hands to harvest the crops. Soldiers had to be brought in from the front. Secondly, it would be dangerous to permit a vacuum to exist between the homeland and the front lines—a no man's land where the dregs of Vlasov's regiment could wreak havoc, along with the Kaminshaks,[2] the

---

2   Brigade of Bronislav Kaminski, who fought with the SS against Soviets, and killed Poles and Jews.

Bandera[3] gang, the Bulba gang,[4] as well as Soviet deserters. Third, those areas were needed to provide food both for the soldiers at the front, very close by, and for the rest of the Soviet Union, which was suffering from starvation. Since all the wagon trains in the country were mobilized into long trains of hundreds of empty cars, the order was given to use them to transport the evacuees.

And that was the beginning of the mass migration in reverse. But everywhere that the unfortunates had fled, thousands of them who could not go home remained in the far-off villages of Kazakhstan, in the mines of the Urals, on the shores of lake Baikal, in the ditches of Sverdlovsk, in Komi, in Bashkiria—just as a river that overflows its banks leaves behind little pools of water everywhere, and some of it seeps into the earth. Some of them had been deported to internal exile, locked in prisons, enslaved in labor camps, or ordered into labor battalions in industries whose production was needed for the war effort. Shattered families—consisting of the elderly, the children, the women, the invalids, dragged themselves across Russia for weeks and months. The long troop trains often waited on sidetracks waiting for locomotives or an opening. Hungry and thirsty, people took shelter in old freight wagons. They walked miles to reach villages where they might buy food. Sometimes elderly farmers would approach the wagons to sell baskets of food, and chaos would erupt over a bread roll. A small bit of yellowed sugar would be bartered for a slice of bread, salt for a cooked potato, a piece of cloth for a herring.

And at the same time, special troop trains rushed along the "Green Road" without stop.

It was called that because all the train signals were always green for them. The troop trains carrying returning evacuees had to wait on sidetracks until they had passed. The masses of returnees were like herds of sheep starving on snow-covered fields that walk slowly, huddled together until they reach spacious green pastures. Then they can spread out and rest. That was how it was with the returning refugees.

From Belarus on, the trains ran half-empty to the German cities. All kinds of other vehicles also followed the path of the trains without

---

3   Ukrainian nationalist Stepan Bandera, some of whose followers massacred Poles and Jews.
4   Ukrainian nationalist Taras "Bulba"-Borovets, whose followers murdered Jews.

stopping. They sped through the small stations, distrustful and scornful, leaving behind station workers and police, surprised and sleepy. If at the start of the war, when the Germans were at the gates of Moscow, the roads of Russia were like the clogged blood vessels of a giant whose blood has stopped flowing, now the roads were like the hot arteries of a roused bear who just woke up after his long hibernation, fully ready and galvanized to attack and roar for joy.

During those March days in the trenches, Menakhem grew friendly with a Jewish soldier who had just been mobilized in Volhynia. He had left Olyevsk at the start of the war. His name was Dobrusz and he was fifteen at the time, working as a shepherd in a *kolkhoz* driving the herd towards the east. They had marched the sheep across Ukraine, through Kuban, all the way to the other side of the Volga River. At night Dobrusz told Menakhem all about his wanderings through Ukraine, its villages and rivers, and about his trips across fields in a wagon covered with the hides of dead horses and sheep. He had spent the winters in *kolkhozes* and summers searching for pasture land in the most remote regions of Kuban. The herd dwindled. They had to pay off the local villages with some of their sheep, and they had to secretly slaughter others in exchange for bread. More than half the herd had died from hunger or disease. New ones were born, but when they returned home only a very small flock was left.

Dobrusz found no Jews left when he returned to his village. Armed gangs were swarming in the woods nearby. Some of them had come to the village and gotten drunk with the peasants. "Run away from here," urged the shepherd elder. "They're slaughtering your people." The gangs had attacked Soviet patrols and murdered the local Soviet activists one at a time. The Soviets punished the farmers and searched for their sons hiding in the woods. Dobrusz went to the train station, about fifty viorsts away. He had brought the herd back home. Now he could leave. But where should he go? Should he try to find Jews? Their language was unfamiliar by now. He only knew the language of the farmers and the cries of his sheep. Dobrusz was tanned; his jaws sunburned, with a head of thick black curls, all the way down his neck. His eyebrows were closely knitted. His voice had become strong and coarse from living outside in the fields, and his hands as tough as chestnuts.

Dobrusz stayed at the train station for two days. He watched people closely, peering into their eyes, trying to guess whether they were Jews. Trains came through with locked wagons and open platforms. There were wagons covered with tarps, trains sending soldiers to the front, and trains with the wounded coming back. Young Dobrusz, now homeless, wandered among the cars. "Take me," pleaded Dobrusz, speaking a farmer's Ukrainian to an officer.

Then he approached the military commander of the station, who ordered him to go back to his village near Olyevsk: "You'll be mobilized from there. Your time will come." But Dobrusz had no interest in going back to a home that was no longer his home. There was a short, stooped farmer standing in the station, a whip in his hand, his fur cap pulled all the way down. Only one puffy eyelid was visible. The other was shut tight. The night before, a Soviet disciplinary patrol had come to his home. The patrol leader had given him three days to turn over his son: "After three days we're deporting you and your family to the land of the white bears. One of your sons is in the woods. We know it. You bring him food, while those gangs attack us." That was what he had said to him.

It was now the third day. They were going to load him, his wife, and little children onto train cars and ship them to Siberia. He had gone to the woods, but his son would not give himself up because he did not want to serve in the Red Army, although there was an amnesty for the people hiding in the woods. His Afanas would have left the forest, but he felt bad for his father and his farm. The leaders in the woods said: "We'll burn down your home and murder your Afanas if he goes with the Soviets." Death was looming both from the Russians and from the gangs in the woods.

So the little, shriveled farmer wandered around, looking with his one watery eye at the long trains and at the people, feeling his world getting smaller and smaller, so that he no longer had a place in it. His poor little horse waited in front of the station. It was noon, and a very long train pulled in. Young soldiers jumped down, all smiles, energetic, wearing light uniforms, and talking loudly. One of them came over and asked, "Little father, d'you have any *makhorka* tobacco to sell? The old man shrugged his shoulders and opened his closed eye. He pulled a withered pouch out of his pants pocket and poured some homemade tobacco into the soldier's palms, "Take it, my son." He shuddered as he said "my son." If only it were! He wanted to weep, but he could not. Farmers do not have tears for weeping. They only weep when they are drunk, and a quiet joy wells up from their belly to their chest, and from there to their eyes, and tears pour out. They wipe away those tears of joy with their warm gnarled fingers.

Dobrusz passed by just then, as he was walking along the train cars searching for someone to help him. The military commander of the station blocked his way and said, "Young man, go home!" The farmer perked up his ears. He suddenly threw down his whip and began to run towards them, the way farmers run after horses that are trampling fields of rye. He threw himself on Dobrusz, embracing him and sobbing, "My son! My one and only! The apple of my eye, come home! You'll be all right with us! I'll give you the best we have! Come home, my one and only! My son, I've been looking for you for weeks! Thought you were dead! Oh dear God, my sole support!"

Dobrusz could feel the farmer's hot tears on his cheeks, his moist lips, and bristly whiskers. He stopped talking and wanted to tear himself away from the strong, gnarled hands of the farmer. But the boy's silence only stirred the farmer's fatherly instincts even more. He now turned to the crowd around him, "Oh, good people, look! My son is back! Let's go home! Let's tell the authorities that you've come home. Dear boy! My sonny boy!" His saliva and tears, his warm breath, and his hands tight around Dobrusz startled him out of his initial shock, and he tried to break loose.

He struggled quietly until he managed to squirm out of the farmer's arms. They stood silently, panting. Dobrusz looked at him cautiously. The farmer approached him again, like a playful kitten, his hands outstretched and beckoning. He bowed very low, as if before a holy icon. He tore off his cap and warmly embraced the boy's legs: "Come home! I'll die without you! Come, my angel! Is this how you return your father's love? Sweet Jesus!" The station police and the soldiers from the train called to Dobrusz: "Go home, boy! Why are you dawdling out here? You fool, obey your father!"

If he did go with the farmer, he would have a room, a bed, as much bread as he wanted. But he feared the farmer's obtuse insistence and he resented his coercive hands on his body. He tore away again, and yelled hoarsely, "Leave me alone, old man!" And with that he struck him in the face with his fist. A trickle of blood slowly ran down his face to the corners of his mouth and into his prickly yellow beard. The sight of the blood stiffened Dobrusz's resistance, and he hit him again. The man fell to the ground, moaning, "People! See how my own son beats his father?! See? Oh, Jesus!"

The locomotive echoed his howling. The wheels turned faster and faster. Soldiers looked out the windows. The train sped towards the front. Dobrusz ran along the track after it, and when he reached the last wagon, he jumped on. He saw the farmer in the distance, reaching out his arms, "My son... See, people?... My son has left for the front."

And that was how Dobrusz had come to be in Menakhem's regiment. And now they were sitting in a trench, where he related his experiences.

Zhillin kept waking up. The night was pitch black, and he was rocking between the clouds. There was a red eye over him. Who was watching him in that nighttime roar? He could see garnet boulders through the window. Suspended between sleep and half-sleep, his childhood came to him: the north country, somewhere near Novogrodsk, on the banks of a cold, rolling sea with chunks of floating ice, a land of roaring rivers and stormy lakes, dense with forests and tundra as far as the eye could see.

The dark garnet cliffs that he saw on the horizon were clouds in the March night. He was in a plane taking him to the front. Its steady hum rocked him to sleep. He saw the cradle hanging in the humble cabin. Frost had painted white thorns on the little windows. His mother rocked the cradle that hung from the ceiling on a rope. The walls were beams of raw pinewood. Green moss filled the spaces between the beams. She sang an old Russian lullaby: "What rustles without wind? What's always green without roots? Turbulent rivers rustle without wind! Boulders grow without roots! And pine trees are always green!" They were coming, those good, gentle, snowy dreams, to drive away the darkness, the shadows that covered his northern heart.

Zhillin's father had joined a Red unit fighting against General Wrangel.[5] He returned to get his family a few years later, and the cradle remained in that empty in that faraway snow-laden cabin. Then Zhillin

---

5   Pyotr Nikolayevich Wrangel, a tsarist officer who led the White Army against the Soviets in southern Russia during the Civil War.

had spent years in Kazan, and later at the military academy, and then came the war. He fought the Finns in Karelia, and the German bastards right after that. Flying in the clouds, he saw it all again. He would have gladly hunted in the mossy tundras with a rifle. He would have gladly gazed forever at the turgid rivers running across forest glades.

Who was it who had pulled him into the stony courtyard of the Kremlin, among the cupolas, the columns, the bright marble steps? Who had instilled that fear in him, that awful terror? Where was the plane going? Zhillin could not tell which direction. Was it to the northern fields, back to the garnet boulders, to the tundras? There he would be thrown onto the mossy banks of the northern sea. It was indeed a strange world! How long had it been since General Chernyakhovsky had invited to lunch the commanders of the Polish partisan units who had helped liberate Vilna?[6] Not one of those Poles came back. A year later the very same general had been invited for lunch—with whiskey—and....

But Zhillin *had* returned from the Kremlin. Now he was flying in a plane, flying to the front. Nothing would happen to him. The day before, someone from central headquarters had said, "Nikolai Feodorovich, why do your hands shake when you raise up your goblet? It's a bad sign, that you have a bad conscience." He had laughed along. That was a pompous fellow! He went on: "You know what the Father of the Nations told me once? You don't? Listen and remember it. Stalin, our commander-in-chief said, 'I choose my enemies myself. D' you understand?' Remember, Zhillin! Those were important words! Repeat them to yourself a thousand times. You need to choose your enemies yourself. Don't wait for them to choose *you* for an enemy. *You* decide who is your enemy!"

No stars could be seen, only puffy clouds. The red eye of the sun was blinding. Something always happened after every ball at the Kremlin. Someone disappeared. Right after the last goblet was drunk, and everyone was tired, and drunkenness was strong, and heads were throbbing, and tongues were loosened, that was when the Father of the Nations woke up. The lethargy in his body wore off, and his piercing little eyes grew animated.

---

6   In 1944 Gen. Ivan Chernyakhovsky invited leaders of the Polish Armia Krajowa to meet with him. They and thousands of others were arrested, many were executed, others deported to Siberia or forced into the Red Army.

Zhillin had once heard a blind farmer in a rural fair in Murmansk sing a song about Kniaz Dmitry. Now the first stanza came back to him. It began, "In his good city... in his Kremlin." The man with the empty eye sockets told of Count Dmitry, who had planned a great ball and invited all the *boyars*. He also invited Domna, a *boyar*'s daughter, to be his love. But when she saw the count's ugly face and heard his alien Karelian language, she disappeared... But he outwitted her and had her head cut off, "So that no one else will have you, and I won't have to listen to your mockery and hatred."

It was now the time to cut off all ties. The man in the Kremlin understood that. The world was still shrouded in the smoke of conflagration. It was scarred with trenches and barbed wire. The Earth was falling apart and the skies had come down low, right over the heads of suffering humankind. Who would even hear a single gunshot in the back, down in a cellar, or even on the front lines? "I choose my enemies myself."

It was not a dream. It was reality. An awful truth. The proof? Night was night. The plane was flying over Prussia, and was now in range of the searchlights, making it as bright as a star. It flew down, sinking along with everything else. Even the red eye of the rising sun.

They had landed. Zhillin walked through damp fields. The airport was huge, with many camouflaged aircraft. The soil was soft and yielding. A sharp wind, undoubtedly from the Baltic Sea, woke him up. Sleep had left him. The dreams were gone. What was more real, the bright lights of the turquoise hall in the Kremlin or the little candles that he remembered in front of the icons in his mother's village house? The man in the Kremlin with the mannequin body or the face of the blind farmer in the market in Murmansk? The drunken chorus of toasts with raised goblets or the trembling of his own lips in the dark? Who could know whether tomorrow someone might show up and tell him, "Zhillin, I've selected you as my enemy, because I choose my enemies myself."

He stopped suddenly, as if a crippling pain had gripped his heart. It probably lasted only a second, or even one hundredth of a second, and then it vanished. He grew angry with himself for that terror, angry at his own weakness, with the black night. He began piling blistering curses that fell on deaf ears in the night: "Devils without horns! Filthy bastards!

What a God-forsaken swamp!" He looked for the orderly who should have been waiting for him. But he only saw shadows in front of him and behind him. Where were the people? Only shadows flitted around him in that stinking land of the German bastards! "Hey! Show yourselves!" he ordered angrily.

But all his cursing and yelling were meant for no one but himself, to build up his own courage. He was trying to dispel the nightmares in the airplane, the spider's web of terror and the spider bouncing at its center with its blood diamond. He wanted to wake up the real Zhillin, the Hero of the Soviet Union.

In the distance artillery was pounding without stop. Searchlight beams scoured the ground, then soared up, shattering the blackness of the skies. Zhillin thought, "It's good that the shooting is far away." He finally found the ordinance and his car. He was suddenly glad, for some unknown reason. It was as if that joy had swept away his sudden terror. The auto flew over the soaking Prussian soil, along secondary country roads. He saw twisted willow trunks, fences made of branches, and a small, dark roadside niche for the Virgin Mary. At every crossroads stood iron or stone crucifixes. Zhillin wanted to talk to the driver, but his words were drowned by the screeching of the wheels and the splashing through the puddles. The car was now on a highway. They came to a guardhouse. "Halt!"

A flashlight glided over the car roof and stopped in Zhillin's face. The soldier suddenly froze. Zhillin laughed to himself. The car continued. He asked the orderly a question but did not wait for answer. Zhillin talked and cursed good-naturedly, lightheartedly. He felt renewed. They stopped at another guardhouse. This was now headquarters. He would be drinking German wine again out of medieval crystal goblets. The tables were already set. They were waiting for him. Plenty of wine was left in the cellars of the Prussian palaces. There would be enough until they had occupied Berlin.

He stood at the head of the table. His hands did not shake now. They toasted, "To the Father of the Nations! Hurrah! To the homeland!"

"How many have we drunk already?"

Then he suddenly saw him again, painted in a heavy frame, the man in the Kremlin himself, stern, piercing. Zhillin downed the whole goblet in one gulp. The old terror crept back like a cat. He wanted to strangle that black cat, and he threw the goblet, smashing it against a marble column.

"Hurrah!" he screamed at the top of his lungs.

That was echoed a hundredfold, as dozens of officers smashed their goblets, too. The orderlies stumbled around, picking up the shattered crystal.

It was a damp and cold March dawn. Menakhem was bundled in his military overcoat. Little Dobrusz dozed near him. Zipunov was awake, gazing into the distance. His face looked like a water stain spreading on the scarlet-gray soil. If not for the war, Zipunov would be waking up now in his cabin, looking down from the bed on top of the stove at the little blue windowpanes. Was it daylight yet? He would hear the creaking of the gates and the bleating of the sheep being driven down the broad street. In the evenings he would sit on the bench outside rolling a cigarette of homemade *makhorka* tobacco. But now he was like a plant that a sharp plow has ripped out of the earth along with its root ball. The plant lies at the edge of the field, not able to grow in the earth but not completely withered. The tiny bits of soil tangled in its dense mat of roots and the morning dew keep it from dying.

How will the farmer Zipunov be able to readjust to his home on his own soil after the whirlwind of war has driven him over desolate roads? His hands would no longer know how to hold a plow. He thought that the blood that had been spilled in the fields would make poppy flowers sprout among the rye. At such moments he prayed to Jesus to forgive the sins he had committed on Polish soil. He gazed mournfully at the sky and was struck by fear. When that fear passed, he felt hollow, and the slightest noise rattled him. It was as if he filled up the trench, sat apart, stayed in the corners, and listened intently. He mumbled to himself, unintelligibly. Was he just humming, repeating what others had said? Or were these stifled sounds choking him? He grew forlorn if a superior looked at him, shrugging his shoulders, turning his head away. His throat seemed to sink into his chest, and his hands were twisted. He never said yes or no.

It was the kind of moan that could be interpreted as one wished: acquiescence, depression, fatigue, sleepiness. It took quite a while to get used to Zipunov's garbled speech. Only at night, in the trenches, when he was eye to eye with Menakhem or Dobrusz, did he liven up and loosen his tongue. And when the troops near him were dozing he would take little watches out of his bags and play with their long golden chains. Sometimes he would wind them up and gaze at the phosphorous gleam of the numbers. He would often hide deep down in the trench and enjoy the brilliance of a gemstone. He did all of this out of sight. He would often wake up and feel with his fingers for the cloth bag on his hairy chest. Then he would laugh quietly into his chest, his mocking peasant laugh.

Dobrusz had a childish face with a little dark fuzz on his upper lip. He was indifferent to the cold at night. In his dreams he was again on the roads of Ukraine. He was angry with the cattle and the sheep. Even now he remembered the distinctive bleating of each of his sheep. He carried the scent of sheep wool, and in his breath was the scent of reeds in the wind. Menakhem once told him, "Dobrusz, you're a Jew. Always remember that!"

"A Jew?" Dobrusz was surprised. "A Jew?"

He crouched down and looked at Menakhem suspiciously: 'Why do you need to remind me that I'm a Jew? It's better if I don't remember it. It scares me. It's like telling me, 'Dobrusz, you're mortally ill. Dobrusz, you're going to die.'"

Menakhem leaned away, feeling tears well up in his eyes. He was devastated by Dobrusz's words. He avoided him for the rest of the day. Dobrusz began to speak when they met again for guard duty at the lake: "From the Horyn River to the Don they kept asking me, 'Are you a Jew?' I hate it when they do that! I wanted to jump down their throats! Whose business is it what Dobrusz is?! I want to talk to them like equals, and they interrogate me?! That makes me nothing! That makes me no one! Like wind, a tree, a piece of earth! This one wants to know so he can pity me. That one wants to hate me and to kill me. I hate them all. After the war I'll go back to the Horyn or to the Sluch River. I'll find myself a farm girl and be like everyone else. Then I won't be Dobrusz anymore. I'll be a real farmer. I'll raise cattle, I'll pull barges on the river, I'll get drunk in the taverns. A farmer once told me how the Germans murdered my parents. I've come here to get revenge. Why are you looking at me like that? I don't care who you are. All I care is that you're at the front like me. But to you it *does* make a difference. *You* have to know who Dobrusz is. Why do you need to know? Tell me!"

Menakhem stroked the lock of hair on Dobrusz's childish face and smiled, while tears stuck in his throat. They spoke no more of it. But Dobrusz did not leave his side from that day on. He knelt down and rolled his own cigarettes. They smoked and gazed to the west, towards Berlin.

The cannons began blasting early one morning. The air was shattered. The booming came echoing in deafening waves. And those echoes were ripped by the roar of aircraft. They flew in formations of nine planes, heavy bombers, in tight symmetry, wave after wave. And at the side of the bombers Jaeger planes swarmed like windblown birds from under the clouds, flying west. Was this the final offensive on Berlin? The night before, the Soviet radio commentator had said: "We have three possibilities. We can attack Berlin frontally. We can go around the capital from the north through Stettin or come from the south. Or, the third option—attack from all directions at the same time."

"Mikhail," wrote Anna. "Why are you silent? It's been a long time since I've had a letter from you. Mikha! Misha! Where are you right now when I'm writing to you late at night? It's so desolate in Praga on the Vistula. The hospital is overflowing. The streets are dense with foreigners. I went to the Jewish Committee to search for the names of your relatives in the lists of survivors. Last week I gathered up a group of Jewish children, homeless, aged eight to fourteen. I'm working to get a home for them in Otwock. In the meantime Yekaterina Yurievna has made them a home in a little apartment not far from the hospital. Our hospital kitchen is feeding them. My mom cried for joy when she heard that you're still alive. She wrote to me: 'Don't lose him again.' I worry about her health. She's lonely on Mokhovaya Street. She sits in her chair for days and listens to the racket that her daughters-in-law make. It breaks my heart when I think about her. Only the grandchildren are friendly. I just can't wait for Berlin to fall! I'm afraid at night, I'm afraid when I hear steps coming to my little room. This is a hard time for me. But I'm ready for this meeting. I'm sorry now that I didn't tell you everything. It's painful to me that I can't talk to the kids in their own language. It would be good if you were here with us. There's a girl here, Hanusz, and a Rokhele, and a Janusz. When I look into their faces I feel that I'm one of you."

"Mikhail, I can hear the wind raging and the rain pouring down the windowpanes. Be strong, Mikha, push on push on! My prayers are with you. We may have to leave Praga. Yesterday was a hard day. But I don't want to remind you of me in the operating hall. You didn't like me then. I know it. You're afraid of the doctor in me. You'd rather imagine me as a nurse. They say that distance brings with it forgetfulness and leads people to regain their calm when relations are strained with their nearest and dearest. Is it true? I stand in the white hall every day. I hold the lives of the wounded in my hands, even when they shake a little. I want to cry because I'll never be the same Anna again. Maybe that's good. Change is the best sign that we're not finished yet. I hope my words of fear and premonition don't disturb you. Perhaps I should tell you everything now. No. It's very late now. You, Misha, Mikhail, have a peaceful night. Your Anna."

Menakhem was ordered to report to regimental headquarters. Over several days the big German village had been transformed into a huge military camp. Spacious rooms housed the various headquarters. Repair shops for freight trucks, tanks, and armored cars were set up in the brick barns. The village was teeming with liaison officers, military engineers, and medics. A long line of supply cars carrying weapons still stretched across the stone bridge. Menakhem ran into a group of German prisoners on the street. Zipunov and Sgt. Sergei Orlov were guarding them. Zipunov was quite cheerful; he would surely discover something good in their pockets. They would surrender their watches. Menakhem perused the prisoners for a long time. He searched each face individually, then he saw their backs soaked in mud. Some trudged barefoot, unbuttoned, their tailcoats in tatters, unshaven, their hair disheveled. Others marched effortlessly, heads held high as if in a victory parade. They passed a wrecked Focke-Wulf bomber brough down in the marketplace. One of its wings pointed straight up to the sky, and someone had clumsily written on it with black paint: "To Berlin! To the Reichstag!" The German prisoners detoured around the wreckage of the plane.

Guards stood in the large courtyard at the iron gate of an aristocratic manor. Menakhem smoothed out the gray-green jacket, pulled the straps tight, and untied the hand grenades from them. He left them with the guards. There were signs hanging everywhere on the stone fence, on the walls, on boards banged into the soil: "Mines!" "Mines!" Other signs had names and indicated locations: "This way to Volodya," "Yekaterina is fifty meters away." Menakhem looked for Yekaterina and saw low buildings whose walls were hung with wild grape vines. He came to another guard post, with inside steps leading to corridors. There were machine guns at the entrance and several soldiers with calm faces. A sign over the door read, "Remember! You are on enemy territory!" Menakhem stopped at the open door and thought of going back. But it was already late. A freckled officer came up to him. A picture of Stalin, not framed, hung slightly crooked, as if temporarily. On the table lay a bomb fragment used for an ashtray. The whole room was carpeted, and the walls were bedecked with silk hangings.

"Sit down," said the officer. His tone of voice did not suit the freckled face and the heavy body. Thin sounds came from his throat like cut glass. He took a silver cigarette case out of his bag and laid it on the table. "Want a smoke?" Then he opened a drawer, pulled out some papers and leafed through them.

Menakhem had realized right away that he was not in the operations department of headquarters, but in the Special Section. He knew it from the open door, from the quiet, from the emptiness of the room, the lack of military maps. He could tell from the lines in the officer's face that this was not a frontline soldier. He was from the NKVD, highly suspicious of everyone. Invisible threads connected this man to every trench, every position on the front line.

"Yes, yes, yes, Mikhail Isaacovitch..."

It seemed like he had not decided how to begin the interrogation. "Yes, yes, yes" was just a tactic to gain time.

How Menakhem knew all this already! You couldn't know how they would do it, you just couldn't know. They had a thousand ways to do it, each one different, but all leading to the same black end. He looked at this well-rested officer with hidden scorn, the kind of scorn that only a soldier who is just back from the advance point of the front line—and was wounded more than once—feels for a man in headquarters who reeks of eau-de-cologne. The fear and depression that Menakhem had felt at the Vistula vanished. Just stepping onto German soil had filled him with assurance and boldness. Here in Germany he was face to face with the enemy, in the lair of the beast. Back in Poland he had been up against not only Germans and Vlasov's army, but part of the Polish population, too. That was depressing. Here he faced only one enemy, the Germans. Back then his enemies were massive. They had all been against him: his neighbours at home, the Ukrainians, the Lithuanians, the various marauding gangs. Even the night itself and the soil of his own village had betrayed him.

Menakhem did not have enough contempt and hatred in him for such a big world. His hatred now was concentrated on one target, Berlin. The unfriendly soil on which he trod gave him strength. He strode across it with his head held high. Here he was the victor. No one would be able to take from him his part in the victory that he deserved.

Menakhem's voice was loud and clear: "I hear you."

"I'm very pleased to meet you, Mikhail Isaacovitch. My name is Sabayev, Vasil Sabayev." The officer struck a match and offered it to Menakhem. "I'm surprised that we haven't met before. I've heard of you."

Menakhem smiled at the sudden switch from his use of the informal "you" to the formal. "Oh, you've heard of me? I guess my reputation precedes me." He laughed and it was obviously a sarcastic laugh, as if to say: "You, look closely at my clothes, at my whole appearance! And you'll know that I'm wise to your tricks! Just wait till Berlin falls. Then maybe the spider's web that your Special Section has woven will fall apart. Maybe things will change, and you'll become decent people again, if there's still a tiny spark of humanity left in your souls. You'll have to take up the plow again." That was what Menakhem thought as he looked at the officer from the Special Section.

Sabayev said, "You're an artist, right? Why don't you draw anymore? I remember your drawings in the army newspaper."

Menakhem thought, "You sly fox, you're real glib with the smooth words." But he just said, "I'm occupied with other things now."

"I just wanted to get to know you, that's all. Someone here mentioned your name, so I wanted to see you with my own eyes. It was an opportunity. Tell me, please…" And here *Politkommissar* Sabayev was choosing his words carefully, then he stopped short. He shuffled the papers in his drawer and pushed the ashtray around on the table. He continued: "Were you at the gates of Moscow and also at the Vistula? Do you remember anyone in command then? Perhaps we have some friends in common?"

"My commanders? I don't remember them clearly... Oh, yes I do remember one." Menakhem raised his eyes to the picture hanging on the wall and nodded to the Father of the Nations.

Sabayev grew serious. His deep-set red-gray eyes turned icy: "Why are you protecting your commanders? Maybe you really don't remember them. That's a bad sign. You were very active in the war. I believe you do remember Nikolai Feodorovich Zhillin, the Hero of the Soviet Union. Right?"

Menakhem turned white.

"Well, I can see that you remember him. He was here and sends you greetings. That is all. You can go, Mikhail Isaacovitch!"

Chapter Three

Prussia, the end of March 1945.

The train tracks and the terminals were crammed with cars from Belgium, Holland, France, along with those from München, Frankfurt, Karslruhe and Berlin. Train bridges and water towers had been blown up. Civilians wearing a dark square on their chest with the word "East" in white lettering were Russian citizens who had been taken from their homes to work in Prussian factories and farms. The roads were scarred with bomb craters and littered at every step with ruined trucks, buses, suitcases, and the carcasses of dead horses whose backsides had been hacked for their meat. You could hear the mournful bellowing of cows that had not been milked for a long time in abandoned farms. Runaway horses ran wild through the meadows, their manes unkempt. Some of them dragged broken harnesses, broken wagon shafts, or wheels. Tens of thousands of Germans wandered with backpacks, the women carrying their children. Some of the men had barrel necks and beer bellies. All of them wore a white armband, the symbol of surrender.

Germran deserters who had quickly changed into civilian clothes mixed in with evacuees. They walked past the farmers' wagons, their heads lowered. "Berlin is burning! Berlin has been bombed without stop for five days! The Gestapo is running the government!" Those were the reports in German on Allied radio. The headquarters of German land forces in Zossen was bombed on March 15th by several squadrons, causing severe destruction. General Krebs and some of his staff were badly wounded. The Germans issued orders to the *Gauleiters*[1] not to allow anything of importance to fall into the hands of the enemy, not anything significant. They must destroy whatever they could not take with them. Bormann ordered evacuation from areas under threat to the central region of the country.

The German "Vistula armies" had already retreated back to the other side of the Oder River. All that remained of their days of triumph was the name "Vistula." General Busse, commander of the Ninth German Army on the Oder, also gave the order to retreat before they were completely encircled. During the last week of March, the Americans crossed the Rhine River and were moving on Darmstadt and Frankfurt am Main. On the eastern front, there was bitter fighting over Danzig, and the Soviets renewed their attack on Küstrin. At the end of March the American General Patton's tanks rolled into Frankfurt.

The German military base in Danzig was destroyed. Their army was still holding out in Königsberg, but their fate was sealed. In Danzig there were endless columns of German prisoners, stretching for kilometers, with all kinds of faces: dull, sharp-featured, chubby, dandified, obsequious, pleading, calm, boyish, dissolute, arrogant, farmers' faces, reserved, gray, desolate, tough, stone-faced.

They wore all sorts of uniforms, including those of the *Volkssturmer* and the black jackets and sailors' caps of the navy's infantry. The "brave" Prussian bastards had not obeyed General Weiss's order, "to fight to the last man." They were marching in their own country and were guarded by troops with machine guns from Tula and Perm, from villages on the Volga River and Lake Baikal. Major Heinrich Landwitz marched at the head of the prisoners.

"They wanted to take over the East?! So let them stay in the East! Don't let one German leave here alive!"

"Where is *Gauleiter* Forster?"

A captured officer shrugged his shoulders: "Don't know him, Mr. Russian."

"You're lying!"

Maj. Gen. Vladimir Leibovich insisted on finding the *Gauleiter*. He had a special score to settle. He was Jewish. His grandfather and father had worked all their lives in the Goldenberg paper factory in Odessa. His father's name was Leib, and he had had nine children. All the others had been murdered. Vladimir Leibovich was going to find the *Gauleiter*.

The Germans put up a desperate fight at the Oder River. Their defenses were impressive: five rows of barbed wire; six lines of artillery; innumerable trenches and anti-tank ditches; huge fortifications, mortars, cannons. But Zhukov's army was unrelenting. A few days later, Zhukov rode around the fortress from north to south and established a stranglehold of steel around it.

Even the smallest movement of the Germans led to losses and defeat, just as a wild horse which, tracked by an experienced horseman, with a noose already around its neck, cannot stop its flight, tightens the rope more and more every time it tries to tear itself away until it can no longer breathe. Then the wild animal falls on its back, baring its teeth in white foam, and its eyes full of blood. The German high command was like that horse, unable to control its rage and stop in time. Its destiny was doomed.

It was springtime in God's world. New grass sprouted along the war roads. Under the yellow rusted iron wreckage colorful little field flowers were germinating. Next to a wattle fence a tree was already decked out in splendid white. The days were bright and clear, the nights were moonlit. Only the Germans wore mournful faces. They prowled at night on side streets, avoiding the highways and the trains, crossing through bushes, sleeping in barns, foraging in abandoned houses and empty cellars for food and civilian clothes. They roamed around alone or in small groups. Complete strangers became fast friends at the first encounter. Defeat and their terror brought them close. Behind a picket fence, in the courtyard of a farm, the body of a German hung from the swinging gate. Slave laborers from "the East" had hung him. Groups of Germans walked through Prussia, trying to reach the Oder River, and to go west from there. Among them, too, were military auxiliaries, traitors who had dutifully served with the German army. Sometimes they attacked each other, with shootings breaking out at night. They robbed civilians wandering on the road that wore white armbands and carried little white flags: "We shed our blood for you, and now you abandon us! With your white rags you've already begun the surrender march!"

They stole their horses, rummaged through valises, and carried on just as if they were still masters in the land. Their leaders passed judgment on terrified old people "in the name of the *ReichsFührer*" and condemned them to death. Their search for civilian clothes took on manic proportions, as they rid themselves of anything that might betray their military service. Some of them put on bizarre clothing: bedraggled sweaters, riding breeches, the black jackets of formal evening wear, worn-out fur jackets taken from Belarussian prisoners, rubber raincoats. Some were bundled up in cloaks, or the remnants of blankets, or dark woolen shawls. At night they looked like scary ghosts.

Some groups were well-organized, with hidden weapons, goniometers, and radios. One such group was camped out in the peat field near the village of Duckwitz and was trying to get close to the front line. Their leader, Karl Ristke, was from Donauwörth, and he still ruled as he had in the good old days. His inn, well-known in Lower Bavaria, was still waiting for him back home. The large brick house with narrow windows stood near the Danube River, huge black letters across its entire width proclaiming "Karl Ristke—*Gasthaus*." Three steps down the street was the beer hall, with heavy oak tables and long benches. The ceiling hung low, and on the walls were displayed deer antlers, brown, twisting, unfurled, fastened to black wooden boards, with a date inscribed on each board. They dated back to earlier generations who had hunted in the woods on the high banks of the Danube. The beer barrels, the beer steins with heavy copper lids, the two sleepy dogs, the wife, and the maid. Ristke could see them all so clearly. He just had to get across the river...

Karl Ristke's long march across Europe had started in the Sudetenland, but where would it end? In the icy waters of the Oder River? In Siberia? He wore his Iron Cross on his chest under his clothes. He would have liked to throw it into the swamps, but he could not. He had to bring it back home. There it would be wrapped in plush and be saved for his children.

At night his radio operator tried to contact headquarters to obtain instructions, but no answer came to his desperate request. Only isolated Russian words came through. They were very clear, reverberating as if they were vibrating against a metal wall. He also heard appeals for help coming from Königsberg, a helpless cry from someone calling himself "General Lersch." Those appeals were drowned out by jazz music and then a coarse voice in Russian! Then suddenly rockets exploded over the peat field. Blinding light spread for several seconds over the swaying tops of the marsh reeds. It was as bright as day.

The Germans hit the dirt. Searchlights were hunting for them, sweeping the blackness with swathes of light, slicing right into the river. A machine gun crackled. Karl Ristke crawled, and then rested. His men crawled behind him like night lizards. But some stopped moving. "Deserters," he called them. They would surrender to the Russians the next day. Better to be a prisoner than to drown in the river or be blown up by Russian grenades. Some of his men disappeared every night. The first to go were the Russian traitors, Vlasov's men. By the time Ristke reached the river, only three men were still with him, all of them from western Germany.

The moon would soon disappear behind dark clouds. The silvery water spread out before them. It would soon turn dark and they would jump in. But before Karl Ristke could raise his head out of the water, a Soviet patrol appeared on the other side of the river. It all happened so quickly and quietly that the Germans were stunned. It was all over by the time their fear had subsided. They were on their knees with their hands up, and a young Russian searched them, while his comrades looked on. The moon crept out from behind the clouds, and again the searchlights turned the river into a silvery road and lit up the tips of the marsh reeds in bloom.

The Russian searched through their clothes and laid everything out on the grass: revolvers, wallets. The radio lay on the side, its metal glinting in the moonlight. Suddenly something happened. Karl Ristke tottered, then fell on his face, howling as if he had gotten a cramp.

"Get up! Get up!" ordered a soldier, hitting him with the butt of his machine gun.

"Don't shoot! Don't, sir!"

When Ristke stood up they could see his officer's insignia on his clothes. Under his unbuttoned shirt they saw a small cross on a silver chain, and an iron cross shimmered at his feet.

"Look how sly this guy is! Threw himself on the ground howling. Wanted to hide this in the grass..."

The soldier brought the iron cross to Menakhem, and said, smiling, "*Kaputt! Kaputt!*"

Menakhem held the cross and looked at the dragoon Ristke standing at attention. And one of the Germans repeated, "*Kaputt! Kaputt!*" like a hesitant echo.

Everything was ready for the final onslaught. They were just waiting for the order. This would be a massive blow against a concentration of very heavily fortified German forces assembled in the Berlin region. Meanwhile reconnaissance missions continued to ferret out the enemy's artillery positions. On one of those nights, Lieut. Lev. Oshanin and another Soviet officer—recently sent by division headquarters—were dispatched across the front line. They were both well-equipped and had radios. Their main purpose was to correct the line of Soviet artillery fire.

Martin Pannwitz, the captured German officer, had made for the Soviets a detailed map of all the military objectives that he knew.

Chapter Three

It was a solid topographical representation of the area on the way to Berlin. The two reconnaissance men were dropped by airplane about thirty-kilometers to the east of Berlin, not far from a highway. Day was breaking.

Oshanin took on the guise of Ristke the innkeeper, and the other Russian had documents proving his identity as a Prussian landowner. They aimed to get to Berlin and start their actions. Both spoke German and could orient themselves on the roads. They spent their first day with German refugees who had stopped in the village of Neuwalden. The villagers were terrified by the nighttime offensive. In the morning they stood in front of the locked church and watched silently as their troops retreated. It appeared that the order had been given for the remnants of the various armed forces to return to Berlin.

The two Soviet officers left for a little forest in the evening and slept in a haystack. Lights were on in Neuwalden. Exhausted German refugees slept in barns. Trucks and armored cars rushed past on a narrow road lined with linden trees. They could hear an artillery barrage coming from the south. "Must be ours," thought the Soviets. Lev Oshanin took the satchel off his back. It was quiet in the woods. An old, dry tree trunk creaked. He looked closely at the little green eye of his radio. He could hear small sounds, like those of peas being thrown against a stretched hide or the ticktock of a wall clock. Suddenly the green light lit up his face. It was headquarters answering! He had made contact! "We're at objective number five... bedlam... chaos... columns of armored... they're retreating." The green light went out. Oshanin was now the innkeeper Ristke. He knew every detail of Ristke's life. There was a small road from the inn running along the right bank of the Danube to Regensburg. The Iron Cross was in his satchel. Karl Ristke... Karl Ristke. He kept repeating his name.

His comrade was silent. Oshanin knew only his "German" family name and his Russian first name. "Call me Valentin," he had told him. The night wore on. It was already spring. It was a mild, starry night. Not far away the glow of huge fire lit up the sky, with black and garnet clouds of smoke. Oil reservoirs were burning. "Atta boy! Nice piece of work!" They heard shooting coming from Neuwalden, then it stopped. "The Fritzes in uniform are murdering the Fritzes without uniforms."

Oshanin admired his friend's excellent German. Only now could he study the features of his face by the light of the moon, but he couldn't read him. It was an unremarkable face, such as could be found among all peoples, a face without any special traits. Although Oshanin looked at Valentin for quite a while, he knew that he would forget his face as soon as he closed his eyes. It was the face of hotel bellhops, barbers, bank officers, a round face, vapid eyes, chiseled nose, tight lips, and sparse hair. It's a face you might see on any street in any city, showing no hint of any nationality. Sometimes they appear plain and dull; at other times they attract your attention without knowing why. Oshanin had been disappointed at first when he had been introduced to the reconnaissance man named "Valentin." He knew right away that it was not his real name, for he himself had been introduced under a false name. Despite the fact that they faced a difficult mission in common, each one totally mistrusted the other. Their mutual ignorance of the other kept them apart, but the enemies around them and their mission drew them together.

Freshly trained troops were arriving from deep inside Russia. They were sent from their trains right to the front line in Germany. These were the youngsters who had grown up during the war and had been mobilized on a mass scale in the liberated territories of Ukraine, Belarus, and Poland. In addition, hundreds of thousands of war invalids took over administrative posts in the army in the hinterland, allowing for the mobilization of those who had not yet served, a new source of manpower at the front. These new recruits were joining an army that was on the advance, which gave them courage. No one now doubted that victory was near. Troop trains ran night and day from distant Siberia to Poland and from Poland to German territory.

These soldiers were well clad in new military dress and leather shoes. Their food was ample and nutritious. They received larger rations of tobacco, zwieback, and American canned food.

On to Berlin! To the Elbe! To the Reichstag!

It was spring, and the days were sunny. When it did rain it was warm and gentle. And the nights were moonlit. The sons of Volga farmers, the lumberjacks from Siberia, the coal miners from the Urals, the steelworkers from Sverdlovsk—could not stop heaping praise on the German roads and walkways, the villages and towns that they saw from the trains: "How well they've been living!" Everything was built of stone: the barns, the houses, the bridges. "All of this wasn't enough for them! So rich! But they just had to invade our humble *kolkhozes*!"

"They wanted our coal from the Donbass and the oil from Baku!"

The Russians attacked German soil with hatred: the bitterness of starving *muzhiks*, the years of misery, the devastated fields, the little wooden cabins, the ruined roads with humble wagons being dragged by decrepit horses, the little oil lamps, the shoes woven from linden bark.

"But here, what a rich country!"

The surge of victory moved them as they drove through German villages. Their hunger and poverty had not been for nothing! "So what if we ate bread made with bran, quinoa, and potatoes? Our commanders have taken us to victory!" They carried Stalin's picture on their regimental flags, on their silver medals. His words had come true: "We will destroy the beast in its own den!"

But instead of a den they found beautiful homes, and bright, spacious cities. Their hearts were inflamed by victory, by joy, by hatred, and bitterness. Their rifle butts forced open gates, their fists banged on doors, and they found themselves standing inside German houses with their sweaty faces and bloodshot eyes. The Soviet soldiers were intoxicated with vodka, with victory, with hate.

But sometimes they felt the decency of common village people, and they happily took the rifles off their backs, loosened their straps, and sat down at the table to drink some tea and admire the clean, high, well-made beds with little nickel angels, the embroidered pillows, the soft divans, the copper kitchen utensils, and the full-bosomed, pale-faced, white-skinned lady of the house.

They would stammer words to the German people to calm them down and were ready to accept them as their brothers. "Are they not people like us?" "D'you see how they work the fields?" And they felt respect towards them. At moments like that they would lie down in barns in the hay and dream of their own homes far away in Russian villages. But those quiet minutes were rare. When they ran into concentration camp prisoners on the road who had been freed—slaves who were half alive, slaves from every country in Europe—and when they heard the survivors tell their tales of horror, their hatred of the Germans would flare up.

They would weep when they heard Jewish women tell of their years of pain at the hands of the Germans. A young Pole led a Soviet detachment to search for the German landowner who had hundreds of Ukrainian girls working for him, and those slaves had been forced to leave with the German army when it retreated. When the Soviets arrived at his house, they found an old man. "That's him!" cried the Pole.

"How can that be?! This doddering old man owns all these fields and woods?! It's all his?! And they didn't take it away from him?!"

The Soviet went over to him and pointed at the fields and barns and asked: "Hey, German, this is yours? Yours?! Speak!" Then he pointed at the huge house, "Yours?!"

The withered old man was confused, and he stammered: "Yes, sir... Yes, *gnädige*..."

The Soviet pointed to the pasture land and the forest: "Yours? Yours?" This was his first encounter with a landowner, the class enemy. He could not understand something. Why was he such a decrepit old man? He shrugged his shoulders and said to the people around him, "I won't stop you from executing a class enemy. But this has nothing to do with our war. You exploited and oppressed people can settle your own accounts." The crowd responded, "Hurrah! Long live the Soviet army!"

The Slavs who had been forced to work for him surrounded him. The Ukrainian

Mitrokhin was doomed. What should he do? He had served the Germans. Where should he go? Back home? He would be shot. To the front? A bullet would get him. He was standing now, facing the landowner and his forced laborers. He looked at the withered old man and at the Soviet soldiers. What if someone asked to see his papers? As he watched, an idea came to him under his shaved head: he did not want to die. One more day and it would be too late. The NKVD would be here and do a thorough investigation. Not one forced laborer would speak in his favor. His heart was pounding and he felt himself strangling. He could already feel the noose around his neck. How many people had he himself strangled with a cord dipped in pitch? That had been back in 1943. He had killed his own people. He tensed up in terror and screamed, "The German is guilty! The German is guilty! Him!!"

Mitrokhin crept up slowly, then suddenly threw himself on the German with a ferocious howl and knocked him to the ground. He seized him around the neck and choked him, all the while screaming and growling unintelligibly. It was already dark. The German and the Ukrainian looked like a sick old wolf wrestling with hunting dog.

Every day they brought new German prisoners. But they were dressed in civilian clothes. Some pretended to be slave laborers who had barely escaped execution. Others claimed to be deserters from the German army. Several of them spoke Polish and said that the Germans had forced them into serving in their army. Lieut. Sabayev called Menakhem to headquarters and relayed an order from the commander that Menakhem should do the first interrogations of the prisoners. And when Menakhem tried to object to the order, Sabayev grew angry: "That's enough of keeping to yourself! Why do you avoid us? You don't speak frankly. You don't answer questions. I've noticed it for quite some time."

"I want to be a frontline soldier, not here at headquarters."

Sabayev blushed. It seemed that those words were aimed at him personally.

"So there's nothing worse than someone at headquarters? You don't like headquarters?"

Menakhem said nothing. He was scornful and indifferent. He thought: "I know these guys only too well. They're all the same kind, the Suzayevs, the Khatshaps, the Zhillins. And this is no longer the start of the war! Now I can see what they're up to! Why did you call for Zipunov yesterday? I know everything. I could see it on Zipunov's fat lips. I'm an old hand at this. Stop playing your games. Just say what you mean!" But he had not uttered those words aloud to Sabayev, but the expression on his face was clear, and Sabayev surely understood it. Sabayev's anger evaporated:

"Stop rolling your eyes like that, Mikhail Isaacovitch…Well, good buddy, you can still get promoted. Sit down. But it's not so easy to get the rank of lieutenant. We know everything, Mikhail. Everything! Nothing is a secret from us. Nothing. Don't do anything stupid. You've already suffered enough…"

Hundreds of Germans passed through Menakhem's interrogation office during his first days there. They were troops from the Sixteenth and Eighteenth *Armees* in the Baltic regions. Among them were also troops of the Third Tank Division and the Fourth *Armee*. Plus there were assorted suspicious characters with no papers at all. Some refused to speak German, only Czech. One of them spoke French. Some of them stood before Menakhem straight at attention, and answered his questions accurately with military precision, and continued to stand at attention until he dismissed them. Others entered nonchalantly, with their hands behind their backs, wearing tattered clothes, and stood before him with their legs apart and their shoulders drooping. They looked calmly at the walls and tried to avoid looking at Menakhem's face. And when they were ordered to leave, they took their time and stood around.

Many of them were terrified when they came in. They mumbled and showed their big rough hands to prove that they had been proletarians all their lives. They would say, "Thank God" after every sentence. One of them said the same word over and over: "Finally." At first Menakhem did not quite get what he meant by "Finally." Did he mean that finally the war had ended? Or the end of Hitler's rule? Or maybe his own end: that he would be shot by the Russians at the bottom of some antitank ditch?

They assembled a small group of prisoners in the courtyard and sent them to special locations. And thus the "master race" passed before Menakhem. He had already faced German prisoners before, when he was fighting in Moscow, at the underground headquarters when Petrov was the chief. On that snowy night the Fritzes in front of him had been freezing, despondent. Now it was springtime. They were in Germany, on the banks of the Oder River. They were brought under guard to *his* office in a fine mansion, and *he* was doing the interrogation. Now he was on *their* territory. In *their* "Thousand-Year *Reich*." He did not now feel the fury, the rage that had seized him when he had first encountered German soldiers.

Now he observed them with steel-cold eyes. He was not disturbed, not by their dullness, nor their arrogance, nor their dejection, nor their servility. He had seen German prisoners weeping at the edge of a ditch before being shot or begging on their knees. But now cold armor gripped his heart.

Only once during the interrogations did Menakhem come near a prisoner. He was tall, long-legged, with a sullen, bony face. He ripped a copper swastika off the German's neck and asked quietly: "How dare you?" He knew that among those who passed before him there were those who had exterminated masses of civilians. He could tell who had done the murdering and who had watched without saying a word. All of them were now fleeing to the west. They lied boldly, gave false names and phony birthplaces, and refused to say in which military units they had served. Sep Dühring, the *Obergruppen*Führer of an SS corps, showed his decoration, the "Knight's Cross With Oak Leaves," and demanded to be treated like an officer. Menakhem leaped up and moved forward, as if a hot wind were pushing harder and harder against his temples and driving him. He felt he might explode. He knew that neither words nor screams would relieve him. He pressed his right hand against his belt, digging his nails into it until they hurt. His left hand gripped the edge of the table and moved it around, his fingers trembling.

Before him stood this SS officer, a hereditary Prussian *Junker*, his face covered with scars and deep wrinkles like the ridges on a tree trunk. He was in his fifties, with a short haircut and icy, deep-set eyes. He looked like an oak tree whose leaves had just fallen off. Only his red neck betrayed the seething rage of this officer with the ghostly gray face.

It was not easy for Menakhem to maintain his outward calm. His natural serenity, his reserve, the profound dignity that he had inherited from generations of impoverished Jewish commoners reined him in. It was a clash of two worlds far apart. Here was the grandson of Jewish villagers somewhere near Sochocin, the descendant of orchard keepers, peddlers, and craftsmen. And there stood Sep Dühring, the Prussian *Junker*. And it was the general who was the prisoner of the Jew Menakhem.

Menakhem wanted to summon witnesses to this meeting, all the Jews from his country who had been murdered, in all its cities and towns: The Jews of Pultusk whom German soldiers had herded into the synagogue and burned alive! The Jews of Ciechanow! The Jews of Makowa! His brothers! His neighbors! Let all of them come! All! Come and see! This is a unique event in our tragic generation! This must be remembered! There must be witnesses to this historic encounter!

Menakhem pressed his fingers to the breaking point. He could see Dühring marching his SS corps into the Jewish towns of northern Poland. In 1939 he had watched the German army's victory parade. Come! Come all you martyrs! Watch him tremble! He is now in my hands, he who exterminated our old Jewish communities in Poland with iron and steel! Look at him!

It seemed to him that his spacious office in the German mansion had filled up. The witnesses had all come, all those radiantly joyous Jews, as if for a holiday, waiting for a great trial. Sabayev sat calmly, carving a five-pointed star and his initials into the table with a penknife. It was quiet in the room. Menakhem looked at the stony German, then at Sabayev. It seemed as if he were the odd man there, as if it was *they* who had summoned *him* to that big black table in that German village between the Soviet army on one side of the river and the German army on the other. What was *he* doing there? There was something unsettling about that silence of those two officers. They were like two rivers that flowed into each other somewhere in a flooded field. But the tree that had been uprooted by the raging waters would never take root again. It would be carried away in the roaring torrent.

Menakhem refused to take revenge on the Germans. He refused to cross a German threshold and refused to accept clothes that the Soviet army distributed from German stocks. He refused to drink from German glasses and to eat off German dishes. Any revenge taken against a German whose personal guilt had not been proven would diminish the immensity of the crime that the Germans had committed against the Jewish people. His scorn for the nation was so great that he stopped conceiving of them as a nation. He saw them as human beings, common people, farmers, farm women, children, the farmers walking slowly to their fields like oxen. He stood at the large window and looked at the fields, the distant villages, the green valleys of springtime, and the tragedy of the Jews dimmed in his eyes.

He asked, "Why did you put up such fierce resistance? Why didn't you put down your weapons?"

Sep Dühring answered in a dry, hoarse voice: "We wanted to protect Prussia from the worst possible fate that could befall it."

"Didn't you see the end of the military operations as a good thing?"

The German laughed sarcastically: "A good thing?! We're talking about the life and death of a nation. My troops knew that if we lost, that would be the end of a culture hundreds of years old. Seven hundred years of German labor in Prussia. That would all be lost in an invasion from the east."

Menakhem paced back and forth across the room. Sabayev stuck the point of his penknife into the center of the star that he had carved in the table and watched Menakhem pacing.

"A culture hundreds of years old?! Culture?! Culture?! How dare you use that word?! Have you no shame?! D'you have any idea how stupid you are, you Junker, you Prussian bastard?"

His anger arose not from his placid ancestors on his father's side, those scribes and scholars, but from the blood of country Jews on his mother's side. He saw before him his uncle Elye, short and stocky, who would storm into the marketplace brandishing a wheel axle, demanding justice. He felt that rage now coming from that side of the family.

"The culture of generations?! I've seen your culture! Your regiments occupied my homeland. I was a witness to what your SS corps did to civilians!" He ran to the map on the wall and ran his feverish fingers over East Prussia: "These are the roads your regiment took. Here's Torun. You slashed through northern Poland like a knife. Then to Wloclawek, Makowa, Mlawa, Plonsk. Come here, you German ObergruppenFührer! Those towns are older than your Prussian seven hundred years! I'm from there! That was September 1939. I was in the Polish army that got beaten by your corps. And now we meet again. A great encounter on the Oder! This is my revenge! I am the son of a nation that you wanted to destroy, that you scorned. I scorn you and your heritage and your land! Seven hundred years of culture?! And what has it given the world?! Auschwitz!! Majdanek!! You SS ObergruppenFührer!!"

Menakhem was silent, like granite. Two guards took the German away. His Iron Cross lay on the table. Menakhem brushed it away in anger. Sabayev mumbled discontentedly.

Tempelhof, near the big German airport, was Lev Oshanin's destination. A place had been prepared for him in the cellar of one of the houses built like barracks. He was expected. But he had some other addresses in case the house was destroyed by a bombing. In a hilly area to the south of the Müggelsee Lake he received the news that Valentin was to head north to Wohlgarten. They had separated on a rainy March day. Oshanin was glad. He had disliked this person named "Valentin" right from the beginning. Apparently "Valentin" already knew that they would split up in that hilly village by the lake.

Their stay in the abandoned inn lingered, and Oshanin concluded that his companion was waiting for a radio message. That message came in a code that Oshanin did not know. It appeared that Valentin had his own separate mission. Searchlights lit up the sky. A reddish fog hung over the western horizon. The evening before their separation they spoke about the Caspian Sea and the Volga River. Oshanin knew the fields along the Don River well. That was where he had done his basic training. But he was from Polesia, humid, mossy green, with stands of white birch trees, silvery willows, and pale poplars.

Valentin asked him nonchalantly, as if he had no ulterior motive, "Are you Jewish?"

"Sure! But you must have known it already. And if you ask a question to which you already know the answer, then it means you want to see how I'm going to answer."

Oshanin's Jewishness was his love for his own family, for the years of his youth, for his warm childhood home. He still remembered how his father had touched his son's new officer's insignia on his uniform and thanked God for allowing the son of a lowly wagon driver to achieve such distinction. As a child, Oshanin had heard stories about the massacre of Jews in Gomel and the self-defense group that his uncles had belonged to. Being a Jew also meant singing Jewish melodies late into the night, mixed with the songs the muzhiks sang as they harvested and threshed the grain. He knew those songs well and often sang them for his army buddies around the campfire on the banks of the Don. He had sung them marching all over Russia, wherever he was with his troops. He was their lead singer.

Being Jewish also meant being a son of the land that stretched from the Dnieper River to the Amur River. His Yiddish was like the soil of Polesia, mixed and knotted with roots, grasses, mosses. The most wonderful plants grow in such soil. He was tightly bound up with his home, his parents, his uncles. Of course he was Jewish! But that was all a personal matter. It was no one else's business. He was not interested in making a show of his Jewishness for others. He spoke only Russian, for that was the language of his gigantic country, and he could speak in that language to everyone. For him, Yiddish was like a cozy shirt against his skin.

He said to Valentin: "Ever since this catastrophe struck the Jews, I mistrust anyone who asks me if I'm Jewish. They have to see me as a human being, and that's enough. And if someone asks whether Oshanin is anything other than a Soviet citizen, then that means..." He did not finish the sentence. They sat, silent, resentful.

Before they separated, Valentin told him: "The Germans have not only slaughtered your people. They've convulsed the peace of mind of every Jew who survived. It will be impossible for non-Jews to live together with Jews. You're full of mistrust, hatred, suspicion, fear, and desire for revenge. Just as someone who loses a lot of blood will be sick all his life, so, too, a nation that has lost so much blood will suffer for generations. You're now a sick nation, and I'm one of those who sympathize with you."

"You sympathize with us?"

That was their last conversation. Oshanin left without turning around. A farm wagon passed by, hitched to two oxen. Some Germans followed it, refugees. "Good mornin'!" he called to them, and he quickly followed the wagon, which was loaded with straw. A sooty lantern hung in the back, swinging between iron-clad wheels. A German with a very flat chin was smoking a pipe. A wounded soldier walked slowly, leaning on the wagon. Some *Volkssturmer* passed them on motorcycles, leaving behind the foul smoke of gasoline. The bedlam on that village road reflected the chaos that reigned in Germany.

Menakhem could not get any rest on those nights. Something big was happening. In his half sleep he imagined the hammering of chisels engraving the judgment against the Thousand-Year Reich onto stone tablets.

During the day hundreds of Germans came through his office: farmers from Saxony, railroad workers from Spandau, a student from Frankfurt, a merchant from Leipzig, a landowner from Prussia. Their faces were already fading from memory. At first he had searched for signs of criminality, and he was relieved when he discovered them. He did not understand why he felt better when he was face to face with a German who had committed crimes. Why was he not looking for signs of decency, or humanity? He resisted the twisted pleasure of having before him a German with a stupid face. Those faces justified the profound scorn that he felt. He thought he had solved the puzzle: Why had they served the Nazis? He flew into a rage whenever a prisoner would start mumbling about having lost his home, about having done his duty to his country, and about his joy at having remained alive, "It's finally over! Dear God!" Then Menakhem lost track of what he was trying to find out. For here was a mortal soul, with fine facial features, bewildered. You could find such people anywhere.

At night he would go to the barns where the Soviet tank troops were lodged. There he ran into Sgt. Orlov amidst groups of soldiers. They were sitting on their cots, playing cards. There was German liquor. They were drinking from pink porcelain cups with gilt edging. *Papavkin* was pouring. When they were done they smashed the cups against the stone wall.

Papvkin yelled, "Real porcelain! You can tell from the sound!" They enjoyed breaking them.

"Mikhailo! You're half German since you talk like them! How'd you like to be my matchmaker? I know a girl, real sturdy, a tank couldn't move her! But I can't make her understand! She just says "Das, was, das," and I don't get a word of it! Can you help out a brother? The liquor's on me!"

"Let's have it!"

Platon Voronka jumped up: "Let's have some snacks."

Dobrusz was drunk. Zipunov shook him by the shoulders: "Hey, sonny boy! Just one drink and already your eyes are closing?"

Zipunov had shown great interest in Dobrusz as soon as he joined the regiment. First he taught him how to use a machine gun. Then he showed the inexperienced Dobrusz how to find his way through all the connected trenches at night. They did guard duty together. Then he took Dobrusz around to all the estates, hunting for watches, silver cigarette lighters, and cigarette cases. By the light of the moon Zipunov displayed all the loot that he had taken on German territory to Dobrusz. He took pleasure in the shiny numbers on the watches, the polished gemstones, the gleam of the silver. They drank German wine together. Dobrusz would doze off right away, while Zipunov stayed awake, rolling cigarettes in very thin paper. At dawn they sneaked into German houses. They looked like a father and son who had found each other again in faraway Germany.

Menakhem knew about this strange friendship between Dobrusz and the sinister Zipunov. "No good will come of it," he thought, watching Dobrusz's boyish head swaying from drink and exhaustion. It pained him to see Dobrusz this way. He had tried to get close to Dobrusz more than once, but without success. It was difficult to talk to the boy. His words had fallen on deaf ears.

Dobrusz was agitated. Every few minutes he would jump up, looking around nervously, up and down. His eyes betrayed mistrust and mockery. Now Menakhem saw him close to tears in his drunkenness, so he went over and stroked his feverish brow. Platon stood in the doorway with a tall German woman.

"Come on, Klara! Let's go! Let them look at you! Let them see your eyes!" He was holding on to the sleeve of her nightgown with dark-colored flowers. Her hair was in disarray, her face flushed. With one hand she tried to hold the nightgown closed over her breast. With the other she pulled her tailcoats down over her knees. It looked like he had brought her right out of bed. "Here's some food and vodka!"

A soldier brought a woven basket full of freshly baked goods and set it at the head of the table. Menakhem turned away to leave. Raucous laughter erupted. "What are you scared of? Hey, hero! Come here! You'll meet our Klara. Shake Mikhail's hand! Get to know him! Why are you just standing there, girl?" Platon gave her a push, and put out his hand towards Menakhem and said, "That's it, German girl!"

She looked at them with big smiling eyes. Her fear had left her. "What's wrong, Klara?"

When she offered her hand the bathrobe slipped down, uncovering her naked shoulder and a lacy nightgown. Wild laughter broke out. Orlov offered her a full glass of vodka. The musician from Leningrad who had spent his free time playing the church organ struck up a song. The drunken, dozing Dobrusz woke up, took a harmonica out of his pocket, and joined in wildly. Zipunov started dancing around the half-naked German girl, clattering on the stone floor with his heels, crouching all the way down, and spinning around madly. The soldiers clapped along. Someone called to Mikhail: "Brother, why are you standing there like a German crucifix? Come on!"

Menakhem turned his back to the girl and took Dobrusz by the arm: "Come!" Dobrusz smiled at him good-naturedly. Menakhem again saw in his face that same boyish scorn mixed with tearfulness. He left, followed by Platon's hoarse laughter and the high-pitched little laugh of the big German girl in the bathrobe.

Menakhem walked through the dark streets, constantly running into guard-posts. Rays of light came from some windows. Voices could be heard. A wayward cannon ball rolled towards the black horizon and exploded over the fields. It would surely be thrown back soon to the Soviet trenches. The tin rooster on a church tower creaked. A tank blocked the way to a side street, and its shadow multiplied itself on a white wall. A door opened somewhere nearby. Frogs were croaking in a meadow. The air was moist, smelling of horse manure, gasoline, and springtime.

"Halt!" Yet another guard. This time it was Kerbaley the Tatar, confident and fearful. Every soldier now knew that fear and confidence were not mutually exclusive. They went hand in hand here on the front line on German territory. More than once Menakhem had seen the natural goodness and decency of soldiers disappear when they enjoyed the fruits of criminal acts. He himself had been tempted by those fruits. But he reined in the intoxication of victory. He did often feel the urge to break free of the restraints that he had imposed on himself. But they constrained him like a rigid, heavy harness. Why should he not walk through the German village arrogantly, laughing, and all liquored up— just like Platon, like Orlov, like the Kalmyk, Gusyev? Why should he not sit at German tables and have a good time with their wives and daughters? Why must he wander around at night among dark houses, like a vagabond who gets no rest? How often had he stood dumbfounded when doors opened and girls beckoned to him! He slept well on those nights, listening to the footsteps of the night watch and the rumble of armored cars.

It was late. The Tatar Kerbaley was singing, a far-eastern melody. It was as if the wind had brought it from Asia. It was a pleasure to hear his singing. But he could not fall asleep. The darkness drew him outside. He went up the steps to headquarters. Alturov was on guard at the entrance. Dawn would break in two hours. A truck passed with blue headlights. He could hear voices calling every few minutes. A telegraph machine tapped away. Communications men ran around like demons. Someone stopped with a long paper scroll in front of the dim light of a car. Col. Gusyev approached him; his tunic slung over one shoulder. The man read him the telegram that had come. The Kirghiz Alturov leaned against the door and put down his machine gun. A commotion stirred in headquarters. Doors opened and closed. Footsteps creaked. An orderly brought in some tea. An old German woman washed the steps outside. Lights went on in the street. A heavy car was started up. The multiple shadows of the tank on the wall disappeared, as did some of the shadows from the church tower.

Menakhem was standing next to the Kirghiz, silently rolling cigarettes. The morning chill was refreshing, and it dispersed his nighttime restlessness. Now you knew that you had another day coming, that God had given you one more bright day. The day was yours entirely. Nothing would happen to you under that bright sky. Only the night was not in God's domain. It was lawless. Now Menakhem could shake off all those night demons that had clawed at him like thorns. Why had he envied the soldiers the day before who were enjoying the fruits of their crimes? In the sharp morning air he regained his composure. He was not immune to the impurity that courses through the veins of all those who invade the land they have conquered from their enemies. Why have You bound my hands? Why have You stopped the mad rush of blood in my veins? Why am I not like all the other soldiers? Let me be free for one hour, God! Turn Your face away from me, for I cannot keep out Your light that overwhelms me! Spread out the darkness around me so that I can run wild over the desolate roads and the blackened footpaths of this evil land. Do not go with me on my impure way. Leave me alone in my hour of victory, just as You leave us alone in our times of defeat, alone among victorious troops face to face with the Germans. Let me enjoy the mad, sweet fruits of revenge and victory.

The springtime earth reawakened in the Soviets their longing for the fields back home. They looked with wonder at the alien soil, which became dearer to them with each bud that opened. At night Sergei Orlov talked of the fields and woods back home: "D'you hear the frogs croaking? It's time to sow oats. Looks like it'll be a good harvest, because the mosquitoes are biting. Oho! That's a western wind with low-lying clouds. Time to get ready for the summer sowing." And when he saw a rowan tree in bloom, it augured a good flax harvest. Once he stopped at an oak tree and smiled: "D'you see, Mikhail? If all the leaves have fallen off in autumn, and in the spring there are no leaves left from the previous year, that's a sign that it'll be a good year both for people and for cattle."

He was now back in the fields at home: "Now's the time to take the tractor down the hard road along the poplars all the way to the little wooden bridge. Once again Akim forgot to put in a new support beam. The bridge to the Redhead's fields has to be mended. Otherwise how can the tractor get across?"

"Who's that Redhead? Your girlfriend?"

Orlov burst out laughing: "Oh, that's an old story. Once upon a time, long ago, we'd often run into a girl with red hair in the fields. She lived in the last cabin in the valley. She'd say she was going over to the next village. That went on for years, and she gave birth to bastards every year. No one in her village knew who the father was. Years later they caught a man who had escaped from internal exile, and the redhead lived with him for about ten years in a ditch in the woods. This was all during the Turkish War. I heard it from my grandfather. Several footpaths lead from her place:

"On the right, towards the big pasture lands. The grass there is low, tangled, greenish brown. When you walk there, your feet get tangled like in rope loops. There's enough there for the sheep to eat. The spring that I pass on my tractor overflows in the springtime, and the water spreads out over the plain. In the summer dry spell you can catch slippery tench fish with your hands and thorny grass pike.

"The path on the left leads to the hay fields, where the grass grows up to your waist. The shepherd Stiopka doesn't drive the herds there. They'd trample the hay. If you come at harvest time, you'll be amazed! The waves of grass swirl like a swollen river. You can watch the colors shimmering, silvery-green here, pinkish blue there, or yellowish-brown, and sometimes it looks like the clouds of white fog before dawn. D'you know what it's like to walk with your scythe through a field like that?! We'd spend weeks there for the harvest, with our wagons, cows, wives. We'd light fires. We'd sit in a circle and we each got a wooden bowl. We ate *ukha* fish soup, and then we'd lie down in the shade of the wagons and the haystacks. What kind of life do they have here in Germany? They say that the Germans have a 'method' for everything. Even when they fall off the oven they have a 'technique.' Thank God, Mikhail, they're losing the war with their 'technique!'" Orlov was beaming with the warmth of the Russian hearth, the good nature of the *muzhiks*.

"I've seen so many things in this world! Listen to what a Russian farmer tells you: I'd give you everything, Mikhail, everything—all the trinkets jangling around in my pockets—I'd give all of Germany, to have a single evening on my porch in my village on the banks of the Oka River. Here I don't smell the earth, the trees. The houses have a strange odor, and the German women have the scent of washed calves. They reek like pharmacies. But our women have the aroma of meadows in bloom, of freshly baked rye bread. When you lie at night with one of our girls, you feel as if you're surrounded by the heavens and the fields, the forests, the meadows. With German women it's the stench of old underwear, dried sausages, awful medicines."

Orlov was embarrassed when he spoke about women. His words rambled, and he would lose his breath. When he talked to the troops about the feminine sex he would use foul language, but he stammered when he talked to Menakhem about them. The two of them grew close after that night of conversation. They could often be seen together. Menakhem would come to watch him working in the shop where tanks were being repaired.

"Say, d'you see how the cranes are flying high up? That's a bad sign!" Orlov had an explanation for every natural phenomenon. He had spent his life in the village. He had worked in the fields from an early age with old men, and he had absorbed the folk wisdom of generations. He could lay traps to capture foxes and knew how to hunt wolves and bears. In the autumn he had collected chanterelle mushrooms in the woods, filling whole barrels to be marinated. He had floated timber down the Oka River and caught fish in huge nets. Sergei had dragged firewood in the winter from the far reaches of the forest.

Once Menakhem told him about African elephants who knew that hungers were upon them and that they had no more strength to fight back. Wounded, they would plunge into the densest part of the forest and keep moving until they reached boulders against which they smashed their tusks. Sensing that the hunters were after the ivory, they refused to let their tusks fall into their hands intact.

Orlov jumped up, amazed and delighted: Did you see it with your own eyes, Mikhail?"

"No, I read it in an account by a traveler. He also described the elephant cemetery. When they sense that their end has come, they go to the cemetery where other elephants have died. They lie down there until they die."

Orlov was very taken with the story. One day Menakhem drew him a picture of an elephant destroying his tusk against a boulder. Hunters stood in the background. Orlov could not believe his eyes: "You drew this with your own hands?!" He looked at the elephant and the boulder sadly and sympathetically.

"Just let this war end, Mikhail, and you'll come and be my guest! You'll go visit the Redhead, you'll see the gleaming waters of the Oka, and I'll take you to the hay harvest. Why would you want to hang around in filthy Poland?"

Menakhem was silent. Only a tiny smile, barely noticeable, came to the corners of his mouth. He remembered faraway Tengushay, Lioska's house, her mother Molkina. It was winter. He was sitting at the bare wooden table. A candle burned in front of the icons. Shadows danced on the walls. The men of Tengushay had been sent off to war. Menakhem had returned for a few days. He was leaving for Murom the next day. Lioska was lying on top of the oven. It was quiet in Tengushay. Suddenly they heard a lamb moaning. Mama Molkina was weary and downcast: "Lie down on the oven, Mikhail. Tomorrow we'll walk you to the train station, like one of our own." Then he watched her kneeling before the icons. Lioska's hands had the scent of hay…

When had that been? Menakhem closed his eyes… Lioska from Tengushay. He could see her carrying the pails from a yoke on her shoulders. She was walking on a snowy street. Her embroidered red sarafan was brilliant… Anna was standing over his bed. There were brightly lit, white rooms. Searchlights scoured the skies… Elderly bearded farmers were going to harvest hay. They took off their caps and kneeled in the still-green hay field, whispering prayers… Suzayev… Petrov… Zhillin… Adrian… Orlov… Sabayev… They ran around in his head wildly, incoherently… the fields along the Volga… the road to Dudnikovo, a village of the Mordvin shepherds… to Aleksandrov with its plowmen… the fishermen of Krasny-Yar…Maidan and its wood-turners… to Atenino and its Tatars… trudging on those roads, end of autumn 1941… thousands of peasant sleds, with whole villages following them to Moscow, to come to its defense. The Germans were at its gates... mines on the snowy fields... rockets... Moscow was like a frozen river whose icy cover suddenly cracks, revealing cold dark waters below it. Would that be the end of his remembrances? The villages on the Volga returned... the German prisoners... Here was Hugo Rudoss again, in the earthen guardhouse outside Moscow... Here was Menakhem's trial again... Sentenced to slave in the mines... Khatshap the Georgian... Abilev the Tatar... Here he was on the banks of the Vistula again... Anna, again...

This swarm of daydreams exhausted him. When he opened his eyes the slight bitter smile vanished from his face. He was grateful that Orlov had resurrected the scent of hay fields in him. Something vital that had escaped from him during the war years was returned to him. He felt disjointed, as if cannon fire and explosions had torn him to pieces. If he were destined to survive the war, a new man would be born from those fragments. And he feared that new man.

On his table there were a number of pencil drawings of German prisoners. It was his favorite pastime. They calmed him down, those agitated, rough strokes on whatever paper was handy. He drew them as he interrogated the men. His left eye grew smaller and smaller, while little wrinkles radiated from it to the left side of his face and brow. His temples gleamed like marble, from the veins. Here was Sep Dühring, SS ObergruppenFührer, in full length; Ristke, with the house on the Danube; the dragoon Dietrich Stulpe; the officer Martin Pannwitz from Crossen; and dozens and dozens of others.

They had odd faces, with broad, flat chins like spades, and angular, distorted jaws, close-shaved heads, rounded skulls, thick necks, and big, hairy ears. Most of the officers were very tall, with big feet and long, stiff hands. They stood glumly at attention before Menakhem. But they relaxed when Menakhem looked at them nonchalantly or indifferently, or if Sabayev showed curiosity or surprise. They would mumble and say they were sorry at every turn. And they really relaxed when they were offered a seat. Menakhem could not understand where their humility came from, those hard German faces with piercing eyes, bony chins, broad mouths and lips that barely hid their large, uneven teeth.

Sabayev leafed through Menakhem's drawings. Once he showed them to a war correspondent from a Moscow newspaper and said,

"See these German bastards? They all came to this office. Mikahil drew them. Only an artist who could plumb the depths of these swine could penetrate their souls." The journalist shook Menakhem's hand: "Good job! One day these will serve as documentation for historians of the Great Patriotic War. You can see the German soul. One look and you can see the whole nation. No, these aren't caricatures. It's the truth. This helps me really see the face of the German nation. We haven't even been introduced! My name's Simonov."

Menakhem asked, "Simonov? The poet?"

Alturov brought in liquor and snacks. Sabayev drank one glass after another, and he was in a good mood. Mikhail's drawings would get to Moscow. They would know that he was serving in Sabayev's general staff and that Sabayev had picked him for it. Simonov was not just anybody. It was said that he was welcome in the Kremlin.

"Hey, Alturov! Where have the devils taken you to? You managed to find your way from Khirgizia all the way to German territory, but now when we need some common sense, you've lost your head!" Sabayev walked firmly, trying to mask his drunkenness. Simonov, too, had drunk, but you could not tell. Sabayev said, "My orderly Kerbaley brought the bacon. Those Tatars have a good sense of smell. He can detect a horse's behind. He brought the bacon, because he himself doesn't eat pig meat. That's why we get to eat a good *zakuska*.[2] Eat up, Mikhail! Oh, you're a faker. You pretend to drink but you don't. We Soviet people, we know those tricks!"

Sabayev often used the expression "We Soviet people." When he was tipsy he put it into every sentence. Now he stumbled on the carpet and fell against the door: "Alturov! You swine! We Soviet people…"

It was dark now. Menakhem walked Simonov to his car, arm in arm. Menakhem struck up a song, the one about the blue kerchief fluttering in a girl's hands. The drink had raised his spirits. He had not sung in many years. A blurred face looked at them through a window. An old German with a pipe in his mouth was walking towards them. They could clearly hear artillery. It was a good sign. Things were moving!

"Simonov, you're a Russian and I'm a Jew. According to Sabayev we're both 'Soviet people.' The enemy—our common enemy—has

---

2   Snack.

brought us together. But what will happen afterwards? I'm worried about the postwar period. German hatred of your people will fade, but hatred of us will remain."

Simonov answered by telling him of his Jewish friends. He mentioned Jewish officers whom he had met recently: "They're heroes, those Jews. Fantastic regimental commanders: Maj. Gen. Krivoshein, tank brigade Maj. Gen Weinrib, Col. Smolin, artillery Lieut. Gen Rozanwicz. Your people have shed a lot of blood. And in defending the Jews we have exalted our weapons. We have washed the blood off our flags."

Simonov embraced Menakhem before he left, and they hugged each other. Simonov gave him some of his poems as a souvenir, and Menakhem gave him some of his drawings.

Headquarters was a mess. Sabayev was snoring on the carpet. Empty bottles and leftovers were all over the place. The smell of liquor was overwhelming. Menakhem opened the windows. The drink had given him wings, and he was pulled outside, barely touching the ground. Near the church he started towards the barns. He ran into Platon Voronka and his girlfriend Klara at a corner near a stone wall.

"Mikhail, you scared us!"

"What a coward! You don't need an interpreter anymore?"

"We're getting along fine without words, for God's sake! She's a quiet little woman. I'll take her back to the *kolkhoz* with me. What do you think? Will they allow it?"

Menakhem left. Kerbaley the Tatar told him that little Dobrusz and Zipunov were spending the night in a German house, where there lived a woman and her daughter. Zipunov and Dobrusz were now "family."

Kerbaley laughed: "That devil Zipunov, goes to the front and gets himself a son-in-law!"

A horse was neighing. The Tatar's nostrils flared. A bat flew by so low that he had to duck down: D'you know, Mikhail, where bats come from? From churches. If a mouse eats up the tallow from church candles, they grow wings and become bats. Ha, ha, ha."

Menakhem could hear him laughing for a long time, the same sharp, ancient laughter of the steppes that had resounded centuries ago in Genghis Khan's Mongolia.

Oshanin was sending regular reports to the headquarters of the Berlin front. There was no word from Valentin. Oshanin had reached his destination. His dispatches were immediately relayed to the artillery positions of Col. Gusyev. A member of the Supreme War Council was coming to headquarters. Dozens of cars were pulling up to the house. The telephone operators were desperately looking for "Col. Ilya." The glass doors were shaking. The rattling of the doors, the din of the car engines, the orderlies and staff running around on stone floors echoed through the night.

Sabayev's drunkenness suddenly evaporated. His short hair bristled and his ears burned. There would be a Party meeting for the officers. Sabayev would have to give a report on political activities. Where were Kerbaley and Menakhem?

The subject of the meeting would be "Political Vigilance." He would have to assemble the commanders of the various units fighting at the frontline. When Sabayev left headquarters he ran into Menakhem near the iron garden gate. A German came running and screaming.

"What does he want?" Sabayev asked Menakhem.

"Two soldiers went into his house last night, forced him into the stable, and locked him in. Then they partied all night with his wife and daughter. They really messed up the house. I'll deal with it, Vasil Akimovitch Sabayev."

Then he left with the German. He was very concerned, because he suspected that Dobrusz had been involved. He ran into Papavkin near the barns. Dobrusz was on guard duty. Zipunov was inside. He woke up Zipunov. The little farmer faced Menakhem half asleep, holding up his pants with both hands.

"Why'd you wake me up? I just got off guard duty."

The German, who had been behind Menakhem, pointed his pipe at Zipunov: "Him! And there was another guy."

"You can go," Menakhem answered in German.

When he was alone with the little farmer he asked, "So it was you who was in the German's house?"

Zipunov buckled the belt on his pants. Foam drooled from his mouth, and he wiped it with the tip of his tongue. His lips curled up as if in pain, and he yelled, "Since when do Jews defend Germans?! You should be ashamed of yourself as a Jew to reprimand me! What's it to you if we had some fun with their women for one little night? You all want to be subservient to everyone. To the Russians, the Poles, and now the Germans!"

Menakhem lunged at him with his fists. Just then Sgt. Orlov showed up and separated them.

"You're disgusting!" said Menakhem. "You have guilt on your hands. You're no better than the Germans. Your pockets are full of plunder. And you have the blood of your Belarussian brothers on your hands."

"I wasn't the only one there! Dobrusz was there. He was the one who took me to the Germans and said we should take revenge. He's a Jew, too. Why are you picking on me? You don't pick on your own! Only on Russians!"

"Coward!" yelled Menakhem as he walked out.

He was summoned to headquarters in the middle of the night. The member of the Supreme War Council was sitting in the reception hall. Col. Gusyev was also there, along with *Politkommissar* Sabayev and several higher officers who had been called especially from various posts. Sitting off to the side was an older man, gray, with broad shoulders and a gentle Jewish face. Menakhem could not remember where he had seen him, but he recognized the face. He was near the door, waiting, calm, unperturbed.

Sabayev told Menakhem, "Come closer," as he opened a Moscow newspaper. "See, there's an article about you, and here are your drawings. Simonov describes you." Col. Gusyev got up. He was a tall, large man, with deep-set eyes and striking features. His Kalmyk face revealed his good nature. He said to Sabayev: "Don't make things worse for Mikhail Issacovich! Speak clearly, and to the point!"

Lieut. Gen. Shamshin smiled. You've been promoted to the rank of lieutenant. Your rank has been restored. Understand?"

It was past midnight when Menakhem walked to the barns to look for Sergei Orlov. He just had to tell him everything! Sergei was already asleep. The soldiers woke up and congratulated him, then he left with Sergei. It was a mild night. They sat down at the foot of the German stone statue and sang.

"Mikhail, there's no wind. We could sow poppy seeds! The sky is like God's palace. The stars are its windows, through which bright angels fly out." He looked at the moon and continued: "Fire is the *Tsar*. Water, the *Tsarina*. Earth, the mother. The sky, the father. Winter, the innkeeper. Rain, the provider. The sun, the prince. The moon, the princess."

Guards passed them: "Are you drunk? Stand up!" Menakhem got up, and the guards lifted Orlov. They walked back to the barns arm in arm. Sergei pointed to an orchard in bloom: "See, Mikhail? They should have bloomed long ago. It's already April. Back home they used to say that if an orchard bloomed late, it was a sign that the owner would die soon. They're gonna die, those German bastards! That's the proof! They've murdered so many nations. To Hell with their pagan souls!"

A column of cars went by. One of the guards said, "Headquarters is waking up."

Chapter Four

Köngisberg was taken in early April. The huge German military concentration there was destroyed. Infantry Gen. Lösch and his general staff laid down their arms. The Soviets took 27,000 prisoners. A new tide of German civilians, wagons, and carts overran the roads of Prussia. White flags hung from their wagons. German civilians bowed humbly before exhausted, mud-spattered Russian soldiers. Towards the middle of April the Soviet army began its final attack on Berlin from the east and the southeast. In three days they had reached the suburbs of the German capital. A huge battle raged for five days in the fortified region between the Oder River and the Spree. The German general staff had brought together 180 divisions to stop the march on Berlin.

On April 22, at around 10 a.m., the first three Soviet tanks entered Berlin. The commander of the tank offensive was Lieut. Gen. Semyon Moiseyevich Krivoshein, son of Moishe Krivoshein, a watchmaker in Voronezh. His tanks pushed from the Weissensee district down the Berliner Allee to the center of Berlin. His headquarters was in the concrete cellar of a five-story house. His closest advisor was Lev Oshanin.

The Soviet onslaught began with a storm of artillery fire. Rockets and powerful searchlights lit up enemy positions, blinding the Germans. They fired back chaotically. Their cannons and machine guns were erratic.

The Soviet infantry moved in, followed by tanks in tight formation, row after row. But there were trenches and antitank ditches everywhere. The bridges had been blown up. So the tanks found it impossible to maneuver around the obstacles. The Germans had erected barricades on the streets. And they had stationed antitank artillery inside apartment buildings with concrete defenses.

Gen. Zhukov's army had just wiped out the enemy in Frankfurt-an-der-Oder, Wandlitz, Hennigsdorf, and Köpenik, and was attacking Berlin from the south. The Allies had crossed the Rhine! The hour of victory was at hand. Russian soldiers were marching on the streets of Berlin. They looked angrily at the huge buildings of banks, businesses, and corporations. They walked through the ruins. Fires were burning everywhere. The City Hall was on fire. So was the *Tiergarten*. The Soviet cannons flew huge banners: "To Berlin!"

Capt. Israel Mirkin's troops aimed their cannons on their targets and fired the first salvo at the enemy, unleashing a barrage of cannons after them. The fields around Berlin were all trenches and antitank ditches, and a triple row of ditches surrounded each neighborhood. There was a hilly, heavily wooded area with lakes that stretches from north to south. Soviet, American, and British bombers almost razed that central area to the ground. All that was left of the Propaganda Ministry was a charred skeleton. The Spree River was dark gray, like that of flayed carcasses. It reflected the ruins of the city. Mounds of brick shards and household goods were everywhere, and papers floated from ruin to ruin. The fragment of a poster barely hung on a wall: one wing of a black eagle holding a swastika in its claws.

Ilyushin bombers ruled the skies. The *Reichskanzlei* stood at the corner of Friedrichsplatz. It was the Führer's residence. The Germans were still resisting. With the city surrounded, they built an improvised airport on the asphalt of Charlottenburg Strasse. Lev Oshanin sent a telegram to operations headquarters: "Objective 25. Reinforce firing. Eigthy meters to the right." Reaching the *Reichstag* was a struggle: fortified concrete emplacements, ditches with water, protective trenches.

One night, Valentin sent a report to Krivoshein's headquarters. He had carried out a nighttime raid in the dangerous streets of Berlin: "The Nazi leaders are hiding in the bunkers of the *Reichskanzlei*. Take steps." He had sent the telegram in the middle of the night.

The Polish divisions under the command of Gen. Poplavski had cut off the roads to the west, and were preparing to attack the *Tiergarten*, which protected the *Reichskanzlei* from the west. Hour by hour Oshanin sent news: "There's a provisional airport between the Brandenburg Gate and the Victory Column. The mice in the Reich's cellars will escape from there." Within a few minutes, artillery fire was pounding away.

That night Moscow was celebrating. Colorful fireworks exploded in the air. Fountains of light lit up Spasskaya Tower. "The troops of the First Ukrainian Front and those of our American and British allies have struck the German front from the east and the west, splitting it in two, and have joined forces in the center of Germany in the region of Torgau." Three hundred twenty-four cannons fired twenty-four times in salute.

Oshanin listened to the victory celebration on his radio, mixed with the bombing of the *Tiergarten* and the *Reichskanzlei*. That was *his* victory.

Lev Oshanin had been in good spirits when he separated from Valentin a week earlier, south of the Müggelsee and got on the road with German refugees. He had joined a group of Germans from the other side of the Oder. An elderly man had difficulty managing his little iron cart, and his wife could barely walk, so they had to rest very often. Since the road was narrow, they had to push the cart into the ditch to let the wagons behind them pass. But when they wanted to get back on the road, they could not. There was foul cursing, engines roaring, horses neighing. Insults and chaos ruled the road. The Germans pushed on without pity. Panic swept them with every airplane noise. Oshanin had just left the field for the road, and when he saw the old man and his cart in the ditch, he helped him get back on the road with the endless crowd of people and wagons, and headed south towards Berlin. The old man cursed his wife the whole way for having wanted to flee. It was all the fault of his sons, those Party members, God damn them! "Franz Glubke, my name is Glubke!"

He wore a threadbare leather jacket with a sheepskin pouch that had the keys to his house, his barns, and his cellars: "It won't be long before we can go back." He had relatives south of Berlin. Maybe the Russians would not get that far. There was a wild assortment of people on the road: Germans from Posen and from Wartheland, Ukrainians, *Volksdeutsche*,[1] farmers, officials, firefighters on their fire trucks, a Red Cross car from Danzig, a freight truck from a soap factory in Küstrin, cars and more cars. Oshanin recognized Russian buses and heavy vehicles. They had been plundered deep in Russia.

Evidence of Allied bombardment and Soviet artillery was everywhere: bombed-out warehouses, ruined depots and repair shops. The roads overflowed with people young and old. There was no order. The crowd surged through every fence. They passed abandoned, desolate farms. Poles supporting electric cables were destroyed in some places. Abandoned buses, cars, motorcycles, and all kinds of vehicles

---

1   Nazi term for ethnic Germans living abroad, mostly in Eastern Europe, some of whom collaborated in the looting of Jewish homes and the murder of Jews when the German army invaded.

stood abandoned on the roadside. Their owners had left them for lack of fuel.

Oshanin observed a car full of SS men stopping. They got out to stop a truck, not to check documents but to take the fuel from the tank for themselves. A shootout ensued. When they left, Oshanin saw dead civilians lying in the ditch. He spent that night in an abandoned farm.

Near Berlin he ran into a group of concentration camp prisoners. They had been hurriedly forced to walk to Berlin, these half-dead prisoners. You could not tell what their nationality was. Their SS guards would not let anyone near them. The civilian authorities had abandoned the Russian war prisoners and concentration camp prisoners to the SS. They shot anyone trying to escape. The mob on the road roared, "Why don't you just finish off these filthy swine?" They did not kill them, because if they did then they would not be guards any more, just deserters. Keeping the prisoners alive justified their not fighting on the front.

Oshanin walked proudly on German territory that was in flames. Vetka, Gomel, Minsk, Polesia. That was the region where the Oshanin family had taken root, like an ancient oak tree.

He remembered his uncles: tanners, wagon drivers, cattlemen, orchard keepers. The October Revolution had overturned and disturbed everything. But his deep roots remained, and the old oak grew new branches. The family produced agronomists, military officers, sailors, engineers, tractor drivers, factory managers. The sons of his uncles had taken up occupations that Oshanins had never known. Artsho, the lumberman's son, became a pilot, and the wagon driver's son a lieutenant in the artillery.

He remembered them, those uncles, short, broad-backed, curly-haired Jews who had wandered from Polesie to Gomel and Tchernigov. The mothers had wept bitterly when non-Jews married their sons. Blond, light-eyed grandchildren from Russian and Belarussian mothers played in their skirts. It took them time to resign themselves to their flaxen-haired grandchildren who sat with them at the head of the table for family feasts.

The Oshanins were every-day Jews who no longer went to their synagogue, because the regime had turned it into a club "with red flags" on the walls. But they recited the afternoon prayers by heart, a little incorrectly, in the evenings, behind dust-covered windows, as they pretended to wipe off that dust off the tops of the windows with their fingers. Their Jewishness consisted in respecting the memory of their ancestors, and in their fellow feeling to other Jews.

Oshanin had left home very young. He had joined the army at eighteen. He felt a powerful need to maintain his link to the Oshanin clan, but he could not read the Jewish alphabet. The only prayer book in the house was hidden in a drawer, along with two sooty candlesticks.

He felt his Oshanin family feeling surge on German soil, the seething outrage for the sufferings of his people. If someone had said to him, even half-mockingly, "You're a Jew," he would have slammed his fist down his or her throat. Sometimes he would be filled with pride when he sang Jewish songs. But here, too, his emotions were mixed. Sleeping in a barn, the night before, he dreamed he was standing on a tower watching a procession of Germans. They were coming out of church, carrying holy images and crucifixes. When the procession came near the tower, he could see that they were actually images of Hitler painted as a saint, crucified on a cross.

Oshanin stayed in the four-story house of a German woman. He had money and some gold coins. Even in that Berlin suburb he had enough to obtain food. The woman, Johanna Ostergard, showed him some friendliness. She was a withered woman with a large Adam's apple and big blue eyes. She wore a black velvet neckband with a pair of gilded glasses that rested on her flat chest. When she was nervous she would repeatedly put the glasses on her nose, but they would immediately fall back down. Then her yellowed, bony fingers would feel around for them, and her eyes would moisten. Whenever her long legs took a step, it would make a cracking sound, as if dry bones were breaking.

The brick-walled cellar was divided into a labyrinth with wooden ladders serving as partitions. In peacetime, the landlord stored old furniture and coal for heating there. Now the entire cellar had been transformed into a bunker where each family had its own little space. Oshanin stayed up most of the night, listening carefully to the bombing. When he first went down to the cellar and saw the wooden ladders, it was as if he had stumbled into a traveling circus, with tired, dozing beasts. Near him slept Sigfried Wendtke with his double chin, who wheezed and who stank from sweat. He was the principal butcher at the corner of the street. His daughters lay near him. A few steps away, beyond a wooden divider rested the family of Hosenke, the jurist and justice official. Next was Butke the lawyer, near a little table with a dark electric lamp. Right next to Oshanin was the family of Selditz, a Prussian *Junker*.

Oshanin's generosity alleviated Johanna Ostergard's hunger. She told her neighbors that he was a relative and that he would be staying for only a week. Whenever the shooting quieted down he would leave to buy more food. She ate with great appetite. She took special pleasure in drinking "real" coffee, and she would ask him, "How did you manage to get this, Mr. Ristke?"

Oshanin strode through the huge rooms of the old German house and observed the dark paintings. Generations of German faces looked out at him. Men with puffy cheeks, double chins and stiff pointy whiskers, women with huge coiffed heads and ghastly pale faces—all in dark brown and black frames. One showed a huge oak table with abundance of apples, pears, and various plants, and, at the very center, a dead duck with its head hanging. Its brightly-colored feathers, shimmered, but the dead eye sparkled like mother of pearl, with blood dripping from it. "That was a well-aimed shot," said Oshanin, pointing at the picture.

He touched the old hunting rifles that hung in the great hall, and he read the inscriptions painted in white in flowery Gothic lettering on the deer skulls. The dates reflected the wide reach of the Ostergard dynasty: 1866 Schwarzwalden, 1889 Wartheland. Oshanin lingered at one deer head, and he took it down from the wall: 1916 Bialowieza. "Not far from my home," he thought. A spider crawled out of the head and hung by a thin thread.

Oshanin leafed through gilt-bound books. Here were the six volumes of Johann Gottfried Schnabel's *Die Wunderliche Fata einiger See-Fahrer—Auf der Insel Felsenburg*. He looked mockingly at Agnes Miegel's *Geshichten aus Alt-Preussen*. Who would write about the end of Prussia? Would it also be a woman? Perhaps she would be from Müggelsee, where he had left Valentin? All his years at the military academy in Leningrad, his study of languages and of German military history—all of that was now useful.

He moved about easily among all these furnishings. He hid his disdain, especially for the linens embroidered with rhyming epigram, which contrasted with the cruel taste of the owners for dead stuffed birds that hung in the rooms over the doorways, their wings spread out, their heads down, and their mouths open. Animal trophies were strewn near the tables and the sturdy leather armchairs: bears, leopards, and foxes, their heads stuffed and their eyes replaced with large, fiery red pearls. The darkness of the rooms gave those pearls the gleam of blood.

Johanna Ostergard had remained an old maid until the war. It was only during the war that she had gotten married to an SS officer, a son of farmers and foresters. Her husband was a healthy, common fellow with little education, who wished to climb the social ladder by marrying a "von Ostergard" woman. The Ostergards were *Junkers*. There had been bankers in the family, lawyers, army officers, and even a minister who had been famous in Prussia in the time of Friedrich II. But the family had declined after the First World War. Its holdings had been primarily in former Germany colonies and in lands that were no longer part of the Reich, in Galizien. By the time the Nazis came to power, Johanna was the only one left in the ancestral house, until this country churl showed up, who did not even know the proper way to use tableware. She told Oshanin all of this in the first few days. She was intrigued by his demeanour: "It looks like you must have been raised abroad for some years. It's easy to see. Or perhaps there's foreign blood in your veins?"

Oshanin had a clear view of the streets of Berlin from the top floor. That was where he set up his radio transmitter. He had been carrying hand grenades with him for some time now. He spent the night before reading the Berlin newspapers and monitoring the radio. A wounded soldier down in the cellar told of the huge military effort that the Germans were making to defend the city. They had divided Berlin into nine sectors, each with its own separate garrison. Once Oshanin even helped the Germans dig ditches in the street and construct concrete barriers. Then he observed that the work was being done by civilians and also war prisoners and concentration camp prisoners. The Germans were building bunkers and firing positions among the ruins, hidden behind mounds of rubble. The center of Berlin had a fortified ring around it, which protected most of the government buildings, and which included over 400 shooting positions.

Oshanin made radio contact with headquarters the third night of his stay with Frau Ostergard. They had been waiting for his report. Their nerves were at high pitch, and telegrams flew fast and furious. The red light kept going on and off. Loud rumbling kept interrupting the radio dispatches, as if from a water mill.

"Concrete fortifications are linked by underground tunnels. They're using the metro network, the cellars, the sewer system's canals. Narrow-gauge rails are carrying cartloads of weapons to the artillery."

"Hundreds of factories and workshops in underground locations are supplying the front: Objectives 6 and 9."

"Destroy objectives 71, 102, 103: Nests of the Third Tank Army."

"An army is being concentrated in Ketzin and Potsdam to defend Berlin."

Suddenly a terrible noise shook Oshanin. Three armored cars had stopped near the house. The red light of his transmitter went out. He hid it among old chests in the attic and went towards the stairs. He heard screaming in the street. They broke down the door. Guards closed off the street. Oshanin stood on the roof and watched the shadows of soldiers running in the deserted street. It was a bright night, the moon shining overhead. He heard boots running up the stairs, their heels banging. He only had two grenades on him. He went for the washroom on the roof. A German's scream echoed off the stone walls. He heard footsteps on broken plaster.

He thought: "They've found me now. Or maybe it's a coincidence that they're searching this house. No, it can't be coincidence. They've detected my radio messages, and the transmissions led them here." Oshanin knew that there were special watches that could determine the source of radio transmissions within a few meters. The house stood like a lonely boulder among the ruins. Where could he go? Someone was tearing down the attic door and searching with a flashlight. A blue light slid across the moist stone and walls. Oshanin hid behind an antenna. Armored cars were waiting down in the street. He knew that the slightest motion would attract their searchlights. And then it would be too late. But it stopped two meters away from him. A single cloud rose up to cover the moon, and it grew dark. That would last two minutes. Half the cloud passed through. He was three meter from the edge of the roof. He jumped and threw both grenades at the cars.

"Hands up!"

Oshanin did not answer. The searchlight fumbled among the antenna wires and came to rest on his chest. His little revolver burned in his hands.

Should he shoot first? But before he pulled the trigger an explosion shook the night. Something dark and heavy broke off the building and flew up towards the sky like a black wing. The searchlight went out. Flames rose soared up from the street. The German started edging back towards the staircase. Right then Oshanin lunged through the attic door onto the German's back. The German did not resist. He crouched at Oshanin's feet with his head hunched between his shoulders.

There was shooting in the street and screams for help. People were running on the lower staircases. Oshanin forced open the door to the Ostergard house and knocked into Johanna, who was terrified: "Oh, my dear God! You're bleeding…" His face was drenched with blood, and his hands were bleeding, too. Johanna looked for her handbag and tried to run out, screaming. Oshanin blocked the door: "Don't move! Stay here!"

Her Adam's apple began throbbing up and down. She fumbled for her glasses with her bony fingers but could not put them on. Oshanin's severe tone cowed her. She took him to the bathroom and brought him towels and bandages. She kept whispering, "My God! My God!" Oshanin washed off the German's blood from his face and hands and tracked every movement that she made. Then he lay down on the plush divan and smoked. It was pitch black in the room. The woman stood by the window. There were ambulances, corpses, wounded men. She said, "Yes, dear God, this is now the end!"

Oshanin thought, "Soon they're going to go through the whole house. From room to room." But he could not leave. It was too late. The whole street was being guarded. His radio was still upstairs. What should he do? Maybe he could somehow slip out like a shadow? It would start soon, as soon as they finished with the wounded and the dead.

The woman was weeping. She had fallen to her knees. She wept aloud, hysterically. It was totally dark. Oshanin's cigarette went out. He leaned towards the weeping woman and touched her thin neck: "Frau Johanna, calm down, calm down." She took his hand in her warm fingers and brought it to her lips. He felt her tears and saliva, slippery, sticky. She guided his hand to her neck and he felt her Adam's apple. Then she pressed his hand to her chest, and he felt the cold glasses that hung on the velvet neckband. She stopped weeping. He felt the convulsive trembling of her shoulders, and then something hard and bony embraced his knees.

The First Belarussian Front under the command of Marshal Zhukov began preparing its artillery in the middle of April for a short but fierce attack. It started at midnight. This artillery onslaught was accompanied by air strikes on the deepest positions of the enemy all the way to the outskirts of Berlin. The infantry and the tanks moved in right afterwards, along with more powerful air strikes. It was still night when Menakhem's regiment marched towards the east, towards the Seelow Heights.

The Messerschmitts and their counteroffensive stymied the attack. It seemed impossible to take their objective in one blow. The fighting at night was heavy, for the enemy had assembled a well-organized defense. It was difficult trudging in the moonlit night on hilly terrain among bushes, plowed fields, and deep trenches that the Germans had dug. There was the scent of overturned soil in springtime and of fields beginning to green. "Oh, God! Lead me to the gates of Berlin! May I see the city in ruins! Let me not die in this awful land, among mine fields, in a night of fire! Since You have taken me back to my desolate homeland, show me the desolation of the enemy! Lead me to the lair of the beast and let me see with my own eyes Your wrath and your punishment of the murderers. For I will not be there alone. My whole people will be there. Hear my prayer in this final hour! Hear my strangled cry to You! I will not forget Your grace!"

Menakhem carried a letter to Anna under his jacket. He had written it before going on the attack. Why had he not mailed the letter? Now it was too late. Maybe tomorrow? "Will there be a tomorrow for me?"

Good Sergei Orlov walked next to him, singing something. Menakhem knew it was meant to drive away fear. He wanted to free himself from the terror that gripped his chest and pounded in his temples. Every time he tore himself free from that grip of fear, he would say something to Menakhem and laugh an uneasy little laugh: 'Life and death are so close together that even a flea couldn't jump between them." Dobrusz walked not far away. He was confident. He had drunk some liquor before leaving. Zipunov moved like a shadow. Col. Gusyev was energetic. Three enemy planes appeared from a mountaintop, then were shrouded in smoke. A mine exploded.

"Get down! Hit the dirt!"

The earth was cool. It was good to people, it embraced them. Even the earth of the enemy. Menakhem took Sergei's arm, and they walked together. Suddenly huge searchlights lit up a semi-circle. The beams grew brighter and brighter. They cut through the front lines of the Germans, blinding them with their harsh brightness. The footpaths lit up, the roads, the bushes, the twisted tree trunks, the skies. It was all light and shadow, shadow and blinding light.

"Forward! Forward! Hurrah!"

Orlov stretched up tall and raised his machine gun over his head, then he lowered it a bit and began running with Menakhem. They ran faster and more eagerly downhill, as if they were spurred on by the searchlights through the fields. It was like running through a fire. Their shadows grew gigantic, so it seemed that their heads had already reached the enemy trenches.

"Sergei, there's letter on my bosom. Take it out of there. Don't let... Mail it. The address is on the envelope. Don't forget. On my bosom."

Someone was shot. They could not stop. Everything was rushing with them, the bushes, the roads, the clouds. Everything on Earth was rushing westward. Blazes of light sliced up the skies, the fields, the people, into a thousand pieces. But not the shadows. Your shadow always ran ahead of you, for miles. The artillery was no longer frightful. Now it was the nearby rattling of machine guns that terrified.

Clouds of sand rolled on the sandy road. The branches shook as if a harsh wind were blowing. But the night was calm. It was machine gun bullets. Why did the night not end? The searchlights stopped the day from coming. "Will my elongated shadow come back close to my feet so that I can put my arms around him? Or will I be stuck forever with this ridiculously large shadow? How will he fit into the four corners of my house?"

But that was not his shadow. It was fear running ahead of him. It was terror that spread from horizon to horizon!

"Anna, I write to you hurriedly. We're getting ready for the onslaught. I only have a few minutes. I'm sitting in headquarters. Last week they gave me back my rank of lieutenant. Night is falling. There's a commotion in the street of the village. But I've been ready for a long time. I'm facing towards the west, and if I turn around, it's only to look towards you. I don't know why my life is unfolding before like a parchment right at this minute. I can see myself living among Jews in my village near the Wkra River. A four-year-old boy sits on a wooden threshold in the marketplace. He sees the high church tower, and bright, puffy clouds over it. The street is paved with crooked fieldstones. My uncle Elye arrives from the countryside in his shabby cart.

"A goat stands near a fence. The grasses have a wonderful scent. I've never again in my life smelled such an aroma as when I chased the little white goat we had gotten. I ran through the meadow, the grasses up to my face. Blooms from the grass stuck to my lips. I couldn't catch that rascally goat. They looked for me late into the night, and it was only when the moon rose that they found me asleep in the deep grass, little white goat standing near me. My mother carried me home in her arms. The goat ran after us, bleating, with a big, brilliant full moon over my mother. That was also the only time I ever saw such a moon. I'll never see one like that again, just as I'll never smell the wonderful scent of the grass that was as tall as I was. Perhaps tonight I will, or some night soon, when I'll return to my childhood, lying in the grasses of the field in springtime. My life will again unfold like a scroll of parchment that someone opens for a while. And when I go back to my beginning, to those earliest memories of a four-year-old, my lips will taste the field again, and the memory will return, and that will be the end.

"No, that won't be the end. It'll be a return to the beginning and the start of another existence. I've wrapped a package with my recent drawings. You'll get them. Lieut. Sabayev will send them. When I close my eyes I see the blinding whiteness around you, the whiteness and the quiet bound together. Anna, you'll be the only witness to my war years. Perhaps someone will rise from the ruins and look for me. Tell them the little you know about me. Tell them that I remained a mournful Jew until the end who walked across his destroyed homeland until he reached the gates of Berlin.

"I'm no hero, and my death won't be the result of heroism. I was thoroughly scared, angry, loving, prayerful. Every night sound frightened me, and I asked the Almighty to protect me with every step I took. I wanted to live. I loved the peaceful sky and the sprouting green grasses. I've often picked up branches with flowers in German orchards that bullets have broken off. I've blessed life even on the soil of those who sowed death.

"Everything will be over when you get this letter. We'll celebrate our victory. The flag of the righteous will fly over the Reichstag. Remember me on that day as someone who helped achieve our goal, even if he didn't get there himself. I can see our victory already, and that fills me with joy. The other thing that makes me happy is that you came into my life. I hug you and kiss you as I get ready to go. Menakhem."

A cool wind blew on the far side of the hills. The searchlights outshone the stars and obliterated the sky. The twinkling stars died out as the night receded. Shadows tried to hang on but could not. They lay stretched out on the open field, torn and fragmented.

Sergei Orlov was driving his sled over the roads through the woods covered with frosty bluish snow. He was almost at the edge of the woods. He could see Sorovo, his village, in the distance: a blanket of gray snow on the roofs and dark, bluish smoke rising. It was bitter cold. His poor horse was covered with white frost. The horse stopped suddenly, heavy steam blowing from his nostrils. The sled creaked. The horse stood mutely. The "Redhead" walked across the snow, dressed in a light-colored sarafan with silver lace. Her unkempt hair, fiery red, fell to her breast. The horse neighed. A wolf howled in the distance. The sled crashed into a ditch. Sergei was on his knees, and the redhead was leaning over him closer and closer. Her flaming hair brushed his forehead, all afire. He could not bear the heat she radiated. Suddenly the horse lunged and galloped. He was now alone with her. She held out her hands. He felt himself being carried across the fields. An old wolf ran ahead. Every step of the redhead brought a blaze of heat and light. An owl hooted in the lonely oak tree that he had avoided when he was plowing. The redhead laughed. The wolf's eyes were burning, the snow was melting…

Someone was screaming in his ear: "Move it! Run!" Oh, it must be Menakhem. What's he doing here in the icy fields of Sorovo?

Night was gone, and the sky was pressing down upon him.

"Sergei! Get up!" Menakhem grabbed him by the shoulders and breathed right close to Sergei's mouth.

"Where are we, Mikhail?"

They ran together over rough terrain. Neither a regular plow nor a swing plow had torn up the soil. Mines and cannonballs had lacerated the field, ripping deeply into its red flesh. Something was gnawing at Orlov, but he did not know what. Was it the snow fields that he would not see again? Was it the redhead, who had pulled him to her arms? Or was it the horse, who had run on without him that night on the road home? Would Sorovo be there, when the horse returned, frost on its breath, dragging the empty sled? The horse would pass by the market place and the abandoned church and stop at the gate of his home. His mother would come to the stoop, frightened. His girlfriend Nastiya would come running from the next house. When they saw the empty sled they would wring their hands and moan, "We've lost our beloved Seryozhka! Lost the apple of our eye! Open your doors, people! Sergei is dead! His body lies somewhere among wolves on the frozen field!"

Sergei ran over the ditches. He fell, got up, and kept running, and he could hear the moaning in that faraway village on the Oka. He was weeping to himself with his mother, with Nastiya, lamenting his fate. She will sit at her spinning wheel and sing the song about silky grasses that cover her footsteps, a sign that her beloved was no more. It was good to hear Nastiya's voice again. It was all over. He was far, far away, looking down from the sky, seeing everything, hearing everything. How fast the time had flown since he had fallen all alone in the snow field, until Nastiya's singing.

Now came new ear-splitting explosions. A German tank lifted its cannon, and everything went dark. Who opened the floodgates? A torrential flood was unleashed to the skies, it swirled together, then foamed and swept away. Clusters of clouds dragged the heavens down to the earth.

A distant little island sparkled at the center of a world that was going to Hell. Menakhem was back in Mazowia. Six-year-old Menakhem was standing in the market square. The farmers had already left the fair. The scent of horse manure and hay mixed with the smell of milk from the cows that had just returned from pasture. He was looking at the big red-brick church. Little Jewish houses and miserable shops were crowded around it. The bell ringer walked through the empty streets and opened the iron church gate. Menakhem followed him, drawn by the quiet of the church yard. The bell-ringer, Mr. Franek, patted his head. Two long ropes hung down from the tall tower. When little Menakhem looked all the way up he lost his balance and fell. Mr. Franek suddenly pulled the rope, and bells rang out up over Menakhem's head. The sound echoed, then multiplied again and again, resounding over the evening fields and all the way to the bluish edge of the forest. They reverberated, combining and recombining, but softer, gentler, polished by the beautiful sky. But before they had totally quieted down, still barely hanging on, old Mr. Franek pulled the rope gain, and peals again rang up to God in Heaven. The little boy held on with his hands, because the booming bells shook his little body, and he grabbed at the bell-ringer's coat tails. "Let me pull the rope, Mr. Franek." He grabbed it and swung with it. The world swung with him. The brass peals shook the woods. Flocks of birds flew up and around the bell tower. Uncle Elye had stopped at the open church gate, angry. He picked the boy up and carried him on his shoulder and carried him across the market. Mr. Franek was laughing, his laughter mixing with the clanging bells. Menakhem could hear nothing. He had called the villages to vespers. From then on he was called "the bell-ringer."

Now those bells were clanging once again, and the hills and valleys resounded. Menakhem pushed his face into the ground and covered his ears. The echoing tore at his body. These were no longer brass bells, but a thundering as if the Earth were splitting. Col. Gusyev was running across the field. He yelled at a soldier: "Get up! Run! A hundred more steps! You coward!" He held his heavy revolver against his chest: "Move it! Forward!"

Wings of steel were fluttering over his head. A bonfire was burning, Kalmyk herdsmen sitting around it. The herd stood in the middle of the field crowded back to back. The silvery moon shone, reflecting in the horns of the bull. The flames leapt up to the sky. Suddenly the bird of the steppes called out. The bull was black and so was the forest. The bull rushed out of the black herd towards the night cry of the bird, dragging the cord that was attached to its nose ring. Gusyev the cattleman ran right after the aroused bull. He reached the end of the rope and tied it around himself. The steppe bird flew lower. Now he could see that it was a huge eagle, its wings outspread over Gusyev's head. Gusyev fell, and the bull dragged him over the field. There were the woods, and Gusyev would be smashed against the tree trunks in a few seconds. But he refused to let go of the rope. He tried to grab onto something to hold him. He tried to anchor himself in the earth, but a brute force ripped him away. One more second and he would be dead. The herdsmen sat calmly around the fire.

"Hey! Get up! Move on! Forward!"

Dobrusz was advancing towards the enemy, his head held high. His fear left him when the firing began. He did not belong anywhere anymore, not to the night nor to the day. Not to the Earth nor to the sky. A dull indifference was upon him. There was no home for him in this world. Now he was attacking an unfamiliar, evil world.

Oh God, why did You put Dobrusz on such an indifferent world? Why could he not have stayed in the village Olyevsk like a homeless dog? Why had he not gone with the little farmer at the train station to a new home? He wrestled with the black shadow that wanted to take him on his wings up to the smoky skies. He cried, "No! No!" on that gray dawn and ran with his chest out towards the low clouds. He feared the quiet. It hid a thousand dangers. Quiet meant death. When he heard the artillery firing that meant the evil hand had begun, and it would stop. It was not monotony and loneliness. Shooting made the time fly fast and gave you hope that it would end, and then everything would be different. No, things would not be different! His home was still gone. The farmers had plowed under the humble Jewish farmhouses. He looked into the village huts. He saw the icons at night and their lamps. A dog smelled him and wagged its tail, the neighbor's dog. Dobrusz could feel the heat from its nostrils. The barn door was barred. He opened the door and climbed into the hay. The dog curled up at his feet. He could hear cows mooing on the road and dogs barking far away. The dog's ears perked up. Footsteps were coming through the puddles. Farmers banged on the door, holding lanterns: "Get down from the hayloft, dirty Jew!" Pitchforks shone in the light of the lanterns. The dog howled pitifully. They were coming after Dobrusz with clubs and pitchforks. He broke through the straw roof. He lit one match after another and threw them down. The dry hay caught fire, then the straw roof. He was surrounded by fire. Smoke was blowing, with Dobrusz hidden behind it. He started to roll down, faster and faster until he hit the plowed earth. The farmers opened the stalls and drove out the cattle and horses. The chains of the wells were creaking. Dobrusz was running in the fields. The fire spread more and more. His shadow had almost reached the forest. Just a bit more and he would be swallowed up by the wonderful darkness blessed by God.

Someone at his back yelled, "Forward! Forward! Run!"

"Don't you recognize me? It's me, Menakhem! Give me your hand! Another few steps! Be strong, Dobrusz! We'll be out of danger."

Papavkin remained in the middle of the desolate field and bent towards the earth. He took the pouch out of his pocket and poured tobacco into his black pipe. He went down on one knee and searched for his lighter. A shell flew close by, screaming. The blast sent him flying on his face.

"Swine! Made me spill my tobacco, bastards! Couldn't wait a bit till I had a smoke?!" He opened the pouch again and took some with two fingers. But they were stiff, so it was hard to hold the pouch.

"Get up! Run! Run!"

"What's the rush? I'll get there in time. I won't miss anything. Are you deaf? Let me smoke!" He stuffed the pipe and inhaled. Then he stood up and looked around. Dawn was breaking. It was time to open the gate, time to open the stable and let out the cows and the lambs. Soon they'd be driving the herd down the street. Onufri was already sounding his horn. Lame Vanyushka was cracking his whip. The lambs were bleating. Hey, old woman, why don't you heat up the oven? Planning to spend the winter on top of the stove? You lazy bear! Are you paralyzed? Soon there was a flame in the oven. He heard her pushing the heavy cast iron pots and the clang of the poker against the tin oven. Then he smelled the fresh-baked rye rolls. The leggings were dry. He took them out of the oven. They were of pure gray wool. He strapped them on with leather thongs. He was in the mood to work. He wanted to push the plow. He wanted to cut through the hay field with his scythe. Yegorka, the *kolkhoz* brigadier, came knocking on his window. A bowl of hot cabbage soup was on the table. He stood at the threshold and looked out at God's world at dawn. He shamelessly gulped down the soup. Some old men were hanging around in the *kolkhoz* courtyard. Pitiful horses dragged miserable harnesses around the muddy roads. The roof needed to be repaired with new straw. The walls of the stables were sinking because the wood was rotting. The wool on the lambs was all matted and knotted. They wouldn't make good fur. Vanyushka drove them over thorny fields.

After taking his dun-colored horse for the *kolkhoz* stable, they had sent it away to the city after a year and never brought it back. Papavkin could still not forget his horse fifteen years later. He also remembered the boundaries of his land. He had marked them secretly. Maybe oneday things would again be as they had been. That day must come, and his farm would live again. Now he was running towards his own fate. Brothers, why are you running like demons? Don't be in such a hurry! The herd is already in the fields beyond! Oh, bitter fate! Papavkin marched among tanks and trucks. He trod heavily on German soil. He knew that behind him lay a homeland that was so poor, yet a thousand threads bound him to it. He would go back right then to those pitiful fields. Don't expect anything good when you return, pals! If only it doesn't get worse! God's world is being ruined. If you survived another day, get on your knees before St. Nikolai the miracle worker and thank him!

Zipunov remained lying among bushes, curled up in pain. He was sure that bomb fragments had torn up his body, so what was the point in torturing himself—mortally wounded—by still running over that faraway hill? His howling gradually turned into moans: "Oh, my poor little head! Poor me! What has happened to me? What will my pitiful orphans say?"

He felt himself all over, tore open his tunic, ripped open his shirt, and touched his chest with his fingers. He was alive. His heart was warm. Then he brushed his face to see if there was blood. His eyes glowed. He opened them wide. Circles of light and blobs of wax sprang before him and vanished. A heavy weight pressed on him. Shiny boots with heels were dancing on his back, his chest, his head. Burning rods were slicing into his body. One more blow, and that would be the end of Zipunov. No, he would survive.

Suddenly, he forced his hands open and looked for the linen bag hanging on a strap from his neck. He opened it and poured out little gold rings, gems, watches, silver coins: "Take it! Take it! It's not mine! I'm giving it back!" The gold gleamed brilliantly under the searchlights. Everyone saw the jewelry all around him. A stranger mocked him bitterly. A riding crop whipped over his head. Suddenly the stranger jumped on a black horse and drove off. Zipunov was alone in the bushes. The jewelry was still there, at his feet. He was not going to just leave it there. Why was the night so blinding? Zipunov crawled on all fours. But as soon as he reached for a gold ring he felt something soft, drops of blood! When he touched his fingers to his eyes he saw that they were drenched in blood. He began to lament out loud that he was dying, very soon. But wait! Maybe he was already dead. Zipunov waited for something to happen. He waited for a black wing to flap over him and for someone to close his eyes. That waiting was good. It grew calmer and calmer in the field.

The medics dragged him out of the bushes the next day. His eyes were still closed when they took him to the field infirmary, though they found no wound on him. His hands were closed tight on his chest, gripping his little linen bag. He opened his eyes narrowly and there was both joy and terror in them. Oh, Death was already building its nest in me! Who knows if I'll ever manage to drag my bones back to my village? No, he would not go back! His Belarussian neighbors were waiting for him. They would take revenge. He would quietly find a way to tell his wife to meet him secretly in the hut in the forest. He would leave with her and the children for distant villages. Zipunov was full of self-pity. His whining lament was drowned out by the roar of planes flying low overhead.

"Dobrusz, there's nothing wrong with you." Menakhem looked at the boy with big, fearful eyes. The boy lay on his back, facing the sky. His upper lip was twisted in a grimace, holding back tears. He was breathing heavily. A purplish film covered his lips. The tin bowl of soup that they had brought him an hour ago lay near him. The field kitchen had risked their lives bringing hot soup in a thermos under German fire.

"Why don't you eat, Dobrusz?" He did not answer. His machine gun leaned against his knee, the barrel pointing towards his jaw. For the first time Menakhem realized how young he was, maybe sixteen. Peach fuzz glimmered on his cheeks, and his pupils were large. The whites of his eyes had yellowed. Menakhem touched his hands. He brushed his fingers on his face: "Why don't you answer? Tell me what your father's name was? What's your family name? It's important. Answer me, my good Dobrusz! He undid his straps. Dobrusz's eyes moistened.

"What's wrong? There's nothing wrong with you. Look at me! Why is your head down? Just try to be strong!"

The boy's face was drenched in sweat. It was daybreak. Bullets flew overhead. Clouds of smoke like shreds of torn cotton hung in the air, then dissolved slowly.

"Dobrusz, give me your hand. We have to go." Suddenly Menakhem began to speak Yiddish, the language that Jews spoke on the Vistula and on the Dniepr, the language of their fathers and grandfathers. He spoke Yiddish gently to Dobrusz amid the din of gunfire. He was really talking to himself aloud, and it was a pleasure to Menakhem to hear his own words. Some time earlier when he had spoken to him in Yiddish, the boy opened his eyes wide in surprise. From then on he had spoken to him mostly in Polish, sometimes in Russian. Dobrusz answered in Ukrainian. But this time when Menakhem spoke Yiddish, the boy's eyes filled with tears. Just as a layer of ice thaws out in the sun, Dobrusz's face began to soften. He sat up, grabbed Menakhem' hands, and stammered in simple, plain, country Yiddish mixed with Ukrainian.

Dobrusz wept. He could not hold the dish of food in his trembling hands.

"You're a Jew when everyone hates you, when the Christians look at you in anger and suspicion, and their children scream at you, 'You killed Jesus!' And then the Germans come and exterminate us all."

The first stage of Operation Berlin ended on April 25th. The German forces in Berlin were cut in two halves, isolated from each other, and surrounded by the Soviet military. Then the second stage began, the liquidation of both halves of the enemy, the storming of the city, and the broad push by the Soviets towards the Elbe River, where the forward guard had already made contact with the Allied armies. Before the German military in Berlin was completely surrounded, the Nazi headquarters ordered the Twelfth Army, which was face to face with the American Army, to turn around and march towards the east. In doing that they opened the road for the Americans and launched a bitter attack on the eastern front. At the same time the Ninth German Army, which was surrounded in the forests south of the city, pushed westwards in an effort to join with the Twelfth and combine their forces.

Those days were difficult for Menakhem's division, which was being attacked from east and west. Its positions were raked by fire from two sides. It was a wooded area with lakes and swamps and waterways. The Nineteenth Germany Army fought on two fronts, one trying to reach Berlin from the southeast, the other trying to join with the surrounded Ninth Army.

Anna's letter back to Menakhem:

"Mikhail, we're waiting to hear that Berlin has fallen. This must come to an end! These last days have been very hard. I fear the nights. The most savage beast can be at its worst while it's dying. I've tried everything to calm down. I know that my unease comes from the doubts that I get after difficult operations and from worrying for your safety. I jump at every word addressed to me. I'm afraid to open letters. Only your jittery handwriting on the envelope can calm me.

"You don't know what it is to lie down, exhausted, and look up out the window at a chestnut tree in bloom. The smell of anesthetics is overpowering. I'm in a stupor, half conscious, prey to devils and demons who laugh and mock me in my dreams. When I exhale I don't want to inhale that oppressive odor again. I fight off the swamps of my nightmares until I can see your face. You don't know how many times you chased away my nightmares!

"We talked so little between us! I've never even held your handsome, troubled face in my hands. I've never felt you next to me or even your warm breath. I've often regretted the reserve that I showed you. Our goodbye was only the touch of your trembling fingers and the light brush of your lips. I'm not ashamed to say it, Misha. You stirred new feelings in me. You made my soul thrill with excitement and sweetness.

"The harder I work and push myself during the day, the stronger I feel your presence at night. I wake up in the middle of the night and walk through the wards of the wounded. When I stand over them, I see something of you in their faces. All their faces lead me to you. All their eyes remind me of yours. Every drop of blood makes me shudder and think, 'Has Mikhail been wounded?'

"Don't be surprised. I always write to you at night after a wearying day. I'm exhausted, like you. Yes, the distance, the gunfire, and the blood that separate us also bring us closer. I want to tell you all of this again and again during these fateful days, now, before the end of the war. Maybe my love for you could replace what has been stolen from you—your home. Will you accept my love? Yes, I can feel it. I believe it.

"The children's refuge that I've organized is moving along. I often visit these sad, lonely Jewish children. The house is in a nice neighborhood in Otwock, not far from Warsaw. You can't imagine how they wait for me! I've found some good Russian friends who are helping me to get everything I need for the children. The gratitude of the children towards the Soviet soldiers is very touching. I hope they never become disillusioned! I'm counting the hours till Berlin falls. I'm waiting for you, Mikhail, Misha! How hard it is to wait!"

Was it really Anna?

The last time he had seen her she was in her white medical coat, her hands raised. It was painful to remember her professional, icy, steely eyes. Her face was hard then, sad, and fearful. And there was something vague and alien that disturbed him. The deep stress wrinkles in her eyes bothered him especially.

But he saw a different Anna in her letter. He knew them both. The first one would lead him out of all dangers and wipe the dirt off his lacerated face. The second would give him her girlish heart and brighten his days. He read the letter dozens of times, and each time he found something new that he had not been aware of. Menakhem had never embraced life as he did now. To live meant to see Anna. Oh, God, now I can look upon your veiled face with hope and faith. I've started hearing the twittering of frightened birds during lulls in the shooting, and my eyes look with pity on every little blade of grass. When I see a lonely dog running over the trenches I pray for its life. In the heat of battle, fighting on the east and the west, I can breathe in the scent of trees in bloom. I follow the flight of the clouds. My fingers touch the grasses near the trenches. I take pleasure in recognizing those I knew so well as a boy. I feel Anna's letter in my bosom. The love that bloomed under terrible skies and clouds of smoke has given me back the world, Oh God.

The shooting stopped on the third day. Purple clouds floated down to the swamps and hung from low trees. Sometimes the silver wing of a plane shone through, and you could hear anti-aircraft cannons. Pearl necklaces seemed to shimmer on the clouds. Capt. Rezinko, head of the medics, led his men out to pick up the wounded. The forward positions of the Germans were on the far side of the lake amidst rushes, in a forest of alders and poplars. You might think the landscape was normal and tranquil, if not for the purple pearls dotting the sky and the spirals of smoke floating between heaven and earth. You might expect a farmer driving a village wagon on a dirt road to the fields. His herd might appear from the valley. Crows would flutter over the field, waiting for the plowman to open the first furrow.

But that would be a surface impression. If you looked closer, it seemed that a whirlwind had torn through. The treetops had been mutilated. Smashed branches dangled from them, swaying in the wind. Some trees were left with no tops at all. Only a severed trunk remained. The woods had been desolated. The pine tops looked as though they had been sliced through with sickles. Dark craters scarred the fields. The fresh carpet of new grass was ruined with roots and wood splinters tangled in the dark brown soil. It was a ghastly mosaic.

The Germans were preparing a new offensive. It was quiet except for the roar of Junker and Fokke-Wulf bombers. Menakhem's division was face to face with the German Twelfth Army. Col. Gusyev addressed his troops: "Soldiers! This is the final battle! Then there will be peace on Earth. The road to our homes goes through Berlin. The German bastards are getting ready for their last desperate attack. Are we going to wait here in the trenches until they're right on top of us?"

Gusyev peered through his binoculars and checked his watch. "Get ready, good buddies! Tighten your bootstraps! Pull in your belts! We're just waiting for the rocket signal." And just as he said those words they heard the powerful roar of rockets: "Those are ours!" They were flying in groups of three like wild ducks. They ripped through the clouds, group after group, behind clouds of smoke. Smoke riddled the sky. The troops' nerves tensed up like taut strings ready to break. The air grew so thick, that it was like breathing in metal. Their chins got heavy and their mouths drooped open. Menakhem could not rely on his five senses anymore. Suddenly a piece of the cloudy sky seemed to fall into the lake. It was as if a lightning bolt had split the forest. It seemed that the horizon had somehow collapsed at Menakhem's feet. The Earth rocked with a howl. Signal rockets shot over his head into the heavens.

The end had begun. No, it was not the end. The rockets sent the heavens that had crashed down back up to the heights of God. "Hurrah!"

Gusyev stopped, his face excited. Someone was wringing his hands, "Sergei! Sergei!" A shadow rolled towards a bush, and a terrible cry came from low bushes with roots upended and unopened buds.

They overran the German positions in the evening. Gusyev had led his men through swampy fields, trudged through the enemy's fortified positions, and attacked on the right flank. Air power had covered his attack. It was a daring assault by battle-hardened soldiers with long experience in the war. Menakhem was sitting in a bunker that they had taken. German prisoners with their hands in the air were standing nearby. Their weapons lay strewn on the grass.

He could not breathe. His throat was constricted. His eyes were popping out of their sockets, bleeding. It hurt him to close his lids. He was lying on his back, face towards the evening sky. His hands were stiff, fingers clutching clumps of earth and grass, but he could not open his fists. The good earth was cooling.

Now his back was leaning against the bare, sandy wall of the trenches. It had happened back home in the village. His mother had carried him to that unfamiliar doctor who would plow every morning near the river. That doctor used to come from the big city for his summer break. Little Menakhem was sick. His mother carried him over a plowed field. A farmer with whiskers: that was the doctor. His mother lay him down on the ground. His little hands clawed at the good earth. He gripped clumps of soil.

That memory had already come back to Menakhem when he had returned to Poland, not far from his village. And now it was back again. He looked at the evening sky with blind eyes and did not see it. He felt as if someone were strangling him with powerful hands. "Stop it!" he whispered. His lips felt odd, puffy and heavy. He could feel only the earth. He knew that German prisoners were standing nearby. Someone passed by. A cool wind mussed his hair, bringing the scent of cherry trees in bloom. He remembered that aroma. Aunt Marem and Uncle Elye had managed large cherry orchards stretching from Plonsk and Sochocin. He used to lay there in a straw hut on starry nights, a boy of sixteen.

The black cherries were ripening, and with them ripened Surcza, aunt Marem's youngest daughter. He had taken her in his arms once, that curly brunette Surcza, but she would not hear of it. She fought back. That was on cool straw on a cool evening. The cherry branches were hanging down to the ground, over their struggling bodies. The moon looked through the branches. But Surcza's throat was whiter than the moon. It was the first time that he felt her warm lips. His blind passion welled up in uncontrolled anger towards the girl. They wrestled silently, passion and hatred intermingled. It was his first experience of love mixed with hatred and fear. Then they sat in the doorway of the hut with their backs to each other. And when Menakhem left, Surcza followed him in tears. Now the evening breeze brought back the scent of cherry trees, and with it the weeping of aunt Marem's daughter Surcza.

"What's wrong, soldier?" Familiar words. Menakhem picked himself up, but he still could not breathe. His machine gun hung from his shoulder. His face was filthy, his skin bruised. Before him stood Gen. Shamshin. Menakhem recognized him. He wanted to speak to him but he could not. The words were on his lips, but they would not come.

"Why are you silent?" the general asked him. "Are you wounded?"

Menakhem pointed to his weapon. And a few Yiddish words came pouring out: "I was not silent, general. My gun did the talking." The general's Jewish fellow-feeling was aroused. They embraced and wept together.

"What do you have in your dirty hands?" Only then did Menakhem realize that he was gripping chunks of soil without knowing it.

"This is the soil of an impure land. You haven't recovered from the battle yet. It will pass. You're from Poland? We'll be in Berlin in a few days. The battle is won."

Menakhem climbed out of the communications trench. He hesitated to take a step, fearing that he would lose his balance. The Earth was still wavering, and with it the swamps and the ruined forests. Why were the lakes not pouring out? How can they keep the waters from overflowing the rivers? He put out his hand, looking for support. His knees buckled. He would sit down soon on the ground, like a sawed-off tree trunk. He had to walk. Here was the lake that rocked. He kneeled on the level lakeshore and saw his reflection in the water. His face bobbed up and sank down to the green bottom, but his eyes stayed on the surface.

He scooped up water in his steel helmet and drank. Then he washed his face, the water running down his neck, onto his body. He shivered with pleasure, and it woke him up. A machine gun rattled towards a flock of birds. A soldier was trying to scatter a crowd of birds massing towards the west. Menakhem whispered to them: "That's where there's trouble, that's where there's war. Fly to the east, to our fields and meadows." The birds answered the gun fire with screeching. "See? They've turned towards the east." But they turned around at the woods and were flying over Menakhem's head. They were the starlings from back home. He recognized them. "Fly to the quiet, peaceful villages.

There the plowman is at work now. There you'll build your nests in old poplars and willow trees. Don't stay here in this land, which has been cursed by God!"

It was night at regimental headquarters. Menakhem was sitting in a German cabin on the edge of a marshy field. Vasil Akimovitch Sabayev had just arrived in his heavy car. The radio operator in the next room was yelling, "Pine Tree here! We've gone past objective X! Sixty-meters to the north. Point 12!" Menakhem went out to the front steps. Dew was covering the fields. Nearby a guard patrolled in front of a niche with the Virgin. A forgotten searchlight stayed still in the sky. Its frozen ray of light seemed to be holding up the night sky.

German prisoners were sitting in a clearing in the woods, about 300 of them captured in the fields and bushes. Some had surrendered willingly. An armored car with a loudspeaker drove around into the night. An officer of the German Ninth army, prisoner Walter Höpke was calling on his men to surrender to the Soviets. Soviet planes dropped leaflets: "Nazis come and Nazis go. But the German people will remain." Stalin had said so.

"Pine Tree" was still talking. You could hear his monotone droning across the marshland. The Germans sat huddled together between the field of bushes and the piece of bare earth. The looked like cold, dark blots to Menakhem. Kerbaley the orderly stood near a truck. He would have to drive Sabayev back that night. Menakhem said, "Let's have a smoke." The little flame flickered in the Tatar's hands, illuminating his angular jaws and narrow eye folds, far apart from each other. The puffy pouches under the brows deepened his eyes.

The first interrogations were about to start, and the prisoners would then be sent immediately to assembly points. Transportation was ready for them. Sabayev was well dressed, his face clean-shaven. When he ran into Menakhem and saw the condition he was in, he shrank back and mumbled something that Menakhem could not make out. Kerbaley told him that Gen. Shamshin had just passed through on his way to check on the left flank, where something had gone wrong. The Germans were still holding the far end of the village. The general's appearance at the most forward position of the front line, at the heart of the battle, elicited surprise and admiration. Shamshin had appeared just when fierce fighting was raging. This isolated German attack had to be repulsed.

The general had grabbed a machine gun and had run out of the dugout to lead the company into battle.

Col. Gusyev had been killed. The medical corps could not handle so many wounded. Capt. Rezinko went to regimental headquarters to ask for help. The radio operator sent out an appeal for medics. There were many badly wounded prisoners. Kerbaley announced: "Our men are in the outskirts of Berlin. It's gonna be fun! The bureaucrats have already ordered wagons of vodka and red banners. Half a liter for everyone!"

Menakhem asked, "Where's the medical corps? Far away?"

"Not far. Right there at the crossroads, behind the fence."

"I have to go," he answered.

But as he got near the niche with the Virgin, a messenger came running after him: "Mikhail Isaacovitch, report to the colonel!" They walked silently.

The bright lights of trucks were kept on the prisoners. A unit with machine guns appeared from the village. Maj. Andrei Stanislavovitch Ostrowski, a blond man with fine features, had replaced Col. Gusyev. Though he was tall and broad-shouldered, his face was a bit too small for his height and his girth. Dozens of trucks arrived at headquarters just when Menakhem got there. Sabayev banged his fist on the table: "Too many German civilians are wandering on the roads. They're soldiers in disguise. We have to arrest them all, then we'll decide. D'you know who this old man is? He might be Hitler! They're escaping from Berlin! They take the country roads, through marshes. But here chaos reigns! Three soldiers are guarding three hundred prisoners. We can't let them get away, those Nazi gangsters! We have special instructions about this. Where are the guards?"

It was past midnight. The interrogations continued. They stood in rows. Menakhem wrote down their names and took their military documents. Sabayev mocked each one. "Mikhail! Just look at that face! Isn't that Goebbels?!"

Sabayev grew serious and paused: "See? He limps like Goebbels, and it's his mug!" Menakhem sized up the prisoner with a mocking look, shuffled the documents wrapped in cellophane, and asked, "Name?"

"Hans Bethke. Bethke from Darmstadt"

"Aren't you Joseph Goebbels?" asked Sabayev.

Several prisoners smiled. Only Sabayev stayed serious. He kept watching the German, but often looked at the others.

"Goebbels has the mug of a mouse, but this bastard looks like a dead bird of prey."

Sabayev grumbled, "It's all the same." He was disappointed that this German cripple was not Goebbels. One of the prisoners, a captain, had been in Berlin. He had retreated from there only on April 25th. He was to be interrogated later. Kerbaley led the chubby captain into a separate room and stayed with him, waiting for Sabayev's order.

The interrogation took place in the presence of Maj. Ostrowski. Menakhem knew right away that the new chief of staff was of Polish origin and that he knew German. Sabayev said, "Mikhail, ask him where Hitler is hiding. Where is Goebbels?" He was convinced that there were Nazi leaders disguised among the prisoners and among the civilians. He was afraid that it would later be found out that they had escaped from his hands. He was furious at the quiet, cozy interrogation of the prisoner by Menakhem and the new chief of staff. Who knows what the Devil they're saying, that Pole and that Jew and that German bastard? It seemed to him that those three had something in common, something secret that bound them together, but that he could not discover. He was desperate to put his suspicions to rest, so he crept out unnoticed. "Little Goebbels" was sitting on the floor in the little corridor. The Tatar Kerbalay guarded him. The prisoner pulled his birdlike head down between his shoulders.

Sabayev looked him over with his flashlight. The German did not even lift his head.

"Fritz! Stand up! Fritz!"

The Tatar shoved him with his boot. The little German stretched out his long neck and yanked his head away from the light. He got up, stood at attention, and raised his hand to his brow in salute to "the Russian gentleman."

"Come, Fritz, Goebbels *kaputt!*"

Kerbaley pushed him into a room in which the chief was staff was sitting with Menakhem and the German captain. The lame little German stammered and groveled in fear. Sabayev banged the door shut and stomped over to the captain: "Who is this cripple? Tell me! You know him!" He was speaking Russian, and Menakhem translated into German.

"No, gracious sir officer. I don't know him!"

"You lie!" screamed Sabayev. "You're all lying! A few days ago you were in Berlin in the basement of the *Reichskanzlei*! We know this! You brought his character here from there! He's Goebbels!"

The captain's mouth dropped wide open in amazement, revealing big, gleaming false teeth. That gleaming angered Sabayev even more: "Who are you? We know everything anyway. You won't get away with anything. Every tiny German document is now in Moscow. The whole archive of you German bastards is now in our hands. D'you think you can hide? You'll get a bullet. Why are you staring at me with your piggish eyes? Who is this creature standing here in front of you?"

"I'm Hans Bethke... Hans Bethke, a hotel employee from Darmstadt," said "Little Goebbels."

"Silence!" thundered Sabayev.

Kerbaley went through their pockets again and took their belts, ripped off their brass insignia, and locked them in a brick stall.

It was already dawn when the radioman called division headquarters. In Sabayev's name he reported that two suspicious characters had been arrested and that one of them had been in Berlin a few days earlier at central headquarters. They appeared to be important Nazi leaders, and they were being held under Sabayev's personal supervision.

In the early morning Menakhem learned that Dobrusz had been killed. Platon Voronko, too. A mine had blown off Papavkin's right foot. Zipunov was nowhere to be found. He found out all of this from Sgt. Sergei Orlov. They went to the medics' station. They saw freshly dug holes in the ground on a hill surrounded by lush green meadows. They were the graves of those who had just fallen in battle. On one wooden grave marker Menakhem read: David Abramovitch Dobrusz.

The Soviet Informburo at central headquarters in Moscow reported: "The attacks of the German Twelfth Army were repulsed. They were stopped from getting through to Berlin. The Germans suffered heavy losses. In an effort to prevent total annihilation, their units retreated in disorder towards the Elbe River and across to the other side, where the English and American forces were stationed."

The German forces in Berlin were surrounded, holding an area of about 100 square kilometers. The ring around them was tightening by the hour. Moscow celebrated that night. Rockets flared over the Kremlin.

Showers of light cascaded through the sky. Cannons fired salutes. The cupolas and the Kremlin walls were lit up. In the halls of the Kremlin they were drinking toasts from crystal goblets.

Menakhem was standing on the watchtower. Berlin spread out to the northwest. You could not see the city, but you could sense it from the purple skies and the distant booming of artillery. He inhaled deeply the springtime air. It was suffused with the scent of tree sap from lacerated trunks and the smell of raw earth. It had the sweetness of morning dew and the acrid stench of dynamite. He looked in the direction of Berlin.

In 1939 Hitler had said in the Reichstag in Berlin: "The war will destroy the Jews completely!" Now the Reichstag would burn, Berlin was burning, and in the basement the mad monster Hitler was hiding. Menakhem was at the gates of the city. His veins were taut and his heart was hardened. He could almost see it now, that unnatural city, in the light of revenge. "Tomorrow I'll be in Berlin," he said, his words as tough as steel cutting marble.

Chapter Five

Lev Oshanin had left Johanna Ostergard's house the day after he blew up the armoured cars. Aerial bombing followed soon after, and the main part of the house was destroyed. In the chaos Oshanin fled through the ruined streets. He walked through the city with his military satchel, sure that he would run into forward positions of the Soviets at one of the crossroads. The German tunic, the officer's cap pulled down, and military satchel made him look like an army doctor hurrying to give emergency help after a bombardment.

Valentin had reached his destination, from which he helped pinpoint artillery fire. "Open fire on the bank building at the end of Charlottenburg Strasse. In one 24-hour period Soviet planes had struck thousands times. They had fought German planes hundreds of times. Seven hundred German planes were brought down in that one day.

The Germans had turned into fortified bases of resistance their large bunkers—protected with walls three meters thick of iron and concrete—that had been used to shelter up to a thousand people. The specially trained Soviet shock troops and partisan detachments played a vital role in the street battles. They were mainly machine gunners and explosives men. The shock troops wielded several cannons of middle and large caliber. Occasionally they might get tanks and armored cars with heavy machine guns. The most in danger were the sappers whose mission it was to clear the mines off the route of the attack units. They also had to repair the streets, the roads, and the bridges over rivers and canals.

The Germans resisted stubbornly. But their wild and chaotic firing indicated their weakness. The Soviet regiments eroded their defenses bit by bit, breaking down the unity of their resistance. On April 28th the territory that the Germans controlled in Berlin was whittled away. They held onto a narrow strip down the center of the city that was a target from every direction. Attempts by their air force to help the beleaguered Germans came to nought. The Soviets occupied all the airports and airfields in Berlin and around the city. On April 30th the Soviets launched an attack on the central defense sector, and they reached the Reichstag.

When Lieut. Lev Oshanin entered the headquarters of Maj. Gen. Krivoshein, Krivoshein's tanks had already left. The general already knew about Oshanin's speech in the enemy's hinterland, and he welcomed him when he came in. They looked at each other and embraced silently. There was something meaningful in that silent embrace. Here were two Jews standing in a German cellar from which orders were being sent to tank commanders to destroy the Reichstag.

The phone rang. A German voice was calling, desperate. Oshanin threw down the phone and cursed at the German fool who wanted to give him orders, thinking he was talking to one of his German underlings. He did not know that the Soviets were in the cellar.

The Germans were firing from the metros through the ventilation openings. So the order went out to the explosives men: blow up the metro entrances and bulldoze them with debris. A German poster hung down from a wall, addressed to the civilian population by Gen. Weildling, the commandant of the city. Soviet armored cars patrolled the Frankfurter Allee. Their squadrons flew overhead. White flags were flying in some windows. Cannons were firing in the suburbs. Smoke curled up from a ruin. Civilians wandered through the cratered sidewalks with whatever possessions they could carry. A patrol led a group of prisoners, walking with their hands in the air.

Oshanin looked at the men on patrol, some with broad faces, or angular jaws, or slanty eyes, or with button noses. The soldiers wore threadbare tunics, hand grenades hanging from their belts. They marched through the unfamiliar, hateful city, their faces stony, their lips pressed together, their eyes icy and watchful, their guns at the ready. That was what the men looked like as Berlin fell. Oshanin looked at the streets of the gray stone city with curiosity and hatred. He had a bitter, obstinate need to see the fallen monster's body. He knew that coming generations would remember how Russian soldiers had conquered Berlin.

Just as a hunter who has found the beast in its lair cannot leave until he feels its dead body under his boot—and not see himself reflected in the eyes of the beast—so, too, did Oshanin need to satisfy himself by looking at the stony, foggy, devastated city of the enemy. He felt not only like a victor, but also like an executioner whose duty it is to carry out a just sentence. He had been worried that the homey houses, the promenades, and peaceful windows might soothe the fury in his heart, as had happened when he was going through the fields and villages.

But seeing Berlin only enraged him more. When he looked at the somber barracks, the concrete walls, the huge structures of iron and steel, stone and concrete, he understood where the evil had come from. He whispered: "This is where it came from! From here!"

But the Red Army had not yet dealt the enemy its mortal blow. German resistance deepened Oshanin's hatred of them, and the old feelings came back, the resentment of all those terrible days and nights under fire, the savagery, the plunder and murder. Resentment boiled in his veins, and he lusted for revenge. The crazy shooting from the metros and concrete bunkers, the calculated and well-planned resistance that was useless against the Soviets—all of that welled up in the troops, calling for revenge. Their raised fist would continue to batter the streets and the neighborhoods until deep scorn and commiseration for the enemy arose from the hatred.

Before the war, the strategic principle had been accepted that huge overwhelming power was needed to launch an attack, whereas retreat needed to be done in smaller, scattered groups. Great discipline was required to lead men against fortified positions that could only be taken by tightly close ranks. Groups scattered over woods and fields, isolated from each other, might turn into deserters and bandits. They ceased being an army.

But that rule was not confirmed in this war. The Soviets did not attack only with large, unified armies. It harassed the army of the Reich to its roots with disparate partisan units and small teams of reconnaissance commandos that befell German garrisons and outposts as if from the sky. They spread anxiety on German territory. They supported every possible source of local resistance. When it was necessary they sent huge armies against the German armored divisions.

But Germany did not have the means to wage that kind of war. They could not trust small units on occupied territory. They relied on masses of troops. Entire divisions—army corps—were supposed to smash the power of the enemy like a fist. But after they struck their blow, it turned out that they had not hit the heart of their opponents, and who were already getting new forces ready to fight back, far away. Even in those areas where the Germans ruled, partisans had organized.

Why were the Soviets able to launch small partisan groups, spread out over villages and woods?

Why were those partisans able to maintain discipline and not turn into deserters and bandits?

How had such a well-organized and well-planned resistance come to be?

Why were the Russians able to utilize all kinds of resistance and styles of attack and retreat, whereas the Germans could not?

Was it that the German army lacked discipline? Did the Germans not go into battle of their own free will?

For the first two years of the war, the Russian troops were badly fed, poorly armed, shabbily dressed. Behind them lay a land of hunger, its agriculture in ruins, a dictatorship with slave-labor camps. And yet these starving, oppressed common people showed themselves to be more moral than not just the Germans, but also their own Russian commanders. Why was that?

There are a hundred answers, and they are all true. But one answer was truer than the others. Oshanin and General Shamshin[1] knew it, and so did every common soldier: The Russian soldiers were fighting because they hoped that victory would bring with it a transformation of the country itself, a new era of freedom. They were fighting for life, against dictatorship, against hunger. They wanted to break the ring of coercion and terror that was strangling Russia and all of Europe.

Among the Russians the thirst for freedom expressed a popular rage against a dictatorship that was even more brutal than their own: a dictatorship based on the extermination of peoples, on the mass shooting of civilians, on gas chambers. The Germans were in a war of conquest to annihilate, to rule over others, to dominate them, to enslave them. They did not hide their aims. On the contrary, they proclaimed them!

Individual Russians fought to defend their country, to free the prisoners in the concentration camps, to liberate the occupied lands. They went to oppose the rule of terror. And that was true. And that truth led them to Berlin.

It was early on a mild April morning. Battles were still raging in the center of Berlin. In the eastern district, orders were posted from the Soviet commander-in-chief concerning the normalization of life in the city. The first May Day banners and red flags appeared on the Frankfurter Allee.

---

1 Aleksandr Aleksandrovich Shamshin, commander of mechanized rifle brigades, tank divisions, tank corps, and mechanized divisions.

On linden trees, hanging on a string, were large banner reading, "The Russians have always beaten the Prussians."

Zhillin was in Berlin. The Special Section for political activities of the general staff for the army fighting in Berlin had its headquarters in a suburb of the city. Sabayev was called to attend an extraordinary meeting. Valentin was also there. His real name was Zirkov. This was the same Zirkov who had parachuted down to the headquarters of Vlasov's army at Zelonki airport, not far from Warsaw, where Antip was in control. That was before they had crossed the Vistula. Zirkov's accomplishments were impressive. He had even gone to Nazi Berlin to give a talk on "The Jews in the Kremlin." He had done all of that to ingratiate himself with the Germans. Then he had managed to lead a unit of German auxiliary troops—commanded by Antip, a Russian deserter from Moscow—down to the Vistula, where they were ambushed by a Soviet reconnaissance team.

The meeting was held in the conference hall of a bank. The general staff sat up front in black leather armchairs at little marble tables. Col. Ivan Serov, the special envoy from Moscow, spoke first. Then came Col. Nikolay Feodorovitch Zhillin. He had changed a lot since his reception in the Kremlin, not only his military dress and decorations, but also his face. Something somber and secretive obscured the sharpness that had been his trademark. His speech, too, was less relaxed, less free, than before he had entered the Kremlin gates. A rustle stirred the hall when he began speaking. His eyes scanned the dark armchairs. Zhillin had the feeling that someone he knew was sitting near the marble column. But during his entire talk he could not remember where he had met him. He could not shake off the curiosity that gnawed at him insistently. He slowed down his sentences, and he felt that he was repeating himself and the audience was pretending to be listening. The stranger kept appearing in his concsciousness, then disappearing, like an unknown object bobbing up and down, far away on troubled waters. Suddenly he focused his gaze and was dumbstruck: It was Babadjanin, wasn't it! The wily Kazakh from the airplane!

Zhillin relaxed, and he spoke with renewed insistence: "This is just a part of the victory! Now we have to conquer Berlin and rule it! That is our task!" But he was dissatisfied with the ambiguity of those words. He wished he could take them back. Instinctively, as if pulled by some secret magnetic force, Zhillin turned his head towards Babadjanin. The familiar hazy, vague indifference of the Kazakh angered him.

"We have to rule the city! And that means first of all to change Berlin. We have to destroy the foundations that were laid by the Bismarcks, and the Hindenburgs, and the Hitlers. It's not enough to chop off the trunk. The poisonous roots must be ripped out of the deepest soil, so that they may never grow again. Comrades, I think you understand me. The first task is to close off the roads to the German leaders who are hiding in the cellars of the Reich. Isolate the members and officers of the Nazi Party. Second: Make contact with those Germans who wish to work with us to control public life in those areas that we have conquered. Third: Dismantle those factories and laboratories that will be useful to us. Treat German specialists as prisoners or war recruits for our land. The fall of Berlin must not be allowed to disarm us. Difficult days are still ahead. The Allies are fundamentally our enemies, I mean class enemies. Remember that! Our mission is: Destroy Nazism! Destroy the German property-owning class! Preserve the achievements of their science and technology for our homeland! Organize the transport of those segments of their industry that are useful to us! Keep a watchful Bolshevik eye on the conquered city and its residents!"

Zhillin then turned towards Babadjanin, who seemed pleased. It was time to finish up. Stalin stared down from the stone wall. "We're fortunate to be living in an era when the Great Man, the Father of the Nations, was able to reshape it with his genius…" He could not finish the sentence because dozens of hands began to applaud. He pushed his way through the armchairs and approached Babdjanin: "Good to see you again!" He shook Babadjanin's hand warmly and smiled.

The attack on the *Tiergarten* began. German anti-aircraft artillery fire had ceased for a few days in that neighborhood. But Soviet bombers were hindered by the fact that groups of Soviet troops had wormed their way into many small areas and streets among the narrow strips where the Germans were holed up.

The Soviet commanders were able to learn detailed information about the Germans' central headquarters from their German prisoners. They were even able to obtain the floor plan of the subterranean labyrinth under the *Reichskanzlei* where Hitler and his retinue were hiding. Special surveillance teams were assigned with this objective: to attack and destroy those headquarters. A report was sent to the Kremlin every hour.

Stalin was not satisfied with those reports from his couriers. He strictly insisted on photographs of the *Reichstag*, the *Tiergarten*, and the *Reichskanzlei*. Babadjanin became his personal courier. Special photo and film reporters were sent to take pictures from airplanes. When the news came that Soviet troops were about a thousand-meters from the *Reichstag*, Stalin carefully perused the pictures of the façade of the *Reichstag*, which was already half in ruins. He studied the columns, the ornaments, the black walls. He was totally focused, with no hint of his usual boredom.

Babadjanin waited with baited breath. He realized that the Great Man was about to express his will. He could tell from the nervous movements of Stalin's paralyzed hand, which was hidden in his bosom. One button in his jacket had always been left open, but this time it was not, so it was difficult for him to take his hand out. He used his healthy hand to support his arm as he pulled out the other hand. There was also a slight tremor in the pouches under his eyes, which seemed to be caused by the strain of looking so hard. Stalin pointed to the cupola above the cornices of the *Reichstag* in the photo: "This is where the Soviet flag must be hung! Babadjanin, here!" He took a red pencil from the table and marked the photograph.

One hour later Babadjanin was carrying the flag from Moscow that was to be hoisted on the *Reichstag*. He handed the special flag and the marked-up photo to Maj. Davydov, whose battalion was to storm the Reichstag along with the battalions of Capt. Neustroyev and Senior Lieut. Samsonov. Two days later Babadjanin telephoned the Kremlin with this news: "Today, April 30th, at 14:25, the Russian soldier Yegorov and the Georgian Kontarya raised the flag of victory over the *Reichstag*."

The cagey Kazakh Babadjanin knew full well why it was crucial that a Georgian and a Russian be present. He had staged the scene for the Georgian in the Kremlin. It would raise the prestige of the Georgian nation, and it would please Stalin that one of his countrymen was the first to reach the Reichstag alongside the Russian. It would also restore the poor reputation of Georgian soldiers. Many Ukrainians were traitors. The Belarussians had allowed the Germans to occupy them far too easily. The Tatars were traitors. The peoples of the Caucasus were undependable. And as for choosing a Jew, that would have cast a shadow on the victory. It would have appeared that the triumph was not that of Russia but of world Jewry. Babadjanin understood all of this. There was an implicit understanding not to distinguish the Jewish heroes and commanders in the Soviet military and to avoid public recognition of Jewish heroes, especially those whose names sounded Jewish. Because that would stir up the populace, and it would play into the hands of Nazi propaganda concerning a Judeo-Communist conspiracy.

Sergei Orlov and Menakhem reached the southern part of Berlin. The Germans had managed to get through the siege in small groups. They were attacking the iron ring around the city from the south and the west. It was a battle of life and death for them. Theirs was a desperate resistance in the final hours of Nazi Germany. SS battalions in full gear tried to break through Soviet positions. Sometimes Soviet medical corps and support battalions fought the German groups.

"Buddy," said Sergei, "I'd blow up the concrete, the paved streets, the whole place. Let the earth under these stones breathe again! Poisonous weeds grow in the filth of big cities. The fields and the skies are cleaner and purer the further they are from stone and iron. It's no surprise that the Nazi evil grew in such somber houses and cellars!" Menakhem listened silently.

But when he stopped talking, Menakhem waited for more. Sergei continued: "But our people are just as stupid. Once we were on maneuvers not far from my village, a small group. A Ukrainian from Kiev was the leader, a sly character. One day he sounded the alarm at at night. He lined us up and said: 'Guys, something terrible has happened. A huge fish just came down the Oka River and swam right near us. But because it's gigantic it stretches from one riverbank to the other and the water can't keep flowing. So the water is overflowing and flooding the villages. This is our mission, to chop up the fish with axes to make a passage for the waters to get through. We have to get axes in the village and run to the river. I'm giving you ten minutes!' The village was eight viorsts away. We ran with all our strength. But when we got there we saw that the silvery river was flowing calmly. He had made it all up."

Orlov told stories whenever he was depressed. He was writing a letter home: "Give my best to the Redhead." Menakhem said, "Hey, can't you find a younger woman that that "bride" of the soldier who fought the Turks?" Orlov kept writing: "We're in the heart of Germany, near the city called Berlin. This little war is coming to an end. We'll see each other before too long. I often think of you. The further I'm from home, the more I miss it." Then he said: "Here we're face to face with the Devil. He shows himself in a thousand evil ways. Sometimes he takes the shape of a human and sometimes just a shadow. He follows your footsteps and breathes his poison and hatred into your face. And when you turn around you only see yourself in the shattered glass and mirrors."

The night before the final assault on the Reichstag, several companies of the First Belarussian Front attacked across the Spree River and fought to control the buildings around the Reichstag. They took control of the complex of houses, with only two hundred meters more to the Reichstag. It was very difficult terrain because it was an artillery zone, all dug up with trenches and pits filled with water. A square courtyard paved with gray blocks of stone served as the headquarters for Menakhem's staff and a company. The exhausted troops rested on stone floors up in cool, high-ceilinged rooms with narrow barred windows. The general staff was down in the concrete cellar. Prisoners were kept in another wing of the building.

Menakhem was tense, worn-out, his eyes bloodshot and swollen. He had not been able to eat army food for a few days. He could not swallow. The overwhelming emotion that he felt upon entering Berlin would not let him sleep or rest. He was on edge and jittery, and he did not recognize his own voice, which had grown hoarse. He drank. The liquor temporarily dissipated his fatigue, waking him up for a few hours. Then exhaustion returned.

German prisoners stood before him. He jumped up several times. Once it was a prisoner's ugly skeletal head laughing with all its teeth in humility, a skull with wings. It made him dizzy. Suddenly his exhaustion, the tremor in his lip, and the weakness in his knees vanished. Menakhem now saw the German clearly. He had never seen one like him. His face had everything: brutality, blood lust, the will to power. This here is the source of all evil. I trudged all the way from the Ural mines to find you, and now you're in front of me.

He wrote: "Anna, your letter arrived at a very difficult time for me. Oh, how well you understand my state of mind! But my health shouldn't worry you. I'm worn out from these hard days, and the wound I got in

Warsaw is acting up again. I probably shouldn't be drinking any toasts to our victory. But how can I refuse a little drink with my good buddy Sergei Orlov? Here in Berlin where everyone is delirious with the joy of victory that each of us feels, I felt my joy was somehow marred, and I wept. Will I ever be able to throw off the shadows that have fallen on my face? I have sealed your face in the apple of my eye, and I trudge over this heartless Prussian city with love for you in my heart and so much hatred for it, my soul so divided between the two."

In the conquered streets of Berlin, Germans with white armbands cleaned the pavement. Mountains of rubbish piled up next to the shattered walls of the Reichstag. There were hills of smashed bricks, exploded concrete slabs, columns that had crumbled, military helmets, rifles, and uniforms. Shiny epaulettes glinted from under the debris. Iron crosses. Shredded flags. Portraits of Hitler and Goebbels that had been trampled. The picture of Göring stared with one eye open from a broken frame.

The *Reichstag* looked like a prison: bricked-up windows with arrow holes for shooting. Soldiers had scratched endless graffiti into the dark stone walls. Destroyed tanks lined the Charlottenburger Allee. The linden trees were in bloom. The ground was cratered, the scars of ferocious battles. The Brandenburg Gate was ghastly, gray, and crassly pompous. It was depressing. Posters were already hanging there. On one of the streets, Germans walked arm in arm with their fists raised, singing the song, "The Communist neighborhood Wedding is on the March." They were prisoners who had just been released. Among them were politicals, criminals, and common bystanders who joined the ranks of the procession. A group of concentration camp survivors came out through a gate, wearing their striped prison garb. They were looking for civilian clothes. A young Soviet officer was in the lead. People whispered, "Jews... Jews... The officer is Jewish, too."

A lanky man with an elongated face climbed up a gate and tore down an enameled shield with a swastika. Someone threw a stone at a window. Glass shards crashed down. You could hear the prisoners singing at the street corner. The concentration camp survivors raised their fists in anger. They tried to break down the gateway of a house. "All together, brothers! Let's do it again! Like this!" They broke it down with iron bars and crowbars. A truck stopped suddenly. Two Soviet officers got out.

"What's going on here?"

"We need clothes!"

"Who are you?" asked the officers.

The lanky man with the long face pushed forward: "Who are we? Concentration camp prisoners! We've walked around long enough in these humiliating clothes! D'you see these trenches? We were forced to dig these a few days ago. They brought us to Berlin for slave labor."

"Why didn't you fight back? Why did you help them fortify the city? Who are you, I mean, what nationality?"

"We're Jews."

"Jews? Well, now everything is clear." He gave them an angry look and called over the young officer who had stayed on the side the whole time: "Excuse me, but what are you doing with this mob?"

"They're not a mob, they're citizens who were just freed!"

"You're not answering my question. What are you doing here and who are you?"

"Who am I?! That's none of your business! I only have to answer to my military superiors, not to the bureaucrats."

"To the military? You've got a loose tongue! Oh, so these are your people, huh? A Jew found some Jews. Now I get it…"

The two officers got back in the truck and left the young man with the former prisoners. One said to the other: "See how they take advantage of our victory? The nerve! They're a disruptive element!"

At headquarters, the former history teacher from the Saratov middle school, Nikolay Sergeyevitch Soloukhin, told the general staff: "Russian troops have marched through Berlin three times in the last one hundred and eighty-five years. We beat Friedrich II in 1760. Fifty-three years later we drove out Napoleon, we stormed across the Nieman River, across the Vistula and the Oder. We conquered Prussia and we occupied Berlin. Now Berlin has fallen to us for the third time. One hudred and eighty-five years ago, one hundred and thirty-two years ago, and now! Let us drink to the three victories!"

The staff was rowdy, and dozens of hands raised heavy goblets. Alturov had worked hard to collect all kinds of drinking vessels. He had found a German sport club somewhere, and he brought a whole box full with the silver cups of a soccer team, all adorned with eagles, swastikas, and Gothic inscriptions etched in silver. They sparkled in the lamp light. Soloukhin, wearing glasses, put down his goblet and continued:

"Franz Mehring wrote in his book *The Lessing Legend*: 'In the history of the world it is difficult to find a powerful group as spiritually depraved and as deprived of human decency as the princes of Germany.' The Italian poet Alfieri considered Berlin 'one huge somber barracks.' Our great Russian writer Saltykov-Shchedrin said prophetically: 'Berlin was created for mass murder.'"

Menakhem was sitting with Soloukhin, talking about the German nation. His harsh words about the Germans aroused Soloukhin: "You're a Jew, I can tell from your hatred of them. That was good for us until we conquered Berlin. It strengthened our war. But it's not useful to us now. What I just said about Germany will be the last you'll hear from me like that. We'll have to change our tune after they surrender. We'll have to adapt our words to the needs of the situation. I can do it. But you'll be stuck with your hatred of the German people. That will isolate you."

A Ukrainian was dancing, spinning in a wild *karahod* and shouting out. Night fell. The spring wind brought the smell of still waters. That night German Gen. Hans Krebs appeared at headquarters, along with two officers carrying white flags. The guards let them in and escorted them to Maj. Ostrowski. "I am fully authorized to report to the Supreme Soviet commander that we are ready to surrender. Our Führer ended his life of his own free will yesterday." That news was immediately sent to central headquarters. But it was only a partial surrender, because the Germans were still fighting in other sectors.

An elderly German woman stopped Lieut. Oshanin not far from headquarters, wringing her hands: "Sir officer, they're plundering my house. My daughter is in danger... The Russian soldiers... Not far... The next street... The third house..." She whispered grimly, in desperation.

He looked at her indifferently, but curious. But suddenly a warmth came over him, dissipating his indifference. That made him uneasy. He reacted against that sudden warmth in himself. Yet he looked at her face for a hint of that same warmth in his heart. She was the typical German woman whom you might find at church on a Sunday, with a wrinkled face, two gnarled, waxy hands, and wearing a string of black pearls around her neck. In her desperation and her quiet pleading she was like all the other elderly women in that war-ravaged city. Oshanin looked at her with sympathy. It was a superficial sympathy at someone else's horror and terror, maybe not a deeply felt one that reached the soul. It was as if his feelings were reflected in a dark mirror back onto himself. But this time it was different. The old German woman's pain pierced him, and as much as he struggled against the warmth he felt in his breast, still the icy shield around his heart melted. As if she understood the struggle inside him, she put her yellow, bony fingers on her black dress and said: "She's half Jewish, my daughter."`

Oshanin followed her to the stone steps.

"Here, Sir."

Screams were coming from the open door.

"This is it. My God!"

He walked down a long corridor and stopped at an open door. Three Russian soldiers had wrecked the apartment. They had ransacked the credenzas, smashed the crystals, torn off the bedspreads, and knocked over the chairs. A young girl stood weeping in a corner of the room, wrapped in a thick, dark curtain. One of the soldiers was trying to pull the curtain off her. The heavy curtain rod fell, dragging with it an oil painting in a heavy black frame. Another soldier was standing near a broken mirror, holding a bottle of liquor in his hand. He was already drunk, and staggering, talking to his own reflection in them mirror: "Hi, Fedka! How do you like Germany? D'you like Berlin? Why don't you say anything, Fedka dear? I'm not good enough to talk to? Oh, now you're a victor! So now you won't talk to me! I spilled my blood for you, Fedka from Saratov! And you're too important? Let's drink! Fedka, stop playing your tricks!"

He pushed the bottle to the mirror: "Take it, I say! So you won't?"

The soldier banged the bottle into the mirror, sending down a shower of glass shards: "The Devil take your mother! You swine!" Then he sat on the floor.

The soldiers had first looked at Oshanin when he showed up at the door. Then they ignored him.

The drunken Fedka told him, "It's getting late, pal! We've guzzled everything. There's just a tiny bit left. One little bottle. This German girl, maybe you'll get somewhere with her. You've got your epaulettes."

Another soldier went over to the curtain rod and tried to unwrap the curtain off the girl: "Wait! I'll show you this barefoot girl!"

"Leave her alone!"

"Take your paws off, officer! You'll be sorry!"

Oshanin pushed him away. The two soldiers laughed.

"What's with you, Kostya? You conquered Berlin, but you can't budge this German whore?"

"I saw Fedyas all around, not just one. Hundreds of Fedyas in all the splinters of the mirror. A whole regiment of Fedyas. Swines! Drunkards!"

Oshanin took out his revolver: "Get out, both of you!"

"We weren't afraid of German bastards, and you're not gonna scare us with your gun!"

Kostya raised his hands covered with blood that he had just cut on the broken mirror: "You're spilling the blood of Russians."

"Come," said Fedya, "Enough!"

Oshanin shoved them out of the apartment. They stood a while on the steps and could not decide where to go.

He told the girl, "Don't be afraid. They were just drunk." A blond, disheveled head poked out from the curtain. Oshanin felt the girl's terror deeply: big brown eyes full of tears, her mouth twitching, sobbing as if she were choking. He saw before him a girl about eighteen years old. One of her shoulders was bare and her dress was ripped. An undergarment with lace was visible at her throat, and her chest was heaving from her panting. One leg was bare, with a silk stocking only hafway up the other leg. "I thank you," she whispered, as she tried to cover her nakedness with her hands.

The girl and her mother went to the other room, leaving Oshanin alone. The three Russians stood outside at the gate, arm in arm. Fedya raise his fist towards the window and yelled, "I left my Fedya up there in that German house, ten Fedyas!" They dragged him away down the deserted street. Oshanin watched them until they disappeared at the corner. He stayed for coffee. He sat with the mother and daughter in a side room and drank muddy war coffee from a faience cup. The old woman brought in a photo album and opened the silver lock on the leather covers.

"This is Marion's father. A Jew from Breslau. He is dead." She wiped her eyes and said something that Oshanin could not understand.

Chapter Five

Night was beginning to fall. "I have to leave. My name is Oshanin, Lev Oshanin. If you'll permit me, I'll visit you again."

As he left, he said to her, "I'm Jewish."

Marion had left the room unnoticed. Her mother called, "Where are you, Marion?" And when she showed up, Oshanin saw she was upset. Something was troubling her. Her warm fingers melted the remaining ice in Oshanin's heart. He realized that she had carefully brushed her hair and had hung red pearls around her long neck on his account.

He said, "I'll come again tomorrow in the afternoon. Do you need anything? How can I help you? When he was at the door he looked at the brass plaque on the door with a Gothic inscription. He took a sheet of paper and wrote in Russian with a pencil: "This apartment is under our protection. Lieutenant Lev Olshanin." He said, "Hang this on the outer door. That will spare you any more visits from Fedya's pals."

The flag of victory fluttered over the Reichstag cupola. Menakhem could see it from his window. German prisoners came through his office at headquarters. Several assistants recorded the proceedings of the interrogations. Most of the prisoners had hidden in the cellars of the Reichskanzlei. Reports of the interrogations were sent every hour to central headquarters.

It became clear from the officers of the German general staff that Hitler was dead, and that the principal witnesses to his cremation were Hitler's adjutant, SS man Otto Günsche, and his valet, SS man Heinz Linge. Others who helped burn his body were the chiefs of Hitler's bodyguards; SS man Johann Rattenhuber, and an officer, Harry Mengershausen. His personal pilot, Hans Bauer, had stayed in the cellars until the last minute. Hitler committed suicide when he saw no possibility of escaping.

One officer reported: "The Führer had lost his mind. Those around him had decided to burn his body. If he had tried to leave the bunker, we would have shot him anyway. He knew it. It was good that he chose to leave this world of his own free will." Soon after Menakhem reported his information, Babadjanin telegraphed these attestations of Hitler's immediate subordinates to Stalin. The Special Section was ordered to find those witnesses. An officer was assigned to begin the search, with a company at his disposition. Among his men were Germans working with the Soviets, mostly former Reichswehr officers.

Even before the Reichskanzlei was taken, the Special Section had reported to the Kremlin: "Hitler's grave lies in a bomb crater near the emergency exit of the bunker. We have followed all your instructions." Those instructions had been: Send Hitler's corpse to Moscow in an especially reserved airplane after confirming the authenticity of the corpse with witnesses and experts. Stalin had given that order as soon as he learned that the Führer was dead.

A black curtain fell. The gruesome tragedy was over. Backstage the people of the Dniepr River, the Volga, the Siberian steppes had torn the masks off their rulers, ripped off their black togas, removed their poisonous weapons, and stripped their clothes. The actors' ugly pretense was uncovered. They squirmed like worms under their boots. They begged for mercy. They feared the righteous rage of the people and committed suicide. And some sneaked away from the arena like thieves.

Once Menakhem saw a German dressed in a concentration camp uniform come into his office. As soon as he looked at him he knew that this was no former prisoner: "Why did you disguise yourself?"

"I was afraid I'd be lynched."

"Where did you get these clothes?"

"I found them."

"That's a lie!" Menakhem screamed, interrupting the interrogation. "You murdered a prisoner."

The SS man began to move back. Menakhem jumped at him in a rage: "These clothes are holy! Take them off! You're besmirching them! Take them off now!" He lunged at him with his fists. Then he glowered at him. The SS man remained in his underwear, and the guards jeered at him when he left headquarters.

One night Hitler called his retinue together in the underground bunker under the *Reichskanzlei* and announced his intention to leave this world. This was a poorly directed epilogue to the drama that the madman had performed before his idiot admirers. But it was not performed under God's open skies in a circus arena or sports stadium, with hundreds of thousands of Germans screaming "Heil!" It was performed behind black curtains that were pulled down, dozens of meters underground, under a heavy cover of concrete, under the full darkness of night. And this tragic-comedy—authored and directed all by himself—had all the elements of melodramatic trash. He still had his subordinates in hypnotic thrall. They were the supporting cast in the last performance, among the players being Eva Braun, the exalted photo model from München and the Wasserburgerstrass and Walter Wagner, the head of civil affairs in Berlin, plus several other followers. And the hero playing his own tragic role—that of himself. The marriage of the "Führer" and the "Maid" required witnesses.

"Do you agree, my Führer, Adolf Hitler, do you agree to take Eva Braun for your wife? If you agree, answer 'yes.'" That was how Walter Wagner, head of civil affairs, asked him in a theatrical and pathetic tone. Then there was a suspenseful pause in the show. The witnesses to the "marriage" disappeared from the underground stage one by one: Goebbels, sinister and lame; Bormann the lover of beer-cellars, and his shadowy retinue; then Wagner, who had registered the "marriage" to legitimize it for future generations.

Scene Two: The last conversation between the newly-weds full of pathos and theatricality.

Scene Three: Hitler alone writing his testament. And right after that, the suicide. The conversation between the two had been short.

Eva: "I know your decision, and I wish to die."

"It will be painful," said the mad Führer.

"I want to die. It will be more painful to live without you."

Then he remained alone on stage. He looked over his testament, the personal legacy and the political. His mouth crooked from an episode of paralysis, he read his own words: "International politicians of Jewish origin, as well as those who served Jewish interests, were the cause of this war... I have no doubt whatsoever that Jewry, which is the real guilty party in this war, will be held responsible for it..." The final words of his testament were commands: "I order the leaders of our nation and all our citizens to strictly uphold our race laws and to violently resist international Jewry, the poisoners of the whole world and its peoples."

It is very likely that the testament had been prepared on Hitler's birthday. A week later, Polish divisions had attacked from the north, cutting Berlin in half. News came that same night that the Soviets had taken Spandau, Potsdam, and Tempelhof. Gen. Zhukov's tanks pushed from the Alexanderplatz towards the Spittelmarkt and the Schlossplatz. Leipzigerstrasse led from the Spittelmarkt to the Wilhelmstrasse. But bridges that had been blown up obstructed the path of Soviet advance. That could slow down the taking of the *Reichskanzlei*, the Tiergarten, and all the bunkers by a day or two. Those objectives were being fired on constantly by Soviet artillery. That was when Hitler was preparing his epilogue.

Some time later Hitler's chauffeur provided additional details: "When we arrived at Hitler's underground bunker, we saw the Führer sitting on a small divan. Eva Braun was lying at his side, with her head resting on his shoulder. The Führer was leaning forward a bit. It was easy to see that he was dead. His lower jaw was drooping, and blood was dripping from both temples. His mouth was bloody. Two "Walter" pistols were lying on the stone floor.

It was time to dim the lights on that dark stone stage. The epilogue had ended with a double suicide by gunshot. On the stage were a bloodied "He" and a "She" who was sleeping at his side like a dove. A skeleton waved his hand to summon demons. Black skeleton demons came dancing on the dark stage, whirling in a karahod until day broke. Then they ran away.

On the First of May the Supreme Commander of the Soviet armed forces announced: "Between January and the First of May more than a million Germans died and 800,000 prisoners were taken on the Soviet front. We have captured and destroyed at least 6,000 airplanes and about 12,000 armored cars."

In that announcement he also warned America and England: "Our homeland has built a first-class army during this war, which is capable of defending the Socialist conquests of our people and protecting the national interest of the Soviet Union."

The troops were surprised. They did not grasp who it was aimed at. Later they realized that it was meant for the Allies, who were standing on the banks of the Elbe River, and without whose active help the victory over Germany would have been impossible. Menakhem saw the war years unroll like a parchment in his mind. It was in Nizhny, in the winter of 1941. The first months of the war. Russia was starving. He had gone to the military mess hall. His company had waited outside for hours to get some watery cabbage soup. He had been assigned to work there a few times and had seen how miserable the food was. They would bring rotten potatoes and frozen cabbage peels from the *kolkhoz*.

They would not have made it through the winter if not for the huge American shipments of canned meat. All of Nizhny was fed at the mess hall. Farmers, city dwellers, children, all came in the bitter cold and waited to get a bit of hot cabbage water and American meat in their little plates. That was what had saved the recruits from starvation. But the officers' mess had lots of American food. Everywhere, Menakhem had seen weapons, clothes, and trucks from abroad. The officers' tunics, worn-out and tattered, were quickly exchanged for English-made tunics. Instead of *kolkhoz* horses, it was powerful trucks from abroad with double wheels that traveled the rough Russian roads, carrying necessities from the villages to the front. It was only when they crossed the old border with Poland, where collectivization had not yet been implemented—because those areas had fallen to the Soviets just before the war broke out—that the troops could eat their fill. Those exhausted, badly clothed, poorly nourished soldiers began to live again. Some regiments would come on leave right from the front to areas of western Ukraine and western Belarus.

It was only in Berlin that Menakhem heard about the powerful bombing raids by the Americans and the British on the most vital industrial and commercial centers of Germany. It was there that he learned from an officer about Jewish soldiers in the American army and about a special Jewish brigade of Israeli Jews in the British army.

Right after Stalin's speech on the First of May, Soviet relations with the forward positions of the Allies worsened. Fraternization with Allied troops was forbidden. The Soviets reinforced their guardhouses on their side of the Elbe River. Menakhem overheard an officer saying, "We'll push on further. We can't stop now. Germans who escaped are massing on the other side. If we don't push on, we'll be destroyed from within. Now that we're so powerful we can't stop here. Our strength is now beyond control. It'll push on through intertia."

The Father of the Nations had been prepared to meet Hitler in Moscow, alive and a prisoner. He, too, had prepared a theatrical spectacle. But he would have directed it in a barbaric, Tatar style, mixed with elements of the Soviet Realist stage, helped by experienced NKVD specialists in organizing huge public spectacles. It was supposed to be remembered for generations, like the delivery of Pugachev to Moscow in a metal cage.

Stalin had wished to tear off the Führer's mask and destroy the halo over his head, not only the mask of a ruler, but also the tragic mask of a national leader and a miserable military commander. He did not want to do it with his own hands. The victim himself would have to offer himself to the world for shame and mockery. He had wanted to see the Führer alive and on his knees.

It was not so long ago that he had said to the two great men in Yalta, the American and the Englishman: "It won't be long until my boots will stand on Hitler's neck." No, he had not meant literally "on Hitler's neck." He had imagined Hitler's death differently. First the prisoner would have to denounce his own, entire past history and fame. He would not be permitted to take any of that with him into the grave. All that should remain for history would be his naked corpse and his own self-denunciation. It would take place in a mass spectacle before the people of Moscow and the world.

But now the news had come: Hitler was dead. Stalin was furious. It was not clear whether it was rage or disappointment, or both. Both disappointment and rage against the commanders who had delayed the attack on the Reichskanzlei 48 hours later than planned. The conquest of the bunkers had been prepared from the north, the Tiergarten, the Reichstag, and the south. All escape routes had been cut off. The units had waited, until it was too late. Stalin did believe that Hitler had committed suicide, but he still had his doubts. Maybe he had disappeared with the help of the Allies?

In those days Stalin behaved like a theater director who comes to a gala presentation, the acme of his career, which would bestow eternal fame on him, but the hero is missing! He wanders through the empty theater, he strides across the empty stage, he searches backstage, but he finds no one. No actors, no audience. The stage décor is gone. A floodlight projects a large red circle at center stage. But it is surrounded by complete silence. He pressed his hands together and waited. The red light went out. He clapped his hands and called out. The door opened, and someone bowed low to him.

"Who are you?"

"It's me, Babadjanin. Babadjanin."

Stalin rubbed his eyes. The empty stage was gone! No more emptiness! No more red light! He was back in the Kremlin. The little red light on the telephone lit up, which meant the call was from headquarters. He did not answer. He just had to talk to the Kazakh:

"Hey, you Kazakh devil! Come closer!"

The little red light reflected in his eyes.

"You didn't do your duty, Babadjanin!"

The Kazakh's flabby face fell. He no longer had a face, just a vague blob between day and night on a foggy field. His clumsy body tottered like a tree that is just about to fall, because its roots have already been sawed. Just a little push. The muffled phone rang again, sounding like nickel coins falling on a carpet. The Kazakh tottered, his body almost falling against the edge of the desk.

"I want to see the dead Hitler!"

Babadjanin was saved. His face came back to life. He smiled at the carpet, the walls, the tapestries, the bodyguards. He walked down the marble staircase and smiled at the steps. The bodyguards were not surprised at his smile. They understood that the brilliant aureola of the Father of the Nations had illuminated the Kazakh's face.

General Weidling, the German commandant of Berlin, surrendered with his general staff to the Soviet Gen. Chuikov. In a beer cellar on the Schönhauser Allee, the Soviets were holding Hitler's immediate subordinates. Leading a small company of troops, Lev Oshanin entered the beer cellar. The German generals, the guards, and several civilians in black funeral dress stood up. The officers saluted the Russian soldiers. Lieut. Oshanin stood in the open door, tall, broad-shouldered, pitch-black curls falling on his forehead. His eyes, under heavy dark brows, perused the Germans. He was tense, suspicious, brimming with hatred.

It was dead quiet in the beer-cellar. Oshanin took a step forward, staring at the Germans, his Jewish eyes glaring at the bony, hard, alien faces. Eyeglasses gleamed in the light, a cross, an epaulette, a shovel hanging on a belt, a brass belt buckle. Oshanin walked down between the heavy wooden tables. The German generals were still standing and saluting. He did not respond. He stopped in front of one of them and looked deep into his eyes. He was a tough, powerfully built German with facial scars and tightly pressed lips.

Oshanin sensed the historic significance of this event in his life. His footsteps in that place would echo in the future. That rigidity of the Junkers, their dazzling insignias, their severe, domineering discipline, their military strutting, and their phony code of honor, all enraged him. The heavy, half-empty beer mugs, the half-smoked cigarettes, the waiters in black frocks, the phony theatrical show of submission, all riled up his Jewish feelings. He screamed brutally, commandingly, "Hands up!"

The Germans were shaken. One of them removed his hand from his salute and raised both hands. Others lowered their heads. One of them mumbled something hoarsely. The Russians came in and pointed their machine guns.

"Hands up!"

Oshanin was standing at the table. Only some of them had raised their hands. The rest stood still and did not move.

"Three minutes! Then we open fire! Don't give me 'honor'! You're like all other prisoners! Your lives are in our hands. Any disobedience will be considered resistance!" It was not clear who was obeying and who was not. The Soviets spread out and pushed the officers into the street, searching them at the door. They took their belts, their shovels, their guns, and led Hitler's staff through the streets of Berlin with their hands in the air.

When Babadjanin heard the news that the Reichskanzlei had been taken, he drove there quickly, accompanied by Zirkov. The garden had been cratered by artillery. Near the lower entrance to the bunker, they had found several half-burned corpses in a bomb crater more than two meters deep. The men of the special company assigned to find Hitler dead or alive rummaged through every corner of the bunkers and every bit of soil in the bombed-out garden. Babadjanin and his companion arrived just when they were carrying the burned corpses out of the crater. Zirkov interrogated several officers from Hitler's retinue and immediately began to authenticate the identity of the corpses. It was impossible to distinguish who was who. It was a formless mass, wrapped in blackened, charred tarps. One skull had its lower jawbone with gold teeth.

In a few minutes they had the address of Hitler's dentist. Zirkov flew through the streets. It was hard to maneuver past the barricades and temporary bridges, the canals and the tank craters. He knocked on the dark door. On the plaque was written: Dr. Blaschke.

"Who's there?" asked a woman's voice behind the door.

"Open up! A Soviet officer!"

She poked her head out. Zirkov and his companions went into the dentist's big apartment. They were in his office. "Where is Dr. Blaschke?"

"He's crossed over to the other side of the Elbe."

"Who are you?"

She smiled: "Sirs, officers, have a seat. Why the hurry? My name is Hausmann. I'm Jewish."

Zirkov asked sharply, "Where's Dr. Blaschke?"

"I already told you. He left me his apartment. I'm Jewish, just got out of a concentration camp."

"Not Jewish, but Judas! Get it?"

Zirkov turned his back on her and said in Russian to his companions: "Take her along. She's under arrest. Call the guards. Put this apartment under constant surveillance." When Zirkov returned to the Reichskanzlei he found Babadjanin in a high spirits, pointing to a burned corpse with a twisted jaw: "That's Hitler!"

On the night of May 2nd, 30,000 German soldiers managed to break through the Soviet line. All Soviet units were on the alert. There was shooting on the outskirts of Berlin. The western sector was burning. Marauders were swarming everywhere. Gangs of Vlasov's army with false documents they had taken from the corpses of slave laborers, war prisoners, and concentration camp victims; German criminals; SS men who had left behind hoards of plunder in Poland. Ukraine, and Lithuania; stragglers from the German army, hungry, bloodthirsty, and furious at Berlin residents who refused to open their homes and give them civilian clothes—a hodgepodge of Germans and their collaborators—Lithuanians, Hungarians, Ukrainians, and Volksdeutscher from Poznan, Katowice, Gdansk, Torun, along with Russian deserters, all rampaged through shops and private homes. On occasion Soviet troops just looked on, silent partners in the pillage. And when the patrols did stop them, the looters would scream and wave their false documents, and lament their "misery." And quite a number of these criminals actually pretended to be Jews!

By the time Zipunov was picked up lying in the bushes after the great battle for Berlin and taken to the infirmary, he already had in his bosom the identification paper of a Soviet soldier who had been killed, which he had exchanged for his own. Now the people back home would believe he was dead and would mourn him. The village authorities would thus learn that the very same Zipunov who had worked for the Germans for some time had died for the homeland while storming Berlin.

Zipunov began heading for Berlin as soon as he was released from the infirmary. In one of the southern neighborhoods he ran into a group of countrymen living in wooden barracks near a German airfield. They were former slave-laborers who had been sent to build an airport, just before Berlin fell. A gold coin won him acceptance, and a suit of civilian clothes let him start looting again. The little cloth sack of gold was still dangling around his neck.

The Germans abandoned their allies. Groups of paramilitaries, Ukrainian and Russian prisoners serving as auxiliaries, wandered the ruined roads of south Germany. Exhausted, hungry, and afraid of revenge reprisals, they aimed to reach the Allies, hoping for protection.

Soviet loudspeakers warned their former citizens: "The roads are barred. You will not escape our righteous fury! If you wish to cleanse your guilt, kill your treasonous commanders or turn them over to us!" They dropped leaflets from airplanes: "The Americans will not welcome you! They have agreed to turn over war criminals. Running away now is a greater betrayal than having been forced to serve the Germans."

The nights were quiet. All you could hear was the sound of tanks and armored cars rolling through Berlin. There were guardhouses and patrols. A sudden clatter of machine gun fire and a booming voice: "Vo-ol-lod-ka!" An echo resounded. A soldier was singing about dangerous nights on alien soil and about home.

Menakhem listened to the night sounds. The singing of the soldiers on guard calmed him down. It brought him back to the fields of Russia. He saw before him the three windmills on the high bank of the Moksha River, the little familiar villages nearby: Tengushay, Bashkirtzi, Krasnyyar, Dudnikovo. He had left those villages that first winter of the war. He had walked, wrapped in his black coat, with all the other villagers. And now he had finally reached the destination that the Soviet general staff had designated: Berlin. This was the end of his long road.

All afternoon he stood reading the lists of soldiers and officers who had distinguished themselves in the battle for Berlin. And each time he recognized a Jewish name, his blood would course through his veins. He underlined them with a pencil, then showed them to Soloukhin: "You're so good at remembering history. Surely you won't forget these names?" His fingers pointed to the names, and he read aloud: "Major General Vladimir Leibovitch Tseytlin; Captain Boris Khurgin, killed at thirty years old; Maj. Nikolai Israilovitch Brazgol; Artillery brigade commander Maj. Grigory Dragunsky; Col. David Margolis, Hero of the Soviet Union. Special honors in the conquest of Berlin: Lieut. Gen. Lutchinsky; Major of the Tank Division Veynrib; Lieut. Gen. Shamshin; Artillery Lieut. Gen. Rozanovitch; Maj. Gen. Dobrinsky; Krivoshein, Hero of the Soviet Union; David Abramovitch Dragunsky."

He suddenly stopped reading and looked at the young Russian. Soloukhin said, "So what are you trying to prove, Mikhail Isaacovitch?"

"I'm showing you that we didn't only die passively in Auschwitz. We waged war against the enemy. Our finest sons. The Russian people must remember the blood that we shed. This was the second time that we Jews have given our blood for Russia. We did it in the October Revolution and now in the war with Germany."

"Of course we'll remember! Don't forget that those heroes listed are first and foremost Russian citizens. Right? You can't put their Russianness on a second plane. Why do you need to emphasize their Jewishness? Because they were victorious? So, Mikhail, do you want to take away some of the Russian heroism for yourself? When it's not in your interest to identify as Jews, you identify as Russians. But whenever someone even hints by a hair that you're not Russian, you scream that you are Russians indeed."

"I don't understand you."

"You don't understand? You Jews asked the Tsar for equal rights, but you didn't get it. Only the Soviet regime made you real Russian citizens. But you've not been able to break out of the isolation that the Tsar had forced on you. You persist in being different, and you speak a language that isn't Slavic. What keeps you from being like Russians? You're still aliens in Moscow, in Kiev, in all the republics. The Kazakhs, the Georgians, the Azerbaijanis also complain about the Jews who live in their cities, because in those places you're considered Russifiers. You don't support their local cultures and languages. You have two circles of protection: the larger one is your Russianness, the narrower one is your Jewishness. We're never sure which circle you're in."

All week before the fall of Berlin the German radio had broadcast classical music, Beethoven, Bach, and Schubert, as well as long recitations of the works of Goethe and Schiller. Undoubtedly they meant to tell the world: See, Beethoven and Bach and Schiller and Goethe are dying here!

It was late at night in a stone courtyard of the Kremlin. A truck covered with tarp stood near a massive brick wall with pointy turrets. Some soldiers hung around near the somber walls. The clock rang on the Spasskaya tower, its peals spreading out all over Russia. It was midnight. Steps approached. The soldiers lined up in a row, casting shadows on the wall, huge, and irregular. One man stood apart, his face turned towards the courtyard with the sounds of approaching steps. First he saw a group of shadows in the corner, then people. The man jumped up and gave an order. At that moment floodlights and stage lights turned on. Rays of light streamed across the courtyard, illuminating the truck and the line of guards, who stood at attention, saluting.

Then the lights turned onto a small mound near the wall covered with a black cloth. The men approached it in a semicircle. One of them came right next to the cloth. He was lit up from the shoulders to the head, as if by a supernatural halo. It was the Father of the Nations! He had come with his retinue to see Hitler's corpse. Babadjanin left the semicircle and bent over the black cloth. The stage light went from his face to his hands. He sneaked a glance at Stalin, perusing his face as if looking for something, and suddenly he tugged at the cloth and laid it at his feet. The Kremlin clock rang midnight. No one saw Stalin's face. His guards and his companions saw only his back. He stood alone face to face with the ruler lying on the ground in front of the massive Kremlin wall at night. He stood like a statue carved of granite.

No, it isn't just a dead ruler who lies at my boots. It's Germany. It's the Junkers. It's their conquered territories. It's all of Europe. Right here at the Kremlin walls. You wanted to reach Moscow. Well, you're in the Kremlin now! Your people were loyal. They didn't abandon you until the very end. You were their God. You announced your plans to the world. You clearly said what you wanted and what your aims were. You showed your face and built the "Thousand-year Reich." It was you who abandoned your people, not your people who abandoned you. Millions of Germans are mourning you. Even now you're still their God, crucified by a Georgian with the help of... World Jewry!"

His lips curled in sarcasm. Stalin looked around and saw the silent guards and his silent, somber retinue. He suddenly felt strange, and an

Chapter Five

unknown terror struck him, as if an evil thorn had pierced his temples. It wasn't the dead ruler that terrified him, but Death itself. How was it possible for a cremated ruler to walk on stone floors? He who had held the reins of power, who had given orders, who had judged others and sentenced them? This wasn't just the death of one beaten ruler. It was the death of rulers, the death of rule by one man. This death is a challenge to all my enemies, those who are out in the open and those who are in hiding behind my back. Yes, he had enemies! They were victorious now and they were in mourning. They mourned because he was still alive and they were victorious because rulers did not rule forever. One day they would roll in the dust.

The death of the evil man shook the dictatorship of the Man from the Kremlin. This was just the beginning. A new day was coming. No, it would not come. He would prevent it from coming. Hitler had been a ghost, maniac, soldier, actor, overblown with parade glory and Prussian arrogance, he had played the role till the end. If only Hitler had been a Georgian, then he would have ruled forever. Then the two of them would have divided up the world between them.

The Father of the Nations curled up, and a shudder went through him. Someone was hurling him down a stone staircase. His skull rolled down, way down, like a watermelon. Bells were ringing. The gates were breaking open. A mob surged into the Kremlin courtyard. His mouth twisted and whispered. Boots were stomping on him...

Stalin announced to his retinue: "Hitler is not dead. Hitler lives." He said it slowly, one word at a time, as if needed to give someone plenty of time, until the day came, to engrave it in black marble. His words were neither commanding nor doubtful. It was a declaration that would not be recanted, because behind them stood massive, sinister walls of stone with guards.

He continued: "National leaders don't die so simply. This corpse is not authentic. This is a phony Hitler. He is alive, the real, the true Hitler! What do you think, that it's so easy to bring down a leader? The people are protecting him. His followers are hiding him. He's surrounded by devoted disciples in life and death. Get this cremated trash out of my sight! Hitler must be hunted down. We dare not let down our guard for one minute!

It was one in the morning. The floodlights were turned off. The guards called out. There were footsteps on stone. Babadjanin was in a black mood. He had not done his duty. He would be considered a traitor who had brought some burned corpse into the Kremlin and had tried to dupe the Father of the Nations.

It was the changing of the guard at the gate. The Man from the Kremlin was nervous, tired, and restless. He took Babadjanin's arm as he went up the steps. "I'm saved," thought the Kazakh. His browless eyes radiated joy.

Moscow was celebrating the total conquest of the German capital, Berlin. Cascades of fireworks again lit up the Moscow skies. Cannons fired, and every shot announced more wondrous displays.

On the Brandenburg Gate there hung pictures of the heroes who had first broken through Berlin: Ivan Grigoryiev and Sgt. Aaron Schinder. May 2nd was a cloudy day. The Berlin skies reflected in purple the fires burning the city. At the entrance to the city on the Frankfurter Allee, Soviet troops were erecting a triumphal arch.

Chapter Six

It was the first few days after taking Berlin. The wind carried the scent of springtime and of dead animals. There were corpses of half-skinned horses at the end of the street. There were the ruins of an airplane without wings. German women in colorful kerchiefs, red lips, and painted eyebrows sold themselves in the cellars of ruins for a soldier's bread ration; "Come here, Russki, good, good…"

A Cossack regiment rode by, young men from the Don River, serious, focused. Germans gathered on the sidewalk to watch the riders. A horse reared up. A young girl left the crowd and threw them branches in bloom. A Cossack smiled. An elderly German wearing glasses said to the Cossack: "Comrade! Me Communist. Spartacist. Liebknecht."`

"Are you a Communist?" The Cossacks erupted in laughter. The rider slapped the old man on the back, "Don't worry, little brother!"

A crowd was massing at the gate. A Russian soldier was holding a German by the throat: "Come on! Let's have your watch!"

A woman screamed from the ruins. A soldier with Caucasian features was dragging her through a gate. A Siberian was playing a harmonica. The woman's cries mixed with his music. A dust-covered rider was singing, his words carried over the lawless streets of Berlin:

"On a broad, paved, well-marked street, a girl was walking to get water. A boy followed her and cried, "Stop, girl!"

"Let's have your watch!"

It was evening. It would be a night of drunkenness, of soldiers out of control, a night of plundering, of anarchy in that city of anarchy, of raping the women of the "master race." The next morning a young Pole said to Menakhem: "The Germans murdered us. The Ukrainians tortured us. And I'm gonna rape those blond, blue-eyed 'Aryans.' I'm gonna do everything that Hitler forbade. Their women are calling you. They stand at the corners, at the courtyard gates. 'Come, come', they call to us. And if they don't call to us, well, I'll go to them, to their houses. Germany ran wild over Europe. So let there be wildness!"

Oh, God, why do you erase the fine line between the conquerors and the conquered? How similar they are! How the distinction between them is fading! One small step, and the righteous become unjust, the liberators become the oppressors. Our people have lived on that fine line for so long, until they were drowned by impure waters. Oh, God, keep the Russian people from turning into filthy rapists and rioters! May the victory that we have won with so much blood not be stained! May they tread this accursed German land with pure hearts, pure hands, pure weapons! May the Germans be punished justly, severely, and openly under the bright face of Your heavens.

Menakhem was not worried about the fate of the residents of the conquered city. He was reserved and indifferent. He wanted revenge, and revenge to him meant: destroying their fortresses, blowing up their barracks, their air fields, their weapons factories, the concrete palaces of the corporate trusts, the beer cellars. It meant obliterating the swastikas, blowing up the stone monuments to evil, destroying the Nazis, and punishing their followers. It meant ripping the venom from the serpent, letting it return to its lair, harmless. It meant encircling their land with walls of suspicion and hatred.

He now saw clearly the fine line disappearing between the conquerors and the conquered, their faces resembling each other more and more. And in those days when he saw this, he realized that it would be impossible for him to live in such a world. He would have to leave. Jews would not be able to exist in this new world. The "master race" was on its knees before common Russian plowmen from the fields of Kaluga, before workers from the steel foundries of the Urals, before fishermen of the Volga River.

German prisoner Hauptmann Balder was ready to serve the Russians. He was a third-generation military man: "It's my profession, just like that of a doctor. Do you understand, Sir? Would a doctor not go when he's called?"

"No," said Menakhem. "We don't need such 'doctors.'"

Zirkov was already recruiting thousands of Germans. He needed them for the Special Section, for the civil government, and he needed them to dismantle the factories.

Captain Balder continued: "I'm ready to serve you with all my abilities and all my knowledge, honorably and loyally. I'm not a traitor. This is professionalism, Sir, professional duty under all circumstances." Menakhem received a special order to send the captain to Zirkov's Special Section. The women with painted cheeks at the courtyard gates, the Balders, all those who were servile and courteous—they were the first ones to erase the line between the conquerors and the conquered.

Well before Berlin fell, during the round-the-clock bombings, the German general staff had arranged orgies in their comfortable bunkers, which had special ventilation, upholstered furniture, separate quarters, and a common amusement room. Jazz provided by male and female singers accompanied their binges of drunkenness and debauchery.

There were half-naked dancing women and women wearing low-cut, black evening gowns, drowned in perfume. They were adorned with gold and jeweled brooches plundered from victims at Auschwitz and Treblinka. Blond, blue-eyed women had their hair carefully curled or coiffed up in radiant braids. The place reeked of the scent of women, their sweat, their perfumes, and champagne.

The officers sported crosses on their chest and silver laurels on their collars. They were bare-headed, their closely cropped hair resembling stiff hog bristles. Others were bald. Music played from phonographs or orchestras under the concrete ceiling. Bombs were shattering the skies up above, but down below they were dancing arm in arm, embracing, body-to-body, breath to breath. The lights flickered with each explosion. Conversations were swallowed up in a thick cloud of dust.

Waiters in black frocks with white cuffs and silk bowties slid among the dancing couples, carrying—on hands raised high—silver trays with dazzling champagne glasses. Couples disappeared, staggering down the long, dark corridors: generals with secretaries and telephone operators, admirals of the Navy, SS-StandartenFührer, SS-*Gruppen*Führer, captains, colonels... drunken mugs, eyes blood-red from drinking... and fear... and the half-naked women... and the shadow of Death. The besotted Elsas and Gerdas tottered in their arms.

But the heavy tanks of Zhukov's army were already rumbling a few hundred meters from the bunkers. Fire and steel rained down up above them. And SS men were hounding a crowd of concentration camp survivors on the southern roads of Germany through the Bavarian forests. They were driving them mercilessly on to Tyrol, leaving tormented corpses all along the way. The Führer's command was still in force. American artillery was already booming in the Bavarian hills, but columns of SS victims were still being dragged on the roads. Who will stop this massacre? Berlin has fallen, but Death still reigns on that soil.

It finally happened. Soviet troops broke into the bunkers. They came suddenly. A *Schlagerlied* was still playing somewhere on a gramophone. It was a woman's voice singing, and through the doors the Russians barged in, with their Asiatic eyes, their flat noses, their hardened faces, their gleaming bayonets. They found the German generals, the half-naked women, the drunkenness, the black frocks, the faces sweaty like melted wax, the reek of women's bodies, champagne, perfume, and smoke.

And here were the Soviets who had stormed across the Dnieper River, the Nieman, the Vistula, and the Oder. They had lain in snow-drenched weeds, in torrential rains, in ditches. They had been torn away from their homes, their fields. They were hard as steel. And it was precisely that contrast between their life amid exploding bombs and the jazz music that greeted them, between the stink of dynamite and the scent of perfumed women, which overwhelmed them and ignited their outrage, their fury. Hobnailed boots crushed the faces of the generals and their women. They stomped on them and stomped. The ancient instinct of the eastern steppes had been aroused by the ancient worship of Germany's pagan gods.

Oh, God, don't punish these men of the Volga for that wanton night of murder and rape. If You had been there that night, You would have covered your face and been silent, like me.

Lev Oshanin often visited Marion's house. He would come haphazardly several times a day to her upstairs apartment and bring packages of food. Her mother could not thank him enough. The house, the mother, and the daughter were under the protection of the Soviet lieutenant. On rowdy nights the Tatar Kerbaley often stood guard at the courtyard gate to stop drunken soldiers from breaking in.

Oshanin was drawn to the dark house. He would sit in the great armchair, his head resting on his chest, listening to Marion playing the piano. Sometimes he would glance at her girlish neck or her fine, graceful fingers. He watched her under his bushy eyebrows. Once, on his way to her house an hour earlier, he had run into several drunken German women, probably coming from some revelry with soldiers. They had stopped at a gate with some German men. The women were only wearing coats, so that parts of their naked bodies and knees were visible. "They're drunk," thought Oshanin. That was easy to tell from the way they were yelling.

And when he got nearer to the gate, he could hear one of those scantily dressed women screaming: "You've got it easy, you German men! You lie hidden in the cellars! Cowards that you are! You let Germany be defeated! Better to have ten Russians on my belly than nothing in my belly! You parade ground heroes! Why are you hiding?" They were laughing and weeping and cursing each other. They smelled of liquor. The waved their arms about menacingly, then disappeared through the gate. The men followed, like shadows.

Marion's father had been a merchant from Breslau. He had been murdered in Dachau. Her mother was an "Aryan" from Oberpfalz. They had hidden in the villages of Niederbayern to escape Nazi persecution. Marion had been arrested and was sentenced to Auschwitz, but she escaped from the assembly point for deportation. They hid with her mother's "Aryan" relatives. Their apartment had belonged to a doctor who had fled.

Marion was a pianist. She had completed secondary school in Breslau. Her voice was pleasant, and it sent a sweet shiver through Oshanin's back when she sang. She awakened subtle, long-suppressed feelings in him. He appreciated it that she sang quietly, for her voice gently rocked him like leaves in a mild wind in the spring. You just could not sing loudly in the midst of ruins, with the stench of corpses in the street. The hours became dear to him in that house with Marion playing the piano and singing softly.

Time stopped, severing itself from the chaos and nightmare around them, sending rainbows like bridges to the fine days of the past and to even more wonderful days ahead for a world reborn. Suddenly her fingers began fluttering like butterflies. She was playing a familiar tune, the song of the Volga boatmen. She had heard it from a Soviet soldier's accordion passing by her window after midnight. Oshanin sang along, and the voice coming from his chest was unknown to him. That strangeness depressed him.

Oshanin had not been born only to hate. He had been unable to completely suppress the love that was in his heart, and it searched for a road into the hearts of others. The stronger his hatred grew, the more his love sought a way out. Oshanin took Marion's hand. Her eyes opened wide, dazzling. Was it fear? Her big white teeth shone in laughter. Was it embarrassment? Her lips whispered. Was it an entreaty, or perhaps an appeal for compassion? Her shoulders shuddered. Was this resignation, was she giving in like all the other German girls? Or was she merely repaying all his kindnesses, the bread, the coffee...?

Her mother left. Oshanin heard her close the door. He was disturbed by her sudden departure. His throat tightened up. The light in Marion's eyes troubled him, her laughter, her whispering. He was standing at the door. He wanted to leave, to get away from her fear, the entreaty in her face, the resignation to repay him his kindness. He just had to leave. He could not bear to watch Marion turn into one of those other German women. He would not come back again. His orderly, Kerbaley, would take care of them. Oshanin would not buy "love" so cheaply. She said, "Don't go. Stay a bit."

He knew that the slightest motion towards the girl would unleash his hands and lust. He wanted it and he did not want it. When he closed the door behind him he was still agitated. The street was quiet. A patrol passed and German civilians wearing white armbands. An old woman was carrying a pail of water. The ruined bridge was well lit. Floodlights illuminated the iron girders. They were working on it at night. The canal was dark, with floating chunks of wood, papers, and trash. It was a cool and windy May evening. Oshanin asked himself how young Marion had managed to drown out the detonations and the shrieking steel splinters with her gentle voice. He had been full of the horrors of war, then suddenly she had calmed him. Those hours of Marion's music were like polished, mounted gemstones that radiate a glow, a brilliance. Those times with her had a beginning and an end. They had a separate existence totally apart from everything that was happening and that was going to happen. He was deeply grateful that the girl had taken him to such heights.

That night, when the officers went to amuse themselves in German houses, Oshanin stayed in the barracks. Sgt. Sergei Orlov was on guard duty in the Strasse Unter den Linden. The city spread out before him: ruins, white armbands, columns of German prisoners, unshaven, tattered, filthy, hungry. German women and children sat in small groups and watched them. Orlov strode back and forth. At his feet lay piles of debris and crumbled pillars. He could hear Russian soldiers singing nearby, as they walked towards the Brandenburg Gate. Smashed metal heads rolled on the ground, and the Angel of Peace stood with its wings broken. There were charred ruins of stone columns and housing blocks that resembled meteorites that had just fallen from the bright skies. There were corpses wearing filthy SS uniforms, others in Navy dress. Swastikas littered the cratered pavement. Prussian Junker arrogance lay under the marching boots of Russian troops.

Orlov yelled, "Where are you going? Get back!"

He had been ordered not allow the mob near the bridge. So he stood there gesturing with his hands for the mob to stop. His gaze softened. His hatred for Germans had begun to recede. He despised them and he pitied them. Orlov had seen Russia and Poland devastated from Smolensk to Bialystock to Warsaw. The Germans are to blame for it, and for the fact that people are starving in faraway Siberia. It was the Goddamned German bastards who forced us to leave our homes, our fields, our forests—and to wander on the terrible roads of war.

The night before, he had walked the length of the canal. Thousands of homeless Germans were sleeping in the metros, among ruined pillars. They wanted to cross the Elbe River and get away from Berlin. They were coming from the Oder, from Wartheland. Orlov gave away his bread. A woman was sitting among piles of rocks. He stared as she bit into the bread with her white teeth. Her hunger brought her closer to him. She did not weep, nor did she beg, but he was deeply moved by the hunger that he saw in the way she ate the army bread ration.

He patted her hair and said kind words to her in Russian. He wanted to tell her about his bitter years at the front, about the desolation in Russia, and about the Oka River. But he could not make himself understood in Russian. His gentle hand caressed her neck. The star-lit springtime skies over Berlin were gentle, too. The woman let Orlov caress her arm and her shoulder. Perhaps it was because her hunger was somewhat soothed by Russian bread, perhaps it was the gentle Russian farmer's hands, perhaps it was the skies over devastated Berlin, perhaps it was fear mixed with heightened human instincts that brought their bodies close together among the ruins of Berlin, not far from the black Brandenburg Gate—that German woman and that Russian soldier. "Back! Get back!" he warned the mob again the next morning, the women and the old men, as he held the machine gun, cold and terrifying, in his hands.

On one of those May days, NKVD Col. Nikolai Zhillin—the decorated Hero of the Soviet Union—showed up at the headquarters where Menakhem was working. He had become one of the most powerful officers in Soviet-occupied Berlin. There were preparations for his arrival. Maj. Andrei Ostrowski welcomed him personally in his office, where they had a long conversation.

Zhillin came with several soldiers. With their short jackets and the black revolvers on their belts, Menakhem saw right away that they were NKVD men from the Special Section. And when he looked closer at their faces it was obvious that most of them had not fought at the front. They were well-rested, well-fed men who had just recently arrived in Berlin only after it was conquered.

Menakhem at first had not wanted this meeting with Zhillin. He remembered those winter days outside Moscow, in their underground bunker. He remembered that German war prisoner who refused to answer Menakhem's questions because he was Jewish. And he remembered Col. Galinkov's fish-like eyes at his trial. But why should Menakhem avoid meeting Zhillin? Let the Soviet officer see that Menakhem had battled his way all the way to Berlin, and that the Soviet victory over Germany was also Menakhem's victory.

"Hello, Nikolay Feodorovitch!"

Zhillin stopped. They looked each other over. Zhillin still looked young and fresh, but deep creases had grown where his eyebrows met. Whereas Menakhem had changed greatly since that winter in Moscow, his face more bony, his black hair streaked with silver, the chiseled mouth even more sharply defined. His dark eyelashes and deep brown eyes darkened his face, worn-out, restless, troubled.

"Mikhail Isaacovitch!"

They embraced. Zhillin was very glad to see Menakhem.

"What great luck running into you! Congratulations, Mikhail! Great job! Come, sit in my car. We'll ride over to the officers' mess. And I see you got your epaulettes back!"

They rode past the Tiergarten, a bombed-out train station, the burned down Excelsior Hotel, across the Potsdamer Platz, and went around the headquarters of the Gestapo and the German Air Force. They sat silently, taking in the ruination of Berlin.

Zhillin's pleasure at seeing Menakhem again soon dissolved. Every once in a while he would glance at the Jew, and in that glance there was something inquisitorial, curiosity mixed with suspicion. The night before it had been reported that two soldiers had disappeared. They had searched the entire sector, as well as in the Spree River. On Zhillin's desk that morning lay a more detailed report of the case. It turned out that both men were Jews. "Now everything becomes clear!" he said to his adjutant. "Why didn't you say right away what their nationality was? They're probably already on the other side of the Elbe River! This isn't an isolated case. It's a bitter twist of fate: Nazis, SS men, Vlasov's army—and Jews—are escaping to the other side. It goes against common sense!"

Zhillin wanted to tell Menakhem the whole story. The car stopped. The officers' mess was deserted. They sat at a little table, and a German girl served them. Menakhem was surprised: "What? They're serving us so soon?" Zhillin's look said "You can count on us." They understood each other completely, the Russian from the south and the Jew from Plonsk. The waitress served Moscow vodka, American cognac, old Prussian liqueur, and French vermouth.

"Take your pick," said Zhillin. "We have a choice."

Menakhem took the bottle of vermouth. Zhillin laughed. His hand lay on Menakhem's arm as he said, "I just knew you wouldn't take the Moscow vodka!"

They drank a couple of glasses, toasting to brotherhood. He continued: "The Soviet government knows how to punish. But it doesn't just punish. After all, you got your epaulettes back."

Menakhem closed his eyes and again he saw that forest in the snow... Frolitch near the little stove in the dugout... Anna. He told Zhillin: "You remind me of those terrible days near Moscow. Nikolay Feodorovitch, you did me wrong then, with what you said at my trial. You remember?"

"Tell me, Mikhail, where will you be a month from now?"

"I don't know," he answered.

"Why don't you know? You have to know, Mikhail!"

Menakhem did not get what Zhillin was getting at.

"I'll be with my unit."

"You're not leaving? What I mean is, where will you go when you're discharged? Where to? Over there?" He motioned towards the west.

"I'll go back to Poland."

"Why not Tengushay?"

Menakhem was surprised: "What a memory you have!"

"My memory has made me what I am. But one thing isn't clear to me. Why won't you stay with us, in Russia? You can become something. Why drag yourself around in that wasteland Poland or in the capitalist jungle of the west?"

"Stop it, Nikolay! You're wasting your time on nonsense at such a table. Don't worry about me. I'll manage. Better if you leave us alone. There are more serious problems in Berlin." He lifted his glass and continued: "Nikolay, let's drink to victory!" Then he called over a soldier who was passing by, and he offered him the bottle, "Come here, Russian!"

Zhillin walked Menakhem to the car and said: "This soldier will drive you back. Don't get lost in the ruins!" When he was sitting in the colonel's black Mercedes and was looking at the driver's short leather jacket, Zhillin bent over to the open window: "Do you get letters from Mokhovaya Street?"

"You mean from Moscow?" Menakhem knitted his brows

Zhillin whispered close to his face, "From Anna Samuelovna."

Menakhem could smell the liquor on his hot breath. He felt Zhillin's burning hand on his fingers. The mention of Anna's name turned him pale, and his head was pounding. His face turned red. He repeated after Zhillin, "Anna, Anna Samuelovna."

And joy erupted from deep inside Menakhem, a spiteful joy breaking through, the way the clear light of day dissolves the fog: "Anna? She's alive! She's in Warsaw! At the military hospital! A doctor!" Menakhem wanted to add something, but Zhillin's look had suddenly changed. His forehead had wrinkled up, and his eyes were shimmering with an eery iciness.

The car flew over the evening streets. At the gates of the Soviet occupation headquarters stood the tall, blond Zhillin, wearing a smart officer's uniform with gilt medals and epaulettes. A light spring breeze blew through his hair. He was still watching the broad avenue down which his Mercedes had taken Menakhem.

Birds were swaying on the linden trees in bloom. It was spring in his bosom, too. Verdant spring was wending its way through conquered Berlin, between death, hunger, the cold, the rapes, and the white flags of surrender, to every tiny bit of earth, to every savaged tree trunk. And Zhillin's heart, too, broke open, like the ruined bridge. "Anna," he said to himself. And he felt as if that Jew Menakhem Isaacovitch had stolen her away and left him standing there at the guarded gates of headquarters. And when Zhillin crossed the cobblestoned courtyard towards the guards who presented arms, his pace became quick and energetic, like those of someone who knows that people are waiting for him.

Menakhem slept badly that night. First he stood at the open window and stared out at the blackness. Clouds of smoke were rolling in the west, and part of the sky was hidden behind a curtain of fire. When the wind blew apart the clouds, silhouettes of burned ruins appeared.

Branches swayed near his window. Part of the tree was charred and bare, while new leaves had grown on the rest of it. Assorted chunks of cornices littered the courtyard, as in an old cemetery. The wine had left a burning in his temples and a thick foam in his mouth. Zhillin had made him uneasy. Menakhem went down to the yard. Kerbaley was on guard duty.

"How's Oshanin?"

The Tatar tried his best with his broken Russian: "Ha, ha! Lieut. Oshanin is a good man. A good man. He's seeing a Fräulein. A beauty. A German girl. Pretty like the sun itself. He's totally changed. He's protecting her from our Russian guys. She's turned his head all around. The way she sings, whoa, mama, she melts his little heart like the snow in springtime. But he stopped going there recently. She invites him. The mother and the daughter. But he's stubborn.

Menakhem left the talkative Tatar and went into the great halls equipped with army cots, where the battalion was quartered. The Kirghiz Alturov was there. He was sitting at the edge of his cot, writing a letter. He was concentrating hard, focusing on the letter and wiping the sweat from his chin and neck. Now he was in another world, in an *aul*[1] in Kirghizstan, or in a shepherd's *kibitka*.[2] His young wife would come out of the shadows and he would say sweet words to her. Menakhem watched Alturov's lips move, and a warm glow spread across his tanned Kirghiz face. He felt so close to those frontline soldiers, as if they had

---

1   Tent.
2   Nomadic yurt.

been his friends since earliest childhood. It would be hard for him to leave them for distant, unfamiliar places.

Sgt. Sergei Orlov was downhearted. He held his head in his hands, propped on his knees. Menakhem said, "Sergei, what's worrying you? Have they stopped writing?"

"No, it's nothing. I'm just depressed."

Menakhem sat next to him, but they said nothing. When the others left for guard duty he spoke quietly to Menakhem: "Yesterday when I was on guard duty, a Ukrainian called me over. I followed him to an abandoned bunker, and there were half-naked German women and lots of our guys. The Ukrainian says to me, 'Take your turn.' I didn't want to, so I left. I was hanging around near the bridge. Hundreds, thousands of Germans were waiting there to try to get across the canal. Our men wouldn't let them. I was walking around, and I saw a German woman among piles of stones, all by herself. I bent over and gave her my bread. I patted her arm and her head, and I talked to her in plain Russian. When I was ready to leave I felt her cling to my hands. Such big eyes! Such an inviting, unusual breath! Such a bright face! It was as if I were in another world, and that world was calling to me. It was pulling me. I wanted to pick her up and carry her in my arms, and take her far, far away, to the fields back home, to my village, to the Oka River. She clung to the earth and to the stones and to me. Then the moon vanished. And she was mine in the darkness. But I had to go on guard duty. I came back to her at dawn, but I couldn't find her. I searched for her in that crowd that was mobbing at the bridge. I screamed, 'Halt! Get back!' and I aimed my machine gun. I was looking for her and I thought I saw her, but it was someone who looked like her. I was so upset that I just wanted to shoot. I have to find her! Where is she? Why are they running away? Won't I ever see her again? Tell me, Mikhail! I can't get it out of my system! Where is that young woman with the wonderful eyes?"

Menakhem thought, "Oh, God, see how close lust is to rape? A mere spider's web separates them. And how close life is to death! Even there where life and death walk arm in arm, love can bloom unexpectedly like the roses of the steppe!" What could he possibly say to Sergei? He did not wish to besmirch the wondrous rose of human beauty that had sprung up among the ruins of accursed Berlin. He consoled Orlov with the assurance that many more wonderful experiences were in store for him. When the skies had regained their peace, when the curtains of smoke had cleared off the ravaged earth, when the plows did their work again, when the fields of rye turned gold again—then he would surely find again those big, warm eyes that he had been so fortunate to encounter.

Politkommissar Vasil Akimovitch Sabayev called Menakhem for a meeting right after Col. Zhillin's visit. They talked about the German prisoners, about the civilian population, about the destroyed museums. Sabayev showed Menakhem old paintings of the "Münchener School" that had been found in a cellar. The orderly brought them tea. The sergeant then checked the weapons of the guards on duty.

Sabayev asked, "Do you know Col. Zhillin from your days in Moscow?"

"Yes, from the Winter of 1941," answered Menakhem.

"Yes, yes. He's interested in you... He said good things about you. You're a painter? It's important. Very important... Changes are coming to the general staff..."

Menakhem sensed that Sabayev was getting at something.

Sabayev continued: "What do you think of these paintings?"

"They remind me of our own painting... but our painters have ideas, whereas they, the Germans, didn't... dead subjects... overdone still-lifes... colors of the evening dusk. Now take our Gerasimov..." Menakhem had said these words with hidden mockery. Sabayev realized it, but he was not sure who was being mocked.

He said, "I think you're mistaken, Mikhail. The Germans do have ideas. Their idea is to celebrate gluttony for the lazy ones who gorge themselves. These pictures are meant for the propertied class and the princes. They're destined for opulent bedrooms. They'll look very nice hanging over big feminine beds. I once heard a lecture on German art. Those lectures were part of a special course that we were required to attend. And what I just told you I heard from a connoisseur from Leningrad."

Menakhem shook his head in agreement, with the mocking smile still on his face. He knew that the officer had an excellent memory and was repeating word for word what the connoisseur from Leningrad had said.

Sabayev went on: "What you're lacking, Mikhail, is a Marxist education. If only you had that, you could really be something! You simply must read the fourth chapter of the short course. Your lack of knowledge confuses your thinking."

That is how the conversation ended. But something had been left unsaid. Sabayev had not shown his cards. Something was brewing.

Soon after, Nikolay Soloukhin stopped Menakhem: "Jewish troops are being moved away from the Elbe River. They're fraternizing with the Americans, and there are Jews among them. And your people are crossing the river. At first we thought that the Germans would take revenge on 'the pitiful Jews,' and murder them. But it turns out that Jews are escaping. Sometimes they take Russians with them. Now units from deep inside Russia are patrolling the Elbe instead."

Sepp Düring, until now an SS-*Obergruppen*Führer, was named head of the German police that the Soviets had just organized in Berlin. When Menakhem found out, he immediately remembered what the Jews of Volhynia had told him that all the Ukrainians who had collaborated with the Germans had become the heads of the new police set up by the Soviets. Men who had shot thousands of Jews were now serving under Soviet command.

He asked Sabayev, "Do you know who Sepp Düring is?! Do you know what he did to the Jews in southern Poland?!"

"We know everything," he answered. "The bosses know. You have a personal account to settle, but Soviet interests are totally different. Yours is a narrow grievance. Blind hatred of Germany is disruptive. Did you read Stalin's last speech about the Germans? No? Well, that explains it."

A few days later Sabayev told Menakhem that he had been ordered to transfer him to another unit: "I think the place that they're assigning you to will be more suitable for you. You're being sent to a unit in charge of dismantling factories. It's more your line of work, disarming Germany, blowing up weapons factories, and the German machinery and their specialists that we'll need to rebuild Russian cities. "

Sergei Orlov embraced Menakhem like a brother and wept. "Don't forget to write a few words, soldier. Let me know where you are. I've been depressed since that night at the canal. That beautiful girl with the huge eyes just won't let me be! I'm ruining my eyes looking for her everywhere. I've been to the far ends of the city. Maybe you'll run into her, Mikhail. Tell her Sergei is looking for her. I don't know her name, but I'd sure recognize her. I'd know her right away, as God is my witness!" He had changed after that night, becoming more pensive, more serious. Now, after long years in the trenches, weariness and apathy hit him.

Lev Oshanin came to say goodbye to Menakhem. They fell into each others' arms. Kerbaley mumbled aloud, "Good people... good people," wiping away tears. Menakhem and Oshanin had much in common, and they were kindred spirits. Just being close, working in the same headquarters, had been great for them. Whenever they ran into each other they felt an ethnic bond. There was no need to shake hands or say anything, just an exchange of glances. But even that restraint bound them together, and they were not even aware of it. They realized how much they had meant to each other only when they had to separate.

Anna wrote:

"Mikhail, Mikha. The days have grown harder and sadder. Your letters are short, your sentences disconnected. I can feel that you're troubled. The joy of your victory is being spoiled by lawlessness everywhere. The roads of Poland are in chaos. Jews who return are being murdered. Trains are being attacked. They're hunting Jews and Soviet officers. Gangs are running wild on the highways, in the villages, in the towns. Jewish committees have to house Jews for protection. I've been to them and seen those broken people.

"Only the children bring me joy. I don't have the time to describe in more detail the kids whom we're taking back from Christians. My children's refuge is growing. Each child is a world unto itself. Little Ignacy sends you greetings. He's seven now, but his eyes are mature, full of pain. Hanka asks when you're coming back. We also have little Aniuta. I got her from a farmer's family near Plock. She's very scrawny, but what a clever girl! Yekaterina Yurievna comes with me to the refuge. I can now say a few words in Yiddish.

"I told Aniuta, 'Come here, little girl,' and she came over and hugged me.

"Then she asked, 'D'you want to be my mother?'

'Yes, Aniuta dear, good little Aniuta.'

'I'll be a good child. Take me away from here. I'm gonna love you a lot.'

"My eyes are getting teary as I write these lines. Who could ever have imagined what was going to happen in this country? I fear what the future holds for these children. Mikhail, my Misha, will I see you soon? How hard are these days of waiting! The hospital has moved across the river to Warsaw, but some departments are still in Praga. I was sorry to leave my little attic room.

"When I first got there, the branches of the chestnut tree were bare. During winter nights they banged against the windowpane. Now they're in bloom. I love the broad chestnut leaves, like open palms of the hand. The whiteness of their flowers soars up to the sky. I woke up last night, half asleep, half awake, and the flowers spread out before me like hundreds of white lights in the light of the moon. Don't laugh at me, Mikhail! I know that you may think me strange, a surgeon who's surrounded by the wounded and bleeding by day and dreams of dazzling whiteness and trees in full bloom. Do you remember that winter day near Moscow when I came out of the hospital to see you off? I stared at the snow field for a long time after you left. I remember your footsteps in the snow, the curves in the valleys, the blue-tinged mist over the forest. I kept looking at the fields until it was dark. That's when the whiteness took hold of me. I look for it everywhere, and when I find it I see your face there.

"I just read over what I've written, and I wanted to rip it up. But I can't. I know that tomorrow I'll put on my serious face, and my cold hands won't even shake when I touch the cold sharp steel. I'll get angry at the nurse, I'll say very little, I'll open the opaque glass doors and go into the operating room, where my own life totters between soldiers I don't know, the dead and the living. Then I'll collapse on my bed, exhausted. Don't be bad, Mikha, don't laugh at my dreams of dazzling snowy whiteness. Your Anna."

Soviet man was never so free as when he was in the ditches fighting at the front. It was there that he walked a thin line between life and death, but it was also there that his terror disappeared: the fear of the NKVD, the fear of being sentenced to slave labor, the fear of long prison sentences. The black cloud of dictatorship began to dissolve in the nighttime sorties, in the reconnaissance missions, in the heat of the battle, in the fortified dugouts—everywhere that initiative and boldness were summoned up. During all that time the NKVD men hid far behind the troops, with the regimental secretaries, with the office bureaucrats, at headquarters far from the front line. That freedom from fear turned the Russian soldier into a hero. The hands of the common man were now unbound.

Even his language regained its former richness. It was no longer fettered by slogans and poster jargon. It flourished with Russian wit, parables, ancient epics, tales of the medieval bogatyrs, passionate love ballads, lamentations longing for little Mother Russia. They quietly mocked the *Politkommissars* and ridiculed the Party heroes who had never seen action. The freedom that they tasted at the front would never again be taken from them. A new path had opened for them, which would lead to a renewed Russia without starving villages and bread made of clay.

A chunk of ice does not melt immediately, even near fire. It needs some time to thaw. Some law of nature maintains it until it turns to water, then steam. It cannot happen in an instant. That was how it was with Russia. Government by dictatorship, too, would have to thaw. It was surrounded by the flames of war. In a short time, just a little longer, the homeland would restore itself. After all, it could not be any other way. After all, it was so clear and obvious. Let the *kolkhozes* survive, and the red flags, and the statues of the deity with the crafty smile, and the star high over the Kremlin. But do not take away the freedom won by the soldiers on the front! Who would dare to unleash again the terror of the NKVD? After all, the soldiers had defended the fatherland with their lives. But yes, they did dare!

Berlin was crawling with military NKVD. New headquarters were established for the generals of these units. They came from all over Russia, well-rested, well-armed, well-trained. They took over buildings, factories, airfields, garages, entire streets, and enclosed them with barbed wire. Their special units kept watch over train stations. They controlled neighborhoods with a network of guardhouses and patrols. Their first victims were the frontline soldiers, precisely those Russians—frank and warm-hearted—with their new-found freedom, who had put down their weapons to rest after their victory.

It was those troops who had conquered Berlin. But right after their great victory, Berlin was again conquered—for the Red Kremlin—by whole divisions of prison guards sent from Butyrka

Prison, Sukhaya-Bezvodnaya, and the slave-labor camps in Komi and Temnikov. Marshal Zhukov was not the real ruler of Berlin, nor was Marshal Rokossovsky. The real rulers were Ivan Serov, Stalin's personal emissary, the shadowy Kazakh, Babadjanin, and the recently celebrated Col. Zhillin. Those three had a throng of assistants.

The map of Berlin lay unfurled on the large tables of the NKVD headquarters. The battle had begun "to maintain the Socialist conquests of the Soviet Union," as the Father of the Nations had promised in his speech at the May First parade. Ivan Serov was speaking in a conference hall of a former German corporation: "We are starting our battle to rule Berlin as a Soviet, Bolshevik conquest." A storm of applause interrupted him. Who was that Col. Ivan Serov? No one knew him. His face was gray and wrinkled, and marked by two deep creases from the corners of his eyes down to his lips. It was a dark, blank face with no hint of a smile, cold and tough.

Zhillin was his opposite: "Napoleon said that big cities are like women. You can take them, but not control them. We Russians, who beat Napoleon, will now destroy his theory. We will control this city." Someone smiled, but then immediately turned around to look behind him. The iceberg that had begun to melt from the flames of war was already beginning to freeze again.

If the war had continued and if there hadn't been a natural river border separating them from the Allied soldiers, the troops from both sides would have met, and the curtain would have been broken. The freedom that the frontline troops had just won in battle could not have been taken away from them. The NKVD was building concentration camps in Berlin, not just for SS men, Vlasov's men, and German war prisoners, but also for frontline Soviet troops.

Long trains were sent speeding back to Russia, some full of wounded troops, some with machines and all kinds of goods. But others were sealed. They ran at night, carrying frontline soldiers straight to Siberia. When military transports had been sent from the Urals to the front at top speed with no stops, all the lights were green, and it was called "the green road." But now, having conquered Germany, the "green road" carried suspect veterans quickly to labor camps in Siberia. But it was now called "the white road."

It was a brilliant, sunny day at Tempelhof airport. The piles of debris were cleared from the concrete roads. Destroyed hangars spread far and wide. Ruins of aircraft lay everywhere, speckled with green and silver aluminum, twisted propellers, wheels, maneuver fuel tanks. Piles of that debris resembled monuments to the air force of the Reich, erected by German war prisoners under Soviet guard. There was a roar of Soviet bombers. The squadron soared into the sky one at a time, under the command of Maj. Tiulkin. They were on their way to meet up with Allied airplanes at Tempelhof. The Allied high command was to arrive at 2 in the afternoon. Engines roared from the west ten minutes before the time arranged. Two Douglas bombers appeared, then a third, circling over the airport, over part of Berlin, and then landed. A silvery Douglas stopped on the asphalt runway. Chief Air Marshal—and Deputy Commander of the Allied Expeditionary Force—Tedder stepped out. Down the steps after him came the American General Spaatz, commander of Strategic Air Forces, and Harold Burrough, the commander of Allied naval forces in Europe.

They were greeted by Soviet Lieutenant General Vasilev. The flags of the Soviet Union, Great Britain, and the United States flew over the airfield. A few minutes later two more planes landed with the rest of the delegates and members of the press. An honor guard lined up. The flags of Great Britain, the Soviet Union, and the United States were presented. The orchestra played the national anthems of the three countries. Col. Lebedyev reported to Marshal Tedder that the honor guard was ready. The head of the delegation, along with those just arrived, reviewed the honor guard. Tedder said, "You have greatly honored us with this parade." The Red Army responded with shouts of "Hurrah!"

The audience was nervous. Some looked at the sky as the noise of airplane engines approached. Soon they saw a fourth Douglas land at Tempelhof, which was bringing representatives of the defeated German army to Berlin. Generalfeldmarschall Keitel, Generaladmiral Hans Friedeburg, and Generalleutnant Stumpff walked across the airfield, accompanied by American officers, towards cars that were waiting for them. Marshal Tedder spoke through a microphone, his clear voice echoing, metallic. He explained that the Supreme Commander of the Allied Forces General Eisenhower had appointed him to greet the Soviet marshals and generals, and that he was especially pleased to do so in Berlin.

The delegates took seats in their cars and drove through devastated Berlin to the Karlshorst suburb. The French delegation arrived at 2:40, led by General De Lattre de Tassigny. Marshal Tedder gave Marshal Zhukov a white silk flag bearing an embroidered emblem of the Allied Forces. The historic event that everyone was waiting for was to take place in a gray house at the corner of Zwieseler Strasse and Rheinsteinstrasse, the former building of the School of Military Engineering. Long tables had been prepared in a gray hall. The flags of the four Allied Forces hung from the wall. The evening was getting late. Marshal Zhukov entered, along with Marshal Tedder and the delegates of the other Allies. Each delegate took his seat under the flag of his country: Zhukov, Tedder, Spaatz, De Lattre de Tassigny. The middle of the table was occupied by the representatives of the Allies and the war correspondents of the international press. One table remained empty.

Marshal Zhukov addressed the audience: "Gentlemen! We have gathered here to accept the unconditional surrender of the command of the armed forces of Germany. I suggest that we begin the work and invite the authorized delegates of the German command." Then he gave the order: "Ask the delegates of Germany to come in!" With that, *Generalfeldmarschall* Keitel, *Generaladmiral* Friedeburg, and *Generalleutnant* Stumpff walked in with their adjutants. Generalfeldmarschall Keitel and the others took their seats in complete silence. Zhukov continued: "Gentlemen, now we will sign the act of unconditional surrender. I address these questions to the representatives of the German high command: Do they have the act with them? Have they familiarized themselves with it? Do the representatives of the German high command agree to sign this act? Then Chief Air Marshal Tedder repeated the same questions. Everyone waited for the answer.

"Yes, I agree," said *Generalfeldmarschall* Keitel, his voice breaking. He fixed his monocle, then walked towards Zhukov and stopped at the large table. He held the document from the German general staff, signed by *Grossadmiral* of the German navy Dönitz, which gave Keitel the authority to sign the act of surrender. Zhukov then asked the German delegates to approach and sign the act. The Nazi generals signed the historic act one after the other, while photographs and films recorded the event for eternity. The document was signed: Germany had surrendered unconditionally. The document was in Russian, English and German versions. Only the English and Russian texts were deemed authentic. One copy was given to Keitel. Marshal Zhukov announced, "The German delegation may leave."

Lev Oshanin cames looking for Menakhem late that night: "I'm back from Karlshorst. They signed the surrender. I saw them, the German generals. What a wonderful night! I just can't sleep. Something made me find you. I'm wandering around for hours. This is our victory." They walked arm in arm through the streets of Berlin. Everywhere they saw the white flags of surrender and the flags of the victors. Triumphal arches were going up. The next day would be festive.

Moscow celebrated that night. A thousand cannons fired thirty shots. The world had never seen a salute like that. The sky became one huge cascade of fireworks. The light over Moscow was as bright as daylight. Moscow was jubilant! The war was over! Germany had surrendered!

The next afternoon, Zhillin's driver came for Menakhem. The short Mordvin man with a broad face and heavy jaws was pleased that he had found Lieut. Mikhail Isaacovitch:

"I've been looking for you for hours, Lieutenant! I'm supposed to bring you to Col. Zhillin without fail. Something's going on. You have to look nice. There's going to be girls. You have to shave. Here's some eau de Cologne, not easy to find! Let's go, comrade lieutenant! Move it! D'you know what the Colonel said? 'Vavilov, you Mordvin, if you don't bring me Mikhail Isaacovitch, don't show your face here again!'"

"Your name is Vavilov?"

The Mordvin nodded.

"Where are you from?"

"The Tengushay district, Barashovo."

Menakhem embraced him: "I know Tengushay, and I was in Barashovo. That's where I was mobilized."

The Mordvin pulled a bottle of eau de Cologne from his satchel: "Lieutenant, let's drink to this encounter! It's good to drink, but it has a smell. You get used to it. It's tasty." Vavilov was soon tipsy, and his words were garbled: "You can take what's left for shaving. Oh, you don't want to drink? That's all right, we'll take care of it!"

He drove the Mercedes like a madman, almost crashing the car into a wall. He banged into piles of iron and ran up onto the pavement, whistling. Then he knocked into the wooden guard post, refused to show his military papers, and took out his revolver. Luckily Menakhem took hold of his arms. Right from the courtyard it was clear that a big party was being prepared. Loads of bottles and barrels and chests were being brought in. There were army bureaucrats, Russian women in military dress with white aprons and silk headdresses, and a mob of waiters. The courtyard was already crammed, from trucks to limousines.

Vavilov did not leave Menakhem's side: "I have to present you to Nikolay Feodorovitch, then you can do as you please. He has to see me here, my good buddy, my countryman. Come, let's find the Colonel." Menakhem followed him, smiling. The Mordvin reeked of eau de Cologne. He slurped when he talked and kept covering his mouth: "If the Colonel smells it, I'm a gonner."

Zhillin was elegantly dressed, with all his medals. Menakhem saw him standing with a group of commanders, Zhillin being taller and more trim. He was unusually handsome, except that his forehead was too low, and there was something sinister in his eyes. "Well, here's Mikhail Isaacovitch," he called out. Menakhem greeted the officers. Vavilov stood to the side and waited for Zhillin to signal to him to leave. The Mordvin mumbed to himself, staring through yellowed eyes at the long tables decked out with bottles of vodka and wine.

Zhillin introduced Menakhem: "This is my friend, from the battle for Moscow. A painter. Do you remember our posters on the Moscow streets in the first winter of the war? The Red Army trooper trampling on the swastika hydra? The caricatures of the German rulers? That was all the work of Mikhail Isaacovitch." Then he went over to the Mordvin, leaving Menakhem alone with the others.

The reception was to last all night. They were waiting for important guests. Marshals were expected to come. Menakhem spent time talking to Lieut. Karopov and Capt. Prokunin.

"We've got to hit the bottle."

"Let's start," answered the lieutenant.

"They'll give us a sign. Then we'll storm the tables, and I mean storm, nothing less."

Chapter Six

The large hall was decorated with colorful papers, pine branches, and portraits. Over the head of the table hung a picture of the Supreme Commander. Oh, how Menakhem knew that face well! What had been Zhillin's purpose in inviting him? Menakhem did not understand. Was it some nostalgic feeling for those days in Moscow?

Karopov was impatient. His face still bore scars that had not healed yet, and something like dark steel glinted on his neck. He had seen terrible combat. He had broken through the stranglehold of German forces and fought in Kertch and Korsun, and bridged the Dnieper River, the Bug, the Vistula. He was from Krivoy Rog and had been a work brigadier on a *kolkhoz*.

Capt. Prokunin, from Tomsk, had been the manager of a tractor station. He had survived the siege of Leningrad and had led his reriment to Vilna, Königsberg, and Posen. He was a Russian with broad shoulders, big, powerful hands, and a ruddy, smiling face.

Goblets were raised. All eyes were turned to the head of the table. A general, his face in bright lights, stood under Stalin's portrait. Menakhem looked at him carefully, and it seemed that he had met him somewhere before. Someone murmured half-aloud, "That's Ivan Serov." That was a name that was said very quietly, in a whisper. Menakhem repeated it to himself: Ivan Serov. He perused his gray, rigid face, looking as if it were made of wax and ash. Incapable of smiling. Motionless eyelashes. Deadly serious, like lead.

The general began, "We are gathered here," then he paused. His hard, dry voice was like a dull saw cutting an old tree trunk. He looked around then continued: "We are gathered here to celebrate our victory over Germany—here, in conquered Berlin. Let us raise our glasses in honor of the Great Man who led us to victory, the Father of the Nations." He could not continue because of the thunderous "hurrah" that surged like a river that overruns dams.

That ended his speech, and an uncontrolled buzzing swept the audience along with a sense of relief, as if they had thrown down heavy backpacks after an exhausting march. The man with the unpleasant, ashen face would have continued speaking, for he was still standing at the head of the table. But the clinking of liquor bottles and the popping of corks made it impossible. Someone struck up a harmonica. Soldiers waited on the tables, carrying trays of hors-d'oeuvres. Menakhem recognized some Jews among the officers. He looked for Gen. Shamshin but did not find him. Zhillin came over to him a few times. They drank toasts together. While they were drinking, one of the military correspondents said something to Zhillin, then pointed to Menakhem and asked, "Nikolay, who's the lieutenant?"

Menakhem offered his hand and smiled. Not waiting for Zhillin to reply, he introduced himself, "Mikhail Isaacovitch."

"Karasov," answered the correspondent.

Zhillin was not pleased at this meeting, and Menakhem sensed it. Zhillin even tried to pull Karasov away from him.

"Stop it, Nikolay! I want to talk to Mikhail Isaacovitch." Then he turned to Menakhem and asked, "Are you Jewish?"

"Yes, I am."

"I'm a writer. Have you heard my name? Jews are interested in literature. I know Gurman, an editor, and Sheynin, a critic. Are you on the general staff?"

Menakhem detected irony and sarcasm in his words. Karasov smelled of brandy. When had he managed to drink it?

"Mister Karasov," said Menakhem with exaggerated courtesy, in mockery. "Excuse me for calling you 'Mister,' but I don't see an insignia of any military rank. Your questions are such that they don't require an answer. Yes, I am Jewish. Do you have something against that?"

"Oh, Mikhail Isaacovitch, my boy! I like you, by God! I was just joking. You're sensitive. That's good. I'd swear to it that you write poems. I can see it in your face,"

"I'm a painter."

"Well, why didn't you say so? At least there's one respectable person here among these drunken revelers! Don't be shocked. You were ready to think me an enemy of the Jewish people. I know Jews. In my opinion, you bring problems on yourselves. Your deep distrust alienates you from others. You don't trust us. Even the slightest insult enrages you. You seize on every word that anyone says about your people, often without reason. We say the same things about ourselves, about Russians and Ukrainians. But we're not allowed to say them about you. You think you deserve kindness and love, and that's natural, of course. But one wrong word and you lose your reason; you get riled up, obsessive, terrified.

"And you become antagonistic when you're defending yourselves against injustice. It's a pleasure to spend time with you when times are good, but your mistrust of your neighbors the non-Jews, pours out in times of war and suffering. Then you think the whole world is conspiring against you and wants to destroy your nation. You think they've been trying to destroy you ever since there were Jews. Don't you realize that this is an absurd, imaginary fear? If it were real, there wouldn't be any Jews left today. Hundreds of nations have disappeared over the centuries, but your people have survived and they will survive. The Nazis didn't plan to exterminate only your nation. It was a pretext to destroy the Slavs. Why have you asserted that the world hates you? You assume that anything that is said about Jews is hateful. It confirms your worldview. That justifies the hatred of non-Jews that runs in your blood.

"Why are you staring at me like that? Are you going to count me among the Jew-haters? I'm not, Mikhail Isaacovitch. It's the Ukrainians that I hate. But no Ukrainian ever looked at me like that. I have Jewish friends, Moscow Jews. Now this problem has shaken things up. Until now this problem did not exist. It's the Nazis and you Jews who created it. Nazism has unleashed the hatred of the Jews, and that hatred is raging in places where there are no Jews left. This anti-Semitism is no longer directed at you, because you have practically disappeared from the liberated areas of Russia, except in the cities.

"Hatred needs a name, an address, and it must be concrete. The Jews were the springboard to unleash race hatred. And that antisemitism spread in the hearts of men, and, like lava, it expanded against other peoples. Hatred has no borders. We know where it started, but not where it will end. If the Jews could understand that, they wouldn't take it so tragically."

Menakhem interrupted him: "Not so tragically? Do you know what it has led to? The murder of millions! You talk as if there were no Auschwitz and no Majdanek!" He could barely speak. The fingers of his hands clutched each other, as he looked at Karasov with sorrow and regret. Behind them a colonel was laughing so hard that the glasses shook. Menakhem turned around and saw a stereotypical Russian face, wide, shiny, heated, his skin riddled with fine, delicate veins. When he laughed it seemed like those veins were simmering.

Wine glasses were tinkling. A woman soldier from the general staff approached Menakhem. She was laughing. Her front teeth hid her lower lip. Her teeth and upper lip were moist. Her forehead was all freckled.

"This is Zinaida Karpovna, from Zhillin's staff."

She asked, "Why are you young people talking so much? You're practically not even drinking!" Then she left to bring hors-d'oeuvres, and Menakhem saw her exchanging winks with Zhillin. "Looks like my old friend wants me to have a good time," thought Menakhem.

"Let's go," said Karasov. "Let's get away from her with the big teeth. With teeth like that, she'll have eaten you in no time, and the only thing left will be your belt buckle and the soles of your boots. Zinaida Karpovna is one of those women like crystallized jams." And he burst out laughing.

They walked arm in arm through the hall and went into a side room, which was also crowded.

"Mikhail, you're wrong to bring up the murdered Jews. That has nothing to do with it. They died as the result of a war between Germans and Slavs. They're victims of that war. If you believe that the world hates you, then you accept your own death sentence."

Menakhem replied: "Why do you keep harping on the Jews? Leave us alone. All we ask of you is tolerance. Nothing more. You, Russian poet, what compels you to keep talking about Jews, a small and lonely nation?"

The Russian answered: "The Jews are more than a small nation, a minority among others. They're a stream that doesn't merge with the larger river, and when the stream does merge with it, then it reappears somewhere else, even stronger. That's what the Jews are like."

Menakhem grew impatient. He decided not to respond. But his silence only provoked Karasov more:

"Your people have two choices. Either they can merge with the larger sea, or they can go their own way. Your people shook up Russia. They made the Revolution and Communism. Your people were the cream of our revolt. Their experiences let them tap into the highest instincts of our intelligentsia as well as the lowest instincts of the mob. Should I name all the Judases who poisoned Russia? Now they're working in another sphere. They've become our experts in literature and art. They're bright, they're very clever and articulate, and they're on their way again.

"Don't you think that a strong hand that sweeps away the foam at the top will reveal the silent, suffering Russian people? But no, it isn't silent! The waters are boiling deep down; they erode the riverbed and its banks. It's a heroic struggle with a rotten, alien, non-Russian layer. Do you see, Mikhail, that there's no proportion between the foam and the waters. That's how I see your 'small and lonely nation.'"

Menakhem did not answer. He drew Karasov's face on a paper napkin with a pencil.

Karasov continued: "You Jews are good at bringing goods that are needed to the market. What we need now is Russian patriotism. Your Ilya provides it. Who can compare to his brilliant writing? We needed a national anthem? Jews provided it. Poster slogans and articles promoting the Russian war effort? David Zaslavsky! They do their job well. Our guys can't compete. A book about the hajdamak Khmelnytsky?[3] Who can write it better than Natan Rybak? Soulful Russian poems? Ilya again! His sonnets are rich and complex. He can do everything! World-class novels. Pamphlets. Biting feuilletons. Lyrical songs. Russian people, just help yourselves to what modern Jews can offer you! They have a whole store! You were the first to adopt Communism, and I have the feeling that you will turn against it. Or rather, Communism will betray you and trample on you."

Karasov was drunk, but that made him less clear and lucid. Menakhem looked at him and said quietly: "You take individual Jews make it seem as if they represent our entire nation. It would never occur to me, for example, to claim that Smerdyakov is your brother just because you're both Russians. One can take any nation and smear it that way by generalizing. You wouldn't talk that way if it weren't for Hitler. You're right that hatred has no specific boundaries. You're bitter and you're looking to blame it on someone. You're not strong enough or brave enough to blame those who actually savaged your country. And so, out of cowardice, you choose a small, nearly exterminated nation to blame instead. You're attacking victims whose hands are already tied, who are wounded and bloodied. You do it with no compunction whatsoever, no sense of morality at all. Blaming the Jews poses no danger to you. Yes,

---

3   Leader of a Ukrainian Cossack uprising against Polish domination in the seventeenth century. Tens of thousands of Jews were murdered. The term *"hajdamak"* referred to paramilitary Ukrainian and Cossack bands serving under Khmelnytsky.

you feel the need to vent your righteous hatred of your regime, so you pick a target, and—to justify that hatred—you then pick and choose your facts like a ghastly mosaic. I could name dozens of ethnic Russians who would easily represent brutality, treason, and murder in our generation. Do you want to hear them?"

Menakhem started to leave, but on the table lay excellent drawings of Karasov.

"Stop it, Mikhail! Don't get insulted! We were just having a normal conversation. Let's see the drawings, brother! You're too sensitive on the subject. Don't look at me like that! I like you! You're more frank than me, more direct. In your place I wouldn't have said those things about Russians. Do you want to hear my poem? Sit down, Mikhail!"

Karasov used both hands to sit him down. His face changed. There was something of the blue forests in his eyes. He began to read:

"Russia, you are the bare pasture fields in late autumn,

Where a hungry ox runs, his eyes burning,

And a hamlet is cradled between its flaming red horns.

All the horizons are cradled and evening falls.

And I, a son of that melancholy, white hamlet,

Play in the viburnum in the valley at nightfall…"

Menakhem liked the poem. He looked at his stereotypical Russian face and thought how odd it was that vicious, insidious antisemitism could reside in a person with elevated feelings, an average person, a decent person. That antisemitism was like alcohol, which can rot and corrupt a person's mind and heart.

They strolled through the brightly lit halls. Karasov wended his way through the officers and the women. His eyes were not accustomed to the brilliance of crystal chandeliers. A Ukrainian was dancing a kozatchok, holding his hands on his hips, his thick neck stiff, his feet barely touching down, as if they were sweeping the floor, the people, the tables. He was crouched way down, so that only his curly head and shoulders were visible on top, and his black, shiny goatskin boots below.

Karasov said: "Come, Mikhail. I don't like that Cossack dance. It's too primitive. He's turned into a top that twirls of its own blind force. Just look at the mug on that dancing Ukrainian. He looks like an idiot, like a cooked red beet. His eyes are glazed, he's foaming at the mouth, and lust just pours out of him. He's possessed by some unnatural force. It's the Devil that makes him twirl like that. All his movements are out of his control. He can't stop, and he can't control himself. It's a mixture of self-satisfaction and depravity, and the release of very taut muscles. He's not human anymore, just a wound-up spring that suddenly uncoils itself. He'll keep spinning until he's all worn out.

"That dance reflects the Ukrainian character. They rise up at every historical event, sometimes against the Russians, sometimes against the Poles. They had Khmelnytsky and they had Petlyura. But they were just briefly stirred up, a passing movement. D'you see, Mikhail, how he's all done for, out like a light? His eyes are closing, his face is now ash."

Karasov went over to the Ukrainian: "Little brother, you're all spent! Straighten up! You're a rag now. When you dance you look like a rooster who's twirling around and his red comb twirls with him." Karasov was drunk, and he went around slapping people on the back: "Russians dance differently. Have you ever seen how Russians dance? Mikhail, where are you? Come closer. When a Russian dances, you can see his soul on his face. All his dreams are in his gentle eyes."

Suddenly the outside doors opened. Several aides entered, clearing a path. They were serious and tense, and they lined up in an honor guard. Menakhem heard cries of "Hurrah!" Karasov's lips turned pale and turned gray.

"What happened?"

He replied to Menakhem, "Nothing. Must be some parade-ground general. They're carrying on that old tradition of parading around. That's great for recruits, not for veterans."

A member of the Supreme Military Council walked to the head of the table. He was a pockmarked character with a short beard. He looked as though he were wearing three layers of uniforms. He did not seem to be made of flesh and blood, but rather artificially stuffed with some strange padding. Three high officers followed him, looking just like parade-ground horses, very young officers just recently come from the officers' training school near Moscow, where they had studied strategy with German generals who had been taken prisoner.

When the member of the Supreme Military Council had taken his seat of honor, Aleksei Karasov said to Mikhail: "D'you know what his military feats were? During the period of collectivizing the farms, he was sent to suppress the revolt of the farmers in Kuban.[4] He attacked the villages at night, at the head of Kalmyk and Tatar regiments. Later he led the Kuban regiment against Kalmyk villages and hamlets. Then he was named *Politkommissar* at central headquarters of the Army, the Kremlin's watchdog over the troops. Now he's in Berlin. You all paved his way here, all the way to the Elbe…"

"Stop it, Aleksei! There are people behind your back. You've drunk too much. You're putting yourself in danger, and me, too…"

"Are you a coward? Tomorrow I'll write a poem to the glory of our powerful ruler, the Father of the Nations, and I'll give it to Gurman the editor… Ha! I'll write a report on the first day in conquered Berlin. But you won't find a trace of the real Karasov in any of it. Little brother, you'll rub your eyes trying to find that mournful Russian who 'plays in the valley with the red pearls of viburnum.'"

Cries of "Hurrah" rang out again. They rolled in waves, coming together in a roar or unbridled joy. Aleksei joined in the clamor. Marshal Zhukov walked into the hall, the conqueror of Berlin, the commander of the First Belarussian Front, middle-aged, powerfully built, with the face of a plowman. His eyes were piercing, metallic. He had a broad nose, with large nostrils, dilated, looking as if they had just taken a huge breath. Two deep creases ran down to his nose, and he had a chiseled chin, protruding, with a deep dimple. His neck was short and stocky, with folds. His lips were pressed tightly, but half open on the right side of his mouth. His smile was fatherly, but severe.

Karasov applauded: "He's the Kutuzov of this war. Only Russians could have produced such a regimental commander! Mikhail, we haven't yet toasted in honor of the Great Russian nation. Come, let's drink! Look, there's Zinaida Karpovna and Zhillin! Let's all toast!" They raised their glasses full of vodka.

"To the great Russian nation!"

Zhillin said, "Enough, Aleksei! Mikhail! You're neglecting Zinaida. You're not gentlemen!" Zhillin did not have time. He had to be everywhere. Singing was coming from the other rooms. But when it was interrupted you could hear loud "Hurrahs!" and women laughing.

---

4 This refers to the Stalinist campaign to collectivize all the farms in Ukraine in the 1930s, which led to starvation and suicides on a mass scale.

The Russian poet and the Jew Menakhem left the halls at dawn. They ran into drunkards on the steps going out. Some Germans had also been invited to the reception. "Those are our German bastards. They helped us, showed us the way to Berlin. We couldn't have managed to get through the ruins and the devastated streets without them. The map of the city was useless."

Menakhem shuddered. He saw Sep Dühring. They looked at each other. And as Menakhem stood in the courtyard and felt the early morning May breeze, he was overwhelmed with grief. He left, alone, through the streets of conquered Berlin.

Chapter Seven

Anna closed the door quietly behind her. Her room had been ransacked. The bed was a mess. The window was open, the wind blowing through it. On her night table lay a half-written letter, some books left open, and an old illustrated magazine. Her white wardrobe was open. The cold air was pouring in. She had just returned from Capt. Klyuyev, the supervisor of medical personnel. Why was her room a mess? Maybe no one had come to clean up. No, she herself had closed the wardrobe and made her bed at dawn. The skies were cloudy. It was sad to see the sheets of rain slanting down on the ruins below. Anna threw a narrow, white shawl over her shoulders and sat on the bed.

Who were those two people sitting in Klyuyev's office who had said nothing during her interrogation? One of them had been a young civilian, the other a woman soldier in officer's garb without epaulettes. She had not looked at Anna, she took notes. Anna noticed her forehead covered with freckles, her protruding lip, and her big, crooked teeth. Klyuyev had called her once by name, Zinaida Karpovna.

It had taken place in the afternoon. Leszniak, the old Polish doctor, was chatting affectionately with Anna. The head nurse, Yekaterina Yurievna, was in the reception room. She had just escorted a wounded soldier out to the gate. When he had first been brought in, he was considered a hopeless case. Now Anna shook his hand warmly, and when he left she watched him from the window as he walked away. She remembered every wrinkle in his face when he lay on the operating table, his ashen lips pressed together, the marbled veins at his temples. Now he was walking with a healthy stride, and she was beaming with joy. But she was sorry to see him go.

It was just then, as she watched the soldier leave, that the door had opened and a medic walked in: "Anna Samuelovna, Capt. Klyuyev wants to see you. He's waiting in his office."

"Capt. Klyuyev?"

The medic nodded, and Anna detected sympathy in his face.

Klyuyev began: "Doctor, it's an honor for me to see you. Please sit, Anna Samuelovna. Sit."

She did not like his saccharine, courteous voice. She sat down at the edge of the chair and said nothing. Her impatience showed in every movement. She coolly sized up the unfamiliar civilian in the corner and the woman soldier.

He continued: "You're in a hurry? I know that you have more important things to do, Doctor. This won't take long. It's my fault that we haven't gotten to know each other sooner. Totally my fault. You know how it is, so much work, such responsibilities! Hm... hm... Doctor, why haven't you applied to be a member of the Party? Now—with our victory over Germany—there's a big push to enrol members. For me, Capt. Klyuyev, it's a matter of prestige. One of our finest doctors isn't a member of the Party!

Anna smiled: "I'm so busy. It didn't occur to me. I didn't think of it."

Klyuyev turned serious: "Didn't think of it? Never thought of it? That's very interesting. Very..."

He did not finish his sentence, but looked at her long, thin fingers on the edge of the table: "Don't you want to be considered in the leadership of the Soviet nation?"

Anna burst out laughing and walked to the window: "With your permission, Capt. Klyuyev. The soldier Blinov is going home. We fixed him up here. There's the car now." She looked right at Klyuyev and continued: "Do you think I would have fixed him up better if I had the red Party card? You honor me with your suggestion, and I'm grateful for your trust in me."

"So you're refusing to join the Party?"

"I didn't refuse."

"Oh, you'll think it over? Quite right! That has to be done calmly and of your own free will. It speaks well of you that you're not rushing thoughtlessly to join the Party. Good, Anna Samuelovna! I like you. We'll put it off."

Anna did not sit down. She stood at the window in her white medical robe.

"Please allow me one more question," said Klyuyev. "You fell into the hands of the Germans when your partisan detachment was attacked. That's what it says in your file. But there's something that's not clear. Didn't you freely desert and go over to the Germans because you were apathetic? You didn't have faith in our victory?"

Anna's hands began to tremble and she was out of breath: "What are you saying, Capt. Klyuyev?"

"We believe you, Doctor! We're only interested in your partisan commanders. Clearly they made a decision, and you were faced with a fait accompli. But you certainly know that there were quite a few deserters. You're trembling? Stop it! You're a surgeon, and such a trifling question, such a trivial matter makes you nervous? Are you tired? Then we'll stop here for now. Maybe another time... What do you think, Anna Samuelovna? I would be very pleased, very!"

Anna was stunned. Her eyes, now moist, shone from her grave face like flickering candles.

He continued: "Don't you remember the names of the general staff of your partisan unit? Can you mention one, perhaps?"

"I already gave my full report, all the details. Are they in your desk? You can easily check."

"Too bad you can't remember. It's important."

Klyuyev leaned over and rested his fat fingers against Anna's hand. His touch made her shudder. She desperately wished to be gone from there as soon as possible. She answered: "Anton Vasilitch Mikhailov was the commander. He was killed in action."

"But surely there were others? Are any of them still alive?" asked Klyuyev.

Suddenly Zhillin's face came to her. He appeared to her like a shadow on the walls of the office. He seemed to be standing behind Capt. Klyuyev. She could feel his breath, heavy with liquor. His eyes were burning. Hands knocked her down in a field with nettles. The pain was so sharp that she locked her eyes shut, weeping inwardly over her own torn, bloody body. She could hear the snide laughter in that terrible night, the drunken, evil laughing of Zhillin's orderly.

She answered, "I don't know. I don't know any surviving commanders."

The captain got up: "Doctor, I apologize for taking you away from your work. It was a pleasure to see you. We'll discuss these matters another time. You *could* help us discover our enemies, but your answers prove the opposite. You don't seem agreeable. I can sense it. Should we put off your application for membership in the Party for now?"

He held out his hand with its short, stubby fingers. When Anna left his office, she sensed that someone was following her. Then she discovered that her room had been ransacked as if someone had been searching in her wardrobe and her bed. Night had fallen. Anna was lying on her bed. The window was still open. The rain was beating against the pane and splashing on the sill, then onto the floor. Yekaterina Yurievna quietly opened the door. She called, "Anna! Anna!" and turned on the electric light. "What's wrong, Anna?"

Anna was wrapped in her shawl, her head buried in her pillows. The nurse closed the window and called the chambermaid to mop up the puddles that had spilled to the center of the room. Then she tidied up the disorder in the room. She knew about Anna's conversation in Klyuyev's office. She, too, had been summoned the day before and interrogated about Anna: Where was Anna going so often? Who was Marek, the Polish Jew? What did Anna talk about? Who was sending Anna letters? They made the nurse tell them about the Jewish children whom Anna was rescuing and bringing to the refuge in Otwock. Then they made her sign her name attesting that everything she had said was true, and promising to report back every few days on what the doctors were talking about, and which civilians were coming to visit Anna.

Yekaterina Yurievna wept. "I can't take it, Anna. I can't take it anymore. I want to leave. The war is over now, so why are they torturing us?"

Anna got out of bed at midnight. She stepped into the washroom and turned on the faucet. She let the cold water cool down her face and neck. She walked down the dark corridors to the great hall with the wounded soldiers. She had slept for an hour at most. The weather cleared with the coming of dawn. She was suddenly overcome with the need to read Menakhem's last letter again. But she could not find it.

Heavy trucks stopped at the hospital gate. A driver was calling out hoarsely.

A few weeks earlier, when Anna had gone to the dark building of the Jewish Committee in Praga near Warsaw to make inquiries concerning Menakhem's parents, she met a young Polish Jew named Marek. He was the only one with information about Menakhem's home, and she invited him to see her at the hospital. They had once been friends for a while. But they went their separate ways in the Fall of 1939. Menakhem had fled occupied Warsaw, crossed the border at night and ended up near the Volga River. Marek, a blond history student, had remained in Warsaw and had survived the Ghetto. He had been a leader of the 1943 Jewish uprising, then joined Gen. Bor's army in the Warsaw uprising of the Poles a year later. He was sent to Pruszkow along with other Polish prisoners, then escaped to the Kielce forest, and returned to Warsaw with the Red Army.

When Anna looked at his bright face, she thought that his courage did not only reflect only on his small Jewish nation but would be a source of universal pride for an entire generation. He had the face of a Greek warrior hero. How wonderful it was that God had created such a pure soul and such human decency and bestowed them on this man, which was so obvious on his face! She was grateful that Fate had protected Marek. When he showed up among the weary, dispirited survivors in those tiny rooms of the Jewish Committee, he brought light and hope with him. Anna compared him to Menakhem. They were two different blossoms, but their roots were intertwined, growing from the same soil. And it made her, too, feel a part of her people. Her Jewish parents had showed her the way, and her open, warm heart had been receptive. Anyone who could imagine himself on the road to the gates of Auschwitz, even for a second, could call himself Jewish, symbolically. She had once said so to Dr. Leszniak.

She had first gone to see the rescued children a few days later. Marek led her up dilapidated, garbage-strewn steps to a few little rooms where surviving Jewish children were holed up. She was heartbroken when she left them, unable to keep from weeping. They had been found in marketplaces, in ruined buildings, in train stations. They had wandered like little beggars at the gates of churches, and they lived with non-Jewish Poles. They were ragged, sick, worn-out. Non-Jews came to the Jewish Committee every day, asking for money to feed Jewish children. Some asked for food and clothes for them. Dozens of letters came offering to deliver children in exchange for payment:

"We risked our lives by hiding them, we fed them and clothed them. Now you owe us for all that."

"We were assured that we'd get millions of dollars for every child at the end of the war. That was just another Jewish swindle."

Marek showed Anna the letters and asked her to help. He told her that when the first Soviet tanks fought their way into Lublin, one of them stopped. The Russian trooper got out, carrying a Jewish child in a blanket. He called out, "Who is Jewish? I want to entrust him to a Jew." The Russian was from a village near Voronezh. "Anna Samuelovna, couldn't you do what this Russian did?"

That was how she became the supervisor of the children's refuge. She managed to obtain some rooms near the Soviet hospital and to get food and clothes. Nurses and doctors joined in. Even some of the patients helped out. Some carved them toys or shared the packages that they had received from their homes far away. A requisitions officer went with Anna to Otwock and requisitioned a villa for the children in a pine forest. She spent her free time running from bureaucrats to storage magazines to get extra rations for them. When they had finally cleared enough space for the children, and dozens of beds were brought in, Anna rode around picking up more Jewish children living in non-Jewish homes, accompanied by Marek and some Soviet troops assigned to the hospital. Sometimes the children were given up only under threat.

Sometimes the children hid, terrified that they would be harmed or that the people asking for them were Germans in disguise. Those six and eight and ten-year old children had learned that murderers of Jews came in a variety of guises: farmers, or good-natured officials, or Christian women dressed in their Sunday best. And the mayor himself might come with a policeman.

So they looked with a mixture of mistrust and childish curiosity upon this unfamiliar woman in uniform who spoke Russian. But they gradually got accustomed to Anna. She took care of their medical needs. Dr. Leszniak often came along, too. One day a friend of the doctor came to see him at the hospital, Dr. Jabrow, a Jew from Vilna. He was old and gray, somewhere in his 70s, who had survived the German camps. He showed surprised to hear Anna's surname.

"Why are you surprised, Dr. Jabrow?"

"You're from Moscow? Your name is Anna Samuelovna Korina?" he asked again. "I remember your father. Samuel Korin. We were very close, practically relatives. How is your mother, Sara Abramovna?"

She shook with emotion, and she threw her arms around him like a member of the family. Her face brightened and warmth radiated from her eyes: "You knew my father! Oh, God, how thankful I am! How you've made me happy! My mother will weep. Do you know what this means to me? No, you can't imagine. You've taken someone torn from her roots and restored her to her soil. You've returned me to my own suffering people." She held his hands and talked about the death of her father, about the house on Mokhovaya Street, about her old mother, about Menakhem in Berlin, about the Jewish children in Otwock.

That day they ate lunch in her room, then they went to Otwock. Dr. Jabrow said: "I want to stay with the children. I hope I can still be useful. My strength is gone, but I want to give them whatever is left." She kissed him and left. She thought about her father's friend all the way back. Why had she not asked him to tell her about her father? Dr. Jabrow could have told her about her father's childhood years. No one ever talked about him at home, and her memory of him was as if he were a dream.

He had died somewhere in Siberia in a Soviet labor camp. And her dead father had often been an obstacle to her, like a sinister wall. He was a shadow over her dossier, which was always questioned, and which she wished to erase, even now, when she wanted to write home to tell about her encounter with Dr. Jabrow. Oh, how easily he had mentioned her mother's name and her father's! She would have to tell her brothers about it. And she would write to Menakhem. She repeated the name to herself, "Dr. Jabrow," and everything in the world seemed connected: the sandy path through the pine woods to the refuge; the children; Marek, a hero of the Ghetto uprising; Warsaw in ruins; the grief of the Jewish survivors; Dr. Jabrow; the old Polish Dr. Leszniak. She would come back the next day and take Aniuta for a walk. She loved to hold the tiny girl on her lap and talk to her half in Russian, half in Yiddish. Her visits to Otwock helped her forget her conversation with Capt. Klyuyev. But that memory came back at night. She knew that the interrogation had not really ended.

In her dreams Anna still saw that shadow on the walls. She saw him lurking in the corners or standing frozen, as if nailed to the wall. Sometimes she imagined him creeping down the corridors, searching. She dreamt she was trying to see what he really looked like, and sometimes she was sure she recognized him: It was the shadow of the same man who had been following her all the way from Moscow. He had tracked her over huge distances, day after day, until he had reached the corridors of her hospital. Now he was right behind her, haunting her day and night. And when she closed her eyes in bed, he leaned over in the black of night, closer and closer.

Col. Zhillin showed up in Warsaw at the end of May. He was assigned as the liaison between the Soviet garrisons and the temporary Polish government. That assignment was from Moscow. They obviously valued the services he performed when he had parachuted into Warsaw and made contact with the general staff of the Polish uprising, and spent time at Kamler's factory with Col. Bor. The Poles knew of Zhillin's radio appeals for help for the Warsaw fighters, which had been transmitted from Bor's headquarters to London, then from London to Moscow—because there was no direct communication. This gained him their trust when he returned as liaison to the Soviet Army, and a welcome from all the Polish sectors. The fate of conquered Berlin now rested on devastated Poland, on Warsaw.

If they did not succeed in restoring calm to Poland, the normal operation of the railroads and highways, and the free movement of Soviet troops on Polish soil, the Soviets would be unable to maintain control in the territories that the Germans had occupied.

Poland wished to be independent. Its people distrusted the pronouncements of the Soviets, as well as the civilian Soviet commissars who were assuming government positions in Poland. And the huge Russian garrisons terrified them. After all, it was only recently that the same Kremlin leaders had declared that Poland did not exist anymore, and that it would never exist again. There was no Poland on Russian school maps in 1940. The part of Poland that the Germans had occupied and called the *Generalgouvernement* was labeled on Soviet maps as the "Sphere of German Interests." But now they spoke only of the eternal friendship between the Russian nation and the Polish nation. Now the Soviets spoke of building a large Poland all the way to the Neisse River. But it would not be a free Poland. It would be ruled by the Kremlin.

Three days after Zhillin's arrival in Warsaw, the sinister Kazakh Babadjanin showed up:

"Nikolai Feodorovitch! We're back together again! On the ground, as in the air. That's good. Do you remember our flight together? You were very suspicious then. Now we're old friends. I'm glad you're back in Warsaw. But it's different now. Surely you must have Polish friends from that time? They're a brave nation. I mean you'll probably see them, Bor's people. That's not bad. You're not going to stay away from them, are you?

"Some of Bor's men are with us, and some are in the woods, guerillas. Those are making things difficult for us. They blow up transports every day and murder Russian officers and soldiers. They rob trains in broad daylight. Do you know what happened yesterday? The Warsaw—to—Lodz train, a vital communication link, was stopped by armed Poles for half an hour. They killed six Soviets and civilians. I think the civilians were Jews. I recommend that you take a plane. It's the safest way to go. These people are going to give us a hard time!"

It was a friendly chat in the courtyard at headquarters. But Zhillin felt the same way as he had at the Moscow airport, when he held the Kazakh's slippery hand and looked into his big watery eyes with no eyebrows. That same fear slowly crept into him again.

Zhillin drove around Warsaw in his black Mercedes and he did not recognize the city. Were those autumn months of 1944 so long ago? He stopped the car amid ruins in the northern part of Warsaw. It was a vast wasteland. Mounds of debris. Piles of iron. Shattered cornices. An ocean of rubble. A single tree with bare branches like bent arms stretched towards Heaven. It was evening, and the Polish skies were mild. A little cloud rose above Krasinski Garden. A flock of birds flew down on the damaged trees. Sadness and homesickness overtook Zhillin. He dreamt of his home, his village far away. The snow was melting there now. The silvery gray sea was washing over the mossy stones. Patches of snow still shone in the meadows. The wells were creaking in the evening. The farm girls carried pails of water. Their eyes did not have to see burning cities, blood in the streets. They were not being raped by hordes of soldiers. They did not have to sleep in stinking bunkers amidst the starving, the wounded, the corpses. They did not depend on the mercy of troops and officers.

Zinaida, lanky, big-toothed, was waiting for Zhillin at headquarters, having just returned from Capt. Klyuyev with the dossier of Anna's interrogation. Zhillin leafed through the papers and suddenly wanted to rip them into tiny shreds. "Good," he told the secretary. "You can go!" He started pacing across the stone floor. He was angry with himself, with Warsaw, and with the web that was trapping him more and more.

Why must he resort to these filthy methods, these devious ways that would bring him back to Dr. Anna Samuelovna? He lived his whole life in tangle of dark intrigue, terror, night shadows, slipping between suffocating walls. Even when he could have shown himself openly and bared his heart, he chose the path of darkness and secrecy and used his sinister power to bring his miserable self close to Anna.

How would she look upon him? She surely suspected that someone was behind Klyuyev. She knew that. That was why she had refused to name him in the interrogation. He did not tear up the dossier. He heard the typewriter clicking in the next room. The telephone rang and Zinaida answered. Zhillin quickly opened the door and looked at Zinaida with the bony, freckled forehead. When she hung up the receiver he asked, "How does the doctor look?"

"You mean that Anna Samuelovan Korina? Her answers were confused. She was in a hurry. She sat at the edge of her chair and gave evasive answers."

Zhillin grew angry. "You're not answering my question! I asked you, how does she look?" he said severely.

"Not bad. A foreign face, not Russian. I wouldn't say she was beautiful. She's... I would say..."

Zhillin burst out laughing: "Oh, you women! You have a hard time saying anything good about another woman. You begrudge them..." He slammed the door.

The next day he spent more time in front of the mirror. He put on his new parade outfit and ordered his driver to take him to the military hospital. Zhillin wanted to see Anna and to put an end to Klyuyev's interrogation. It might turn out dangerous for Zhillin himself. The web that he had spun all around him could trap Zhillin himself. Klyuyev sent copies of all his dossiers to the higher-ups. Anna might start talking about that night of drunkenness long ago in the village with the partisans. He knew that spies from Moscow were on his trail. He might be implicated in that mess. He had to prevent that. He had to cover the traces that he himself had foolishly revealed. His own mad impulses could be his undoing.

A nurse informed Anna, "An officer is waiting for you, Anna Samuelovna." Anna walked through the great hall, between two rows of white beds. Every step closer to the door upset her more and more.

A wounded soldier smiled. She stopped at his bed and smiled back. But that was just a nervous smile hiding her agitation. She tried to maintain that superficial smile down through the corridor. She was grateful to that soldier for that moment of kindness. Someone was coming towards her, but she did not recognize the face. It was like those burning eyes she had seen in Klyuyev's office. Who was standing in front of her? Oh, it was Marek! "What's wrong with me?" she thought. It had been a rough day. She had needed to remove a fragment from a wound that had healed long ago. The war was over, but the wounds continued. She was exhausted and she was tense. Faces swam before her: the soldier she had operated on, Klyuyev, old Jabrow, Zinaida with the sharp teeth.

"Oh, Marek! Is something wrong?" she looked at him questioningly.

"Nothing. You look upset. I'll come another time. We took in two more children today. I hoped you could come to Otwock. Dr. Jabrow is really like a grandfather to the kids. But I think someone is waiting for you."

Anna turned towards the little marble table, where a Russian officer was sitting. Anna turned to stone. Zhillin stood up and walked towards her. Anna stepped back, stopping against the dull glass panes. She felt the cool panes at her back.

"Anna Samuelovna, don't you recognize me?"

She did not answer. Her hands grasped for something to lean on. Her eyes flashed like a blast of wind that clears the snow off a frozen lake, uncovering black freezing water below. Marek waited on the side, looking at the doctor, then at Zhillin, as if he were expecting something. Anna said nothing. It was an icy silence. Zhillin was sorry he had come. I'm doing one stupid thing after another. How can I look her in the eye? What shamelessness! He felt small, worthless, there in the hospital surrounded by clean, white corridors, facing the surgeon with the proud head, suffused with dignity. Every look of hers stopped him completely. What was he compared to this young doctor? A worthless worm crawling under filthy boots. He would be trampled anyway. But she would stay in the whiteness, the purity. How had he dared to raise a hand against her, that night with the Belarussian partisans? He would bow to her in silence and never see her again.

But he was not brave enough to do that. The Hero of the Soviet Union was entangled by black threads to that crafty Babadjanin and was so terrified of him that it made him stammer. Now he felt powerless before the doctor whom he had thrown down on his cot that night in his drunkenness. Now he trembled in her presence; he was at her feet. This was his fate: debasement. Others thought him almighty. But it was a lie!

Why was she silent? Why didn't she talk? Any words would have relieved him. They would have given him hope, even bitter, angry words. They would have lifted him up from abjection. They would have permitted him to look at her face.

She answered: "I recognize you. I knew you would come." Her words relieved him.

"You knew I was coming?" he smiled. But the ice in her eyes froze that smile on his face.

"Does that mean you were waiting for me?"

Now the snake slithered from Zhillin's eyes. He was not the rabbit that he had seen as a child facing the snake near the granary. He was the snake that slides through the fields, its dark back shimmering, the silvery zigzag on its stomach. Now he paused, with the silvery stripe gleaming.

"I was not waiting for you!"

Her plain speaking sliced right through him like a steel blade. She spoke clinically, like a surgeon. Now the snake in his eyes turned its ugly back, and a poisoned smile spread on Zhillin's lips. He clicked his heels and saluted. Then he took his cap and leather gloves from the marble table.

"Farewell, doctor!"

Anna did not wait for him to leave. She turned around, went back to the hospital ward, and saw the smiling wounded soldier smile at her again. But this time she did not respond. Zhillin did not go right to his driver. For a long time he watched the unknown young man whom he had seen speaking to Anna. Then he waited in the corridor until a nurse came towards him.

"Citizen, please tell me where Capt. Klyuyev's office is." And she took him to the door.

Klyuyev was shocked at Zhillin's visit. Was it good news or bad? They had a smoke and looked at each other.

Zhillin told him: "I'm just passing through. I wanted to see the hospital. My secretary was here. It's a pleasure to meet you personally.

The hospital is well-run. But there *is* one thing. But the security is... for example, I ran into an unfamiliar civilian. He was chatting with the lady doctor. That's curious. Who's in charge of visitors' passes? You need to be more careful! Especially now, in these troubled times."

Capt. Klyuyev rang a buzzer on his desk and a sergeant entered.

"This is the man in charge of security."

"Let's leave that alone for now. I'm in a rush. I've received the dossier of the first interrogation. It's interesting. Don't forget to beef up security."

Zhillin left, relieved.

He saw Poland in ruins, Poles living in the street, with bitter faces, with scorn and hatred. Yes, hatred. He had not felt such hatred in Berlin as in liberated Warsaw. Now our greatest enemies are the Poles, not the Germans. His car had to stop at an intersection, because some push carts and a horse-drawn wagon were blocking the way. It was dark. The Poles pointed to his big Mercedes. They hurried to clear the road. The driver let loose a volley of bitter Russian curses. A young Pole with a mustache raised a fist towards him. The driver pointed his gun at him. Zhillin curled up and cuddled in his upholstered seat. A military patrol appeared and escorted Zhillin through the dark streets of Warsaw.

Menakhem was discharged from the army. At the end of May he went to the Warsaw railroad station, which was half in ruins. He strolled around the wooden barracks. No one was waiting for him. Farmers were swarming in the station, dragging sacks and baskets, making their way towards the freight cars. It was a lively crowd, with crude faces, shiny with lard and vodka. Among them walked frontline soldiers, recently discharged, wearing raggedy tunics, carrying small satchels.

Polish police and Soviet patrols were watching everywhere. All kinds of peddlers sold their wares in the station, like hot tea and boiling grits. There were professional looters with goods plundered from the cities and villages of eastern Germany; smugglers returning from Siberia; peasant families coming from the other side of the Bug River with bundles and bags. Smiling young Polish women with valises and overstuffed leather handbags, who had gained experience in the commerce of war during the German occupation, were all on good terms with the station officials and the police, so they were able to take all the little tables in the buffet.

Carrying his wooden satchel through the mob, Menakhem perused all their faces. He was searching for Jews. Someone stopped him. It was a Soviet patrol: "Documents?!" Apparently Menakhem's Soviet tunic and his officer's insignia must have attracted his attention.

Anna did not know that Menakhem was supposed to come that day. He had written to tell her that a military commission had discharged him, and he was waiting for orders from headquarters. Menakhem wandered the streets of Warsaw on that rainy Wenesday afternoon. It was not his hometown. He had grown up on the banks of a little river in northern Poland among meadows and alder tree forests, fields of reeds and water mills with dams of stone. His grandfathers and uncles had been peddlers in the villages. He had left at sixteen to study in Warsaw. He had fled the city when the Germans occupied it. He could still see it as if it were yesterday. He had found himself among a crowd of Poles on a side street not far from the Plac Teatralny. The Germans had turned the ruined square into their victory parade ground. He could hear the drums beating in the distance.

Now he was again walking across the cobblestones of the huge square. The walls were charred black. Columns stood supporting nothing. Entire buildings were desolated, hollowed out. He did not recognize the people. This was not the Poland he had known. The faces were different. The women wearing kerchiefs and shawls and broad-shouldered army coats—these were not the people of Warsaw. The gruesome years of war were etched on their faces. Their surface dignity dissolved at the first look of a stranger. He could see grief on their faces and also the pride of having been favored by Fate to survive. They walked with the confidence of chosen people. Before the war Warsaw had exuded a feminine charm: the streets, the parks, the boulevards, Menakhem had once sensed it. But now it was gone. Instead the city seethed with feminine outrage, with revulsion at having been violated, and it pained him.

Menakhem had just one address: the address of the Soviet military hospital where Anna worked. Yekaterina Yurievna took him to her door. The nurse had recognized him and she beamed with joy. She waited in the corridor until Menakhem closed the door behind him. He put down his satchel at the doorway. Anna stared at him with big, watery eyes, gleaming with an inner light. He stood silently in the room as evening fell. He seemed taller to her now, and she lay her head on his shoulder and brushed his neck with her warm, moist lips.

Menakhem spent the night in Anna's room. At midnight she put on her slippers and white doctor's robe and went to check on the wounded. When she returned, Menakhem was in a deep sleep. She bent her warm body over him and caressed his neck, his hair with her long, nervous fingers. Her hands on his scars brought her back to that village outside Moscow, buried in snow, where they had met for the first time. Here was that shell wound in his shoulder again, barely hidden under thin skin. She pressed her lips to him as he slept wearily, and she was glad. She again saw herself meeting Menakhem that night. She again took his hands to wrap her fingers around his. But her recent agitation resurfaced: Klyuyev's words, Zhillin's sudden appearance, and her new terror at the shadows that followed her—all of that mixed with her renewed passion, her months of longing, the desire to wrap herself with Menakhem's exhausted body, to give herself completely, body and soul, to him. She leaned over him, this sad young Jew who had come back from the war. She would give him everything.

But her life was not in her hands. Others were in control. All she had left was her love. Everything else could be trampled on some dark night. Did he realize that? The next morning, Anna brought him breakfast on a tray. They sat at her little hospital table in her little room. He suddenly had a foreboding that they would be separated again. It would be against their will. He tried to suppress that premonition, but he could not. Anna's fingers were pale. He pressed his lips to them. He asked himself, "Where did I ever get such an idea?!" But the feeling drilled itself like a corkscrew into his brain. He could not see why this presentiment had taken hold of him. He was sure that Anna was thinking the same thing.

"Anna, what were you thinking just now?"

She laughed. It calmed him down, and he was glad that she had laughed just then.

"I'm leaving soon. I have to do something."

"Marek is coming now, your old friend. I sent for him." The three of them, Anna, Menakhem, and Marek left at noon to see the children in Otwock.

Antisemitism surged in Poland after the war, growing uglier every day. Stones were thrown at trains bringing Jews back from Siberia and from the central Asian Soviet steppes. It was dangerous for Jews to leave their homes after dark. They were being murdered. People who had been seen recently suddenly disappeared, their corpses turning up later in out of the way train stations. The country was swarming with ruthless characters unleashed by the war. They ran wild from the Oder River to the Bug, from Bug to the Dnieper. Remaining units of Bandera's gangs spread out to the Dniester River, from Huryn to the Vistula River and Cracow. There were Vlasov's men; gangs of Polish Volksdeutsche; war criminals; extortionists who had betrayed Jews to the Germans; concentration camp guards; smugglers.

Discharged Soviet veterans who had lost their plunder by playing cards and getting drunk went robbing in Poland to bring back loot on their way home to Russia. Gangsters looking for ways to escape to Czechosolovakia, Rumania, and then further away, stocked up on gold. These scoundrels preyed on Poland, for the gold was there that Germans had plundered all over Europe. Warsaw became the center of the black market for occupied Europe. Drunks and thieves now traded in the possessions that had been stolen from the Jews. Warsaw attracted hordes of people, like locust, from distant corners of the country. When they got to Warsaw, they encountered Jewish survivors from the Soviet Union and the camps, who had gravitated to the larger cities.

Antisemitism flared up among the residents of Warsaw and Lodz. They feared that returning Jews would demand that their apartments, their homes, and their possessions be returned to them. A special emissary from Moscow addressed Zhillin's general staff:

"Our aim is to develop contact with the Polish people. It must be a close and friendly relationship. We cannot take severe measures. The country is still reeling from the war. Every farmer has weapons. We have to stay out of internal conflicts here but keep a watchful eye on them. We need to take advantage of certain things here to use them to our benefit. Antisemitism is one of them. There may be some Jews among you, or not, but I'll be frank.

"Even our Soviet officials of Jewish nationality will understand. We sympathize with your tragic small nation, but we will not stain our Bolshevik morality if we cannot help them. There is a higher interest: the well-being of all the Soviet nations in the whole Soviet Union. It is precisely the turmoil and chaos in Poland, especially the murder of the remaining Jewish survivors, which justifies to the outside world strengthening our military garrisons in Poland. Foreign governments are convinced that the country is not yet capable of independence, and Soviet garrisons are necessary because Nazism is still rampant."

Zhillin paid close attention to the words of the emissary from Moscow. He understood that they were aimed directly at him, and that the words of sympathy for the Jews were mere lip service.

The speaker continued: "As you can see, such negative and regrettable in this country can be useful to us. Keep that in mind and draw your own conclusions. Details and instructions are not necessary. Everything is clear."

Marek was murdered in his apartment in Warsaw. He was found shot to death in the bathroom. He had been killed in broad daylight. A few days later the Jewish children's refuge in Otwock received a threatening letter: "Get out of Poland! If not, we'll blow up this house and all the children."

Old Doctor Jabrow and Menakhem went to the representatives of the provisional Polish government. They sent an investigator and assigned a policeman to guard the house. There was a Soviet garrison not far from the refuge, and Menakhem went to see the commander. They received him courteously and suggested that he contact the liaison officer of the general staff. But Menakhem replied to the commander: "About a hundred Jewish children are threatened. You have to act now. Give us weapons."

He left empty-handed and went to Warsaw with Dr. Jabrow. One of the liaison officers was Zhillin. Anna was against asking Zhillin for anything but did not give a reason why. Even the Poles wanted to ask for his help, especially since there was a Soviet garrison just a few kilometers from the refuge.

Zhillin received Menakhem warmly. He served brandy and snacks, expressed an interest in the children's refuge, and said he would help them as much as possible. Jabrow was touched by this reception: "Only Russians can be so warm-hearted. I remember their goodness and generosity from before the Revolution."

Menakhem was surprised that Zhillin did not mention Anna. But when they were about to leave, Zhillin said: "I heard that a young Jewish hero was murdered, a ghetto fighter. I think Marek was his name. Why don't your people do something?"

"We're powerless."

"No, you're not powerless. You underestimate your possibilities. I have a proposition for you."

Menakhem saw a change in Zhillin's face, now streaked with shadows. His eyes gleamed yellow.

"Your children's refuge needs to make an appeal... No, not just the refuge... The Jewish Committee must sign this appeal to the Jews of the world. It declares that only the Soviet garrisons in Poland can protect you, and that without those Soviet garrisons the remaining Jewish survivors will be murdered. This is crucial for your people. I think you understand?"

Menakhem now realized the game that Zhillin was playing.

Chapter Eight

He heard steps in the rainy night. Menakhem was standing at the window. The panes were clouded over. The steps faded into the black of night. They would probably return. The pine trees cast scattered shadows. An oil lamp swayed in the big hall, its pale, yellow light falling on the children's beds.

Dr. Jabrow was sitting, hunched over, and reading. He was exhausted from visiting one child after another. The rain was pounding on the windows, lighting them up with a silvery glow. Menakhem went out on the street, his collar up, to listen to the night sounds. The dog, Rex, curled up at his feet. He felt the dog's warm breath on his hand, and it felt homey. He started walking around the building. The dog disappeared among the bushes and suddenly started to moan. That is how dogs weep when some unkown fear takes hold of them.

Menakhem had been guarding the children's refuge at night for several weeks. He spent his days in Warsaw getting officials to give him food for the children. In the evenings he would sit with the older children, telling them stories about voyages and deserts and about the intelligence of God's creatures. It was a way to calm the anxiety that gnawed at his heart. Then he would grip the loaded pistol in his pocket and go out to stand guard. Shadows swarmed around the house.

Harvest time brought rain-swept days. It was bad enough that the fields had been half destroyed and wild growth had sprung up on the unplowed soil—a tangle of ugly nettles and wormwood never seen before. And now rain poured down, and the paltry tufts of rye were beaten down by wind and water as if hordes of dancing demons had trampled them at night. At dawn the farmers saw footprints in the damp soil, but they were unable to tell if they had been made by humans or by creatures not of this earth. Sometimes they could hear shooting at night, and they could see farms burning on the horizon. Armed men overran the roads. They held up trains, plundered baggage, kidnapped passengers, and then disappeared. No one knew who they were, what they wanted, or whom they were fighting. They might be dressed as peasants, or Russian soldiers, or religious hermits. They spoke all kinds of Slavic languages. They had only one thing in common, hatred for Jews.

Anna always waited for Menakhem with both joy and dread. When she caressed his forehead and his neck, he always choked up and turned away his moist eyes. But he did not like that weakness in himself. He struggled to control it, and he did. After a sleepless night of guarding the children's refuge, he would sit on Anna's bed in her little hospital room and hide his face behind her long fingers. His shoulders trembled, and his tears touched her hand. Then he put his head under the cold-water tap and smiled. Anna understood that the war was not over for Menakhem. He could not be at ease yet, after what he had gone through. It was still war for him. He was still surrounded by danger. Even there in the hospital, the war was still raging.

How good it was for Anna, to be able to look at his face, the dark eyes, the black hair of the exhausted Menakhem! She loved to see the smile spread from the corners of his mouth while tears ran down his face. She loved their salty taste on her lips. She waited for him to embrace her and hold her tight. She longed to feel his warm breath, his panting, and wanted to breathe it in even deeper. Her lips hungered for his. And he loved her even more for it, and for the arms that welcomed him so freely, her warmth, her big, gentle eyes that were so open to him. It was intoxicating.

As Menakhem left her room, walking with Yekaterina Yurievna, he met Capt. Klyuyev. They looked each other over. Then Menakhem heard a heavy door slamming shut. The nurse wrung her hands and left him. When he was on the street, Klyuyev's inquisitorial stare came back to him. He was sure that something was going to happen very soon. He wanted to suppress that certainty by thinking of Anna. He loved her big eyes. They were always bright, shining even at night. His fingers could still feel the softness of her neck. Klyuyev's eyes had the look of someone who knows another person's fate. No, it was silly to worry about the captain who sniffed around the doctors and patients in the hospital! But Menakhem stopped when he remembered the nurse wringing her hands and leaving so suddenly.

The next day day Dr. Jabrow was summoned to Warsaw. He returned late at night.

He told Menakhem: "We have the possibility of taking the children across the border, to the west. The authorities have promised not to stop us."

Menakhem shuddered, "Leave? Escape?"

He said those words in such a way that he did not know whether he was asking the doctor a question or agreeing with him. They were part of an interior dialogue he was having with himself, but he had voiced only two words aloud.

A Soviet liaison officer had invited Jabrow and had explained that there would be no objection to taking the children to the other side of the German border, to the west: "We can't be responsible for their lives. Anything can happen. Furthermore, foreign representatives have taken steps."

The doctor added: "Those officers have been well paid off. It's worth their while."

Menakhem was silent.

The next day he was playing with the children again. He told them stories about a big, beautiful world on the other side of the sea, a world of perpetual summer. He held little Aniuta in his arms. Rysiek with the bright eyes played at his feet. Freckle-faced Adasz asked him: "Is it true that we're getting ready to go far, far away? Are you coming with us, Mikhail?"

If everything was such a great secret, how had the little redheaded boy learned of the trip they were planning? Oh, how children find out everything!

The night before they left, Dr. Jabrow talked to the children: "I'm going with you. It's a long trip. Don't be afraid. It won't be easy to leave behind these Polish fields and forests. We were born here. We love the Polish skies and the tragic Polish soil…" He choked up and could not catch his breath.

A while later he added: "This land has turned into a stepmother, and the skies have turned against us. The nights have become dangerous. Farewell, Poland!" Then the doctor turned towards the window and lowered his head. Just then a boy began to weep in the corner of the room. Everyone listened to his thin voice screeching like a violin against the silence. The sobbing child was slender, about ten years old. They had rarely heard him speak above a whisper. He was shy and reserved and always stood apart, watching the others play.

Menakhem went over and asked: "What's wrong, child?"

"I don't want to go away from here. Sometimes I can hear my dead mother singing. Over there, far away, I won't hear her. The soil *is* good for everyone. The skies, too! It's the people who are bad. God will make them good. We have to pray to God."

Menakhem wandered through the rooms of the children's refuge all night long. He stepped outside a few times to listen to the rustle of the wind in the pine trees. His eyes scanned into the dark distance, followed the light of fires hidden in the fog, then he opened his arms to take in the night of late summer, and he breathed it in deeply. Once again he smelled the scent of the Polish fields and almost tasted the pine resin on his palate, as he had in early childhood. He still had not decided whether to leave with the children or to stay behind.

Anna's face came to him a thousand times a second. His inner dialogue with her continued without interruption, all bound up with the rustling of the wind, the black of night, the stars, the smell of pine resin. It was one long dialogue with God's world. Little Adasz had asked him, "Are you coming with us, Mikhail?" And what about Anna? Could he leave her behind? Would she go with him to unknown lands? Could she even do it, she who was a surgeon in a military hospital?

Menakhem's conversation with Zhillin convinced him that he had to leave Poland. Anna would also have to escape. Something awful would happen if she didn't. No, nothing would happen to her! But then he remembered that her face had turned pale and her hands shook when she heard about Zhillin's meeting with Menakhem and Dr. Jabrow. Now it became clear why Zhillin had asked such discreet questions about Anna in Berlin that night during the victory celebration. And the night before his death, Marek had told him of the strange encounter between her and some Soviet officer in the hospital corridor. Menakhem now realized that it had certainly been Zhillin.

Menakhem sat half-dozing on the steps in front of the house, with Rex lying at his feet. He dreamt of speeding trains with locked doors and barbed wire. He saw train stations in the black of night. Airplanes were soaring over burning forests. Someone was weeping nearby, someone he knew. It was Anna. She was standing on the other side of the rails. He was running through blackness, his arms reaching out to her. Suddenly a black train roared past, dark wagons, and more dark wagons. When will these wagons end? A black wall stood between him and Anna. When will this black train ever end? Now he could not hear her anymore, only the train wheels clattering, the locomotive howling.

It was dawn when he finally shook himself awake. He shivered in the cold and felt sick and tired. That day, trucks would come late at night to take the children and some adults. He walked to the train station, Rex following. A suburban train arrived. From the window Menakhem could see Rex barking, his ears perked up.

The night before, head nurse Yekaterina Yurievna had knocked on Anna's door after midnight: "Anna Samuelovna, get dressed. They're waiting for you downstairs in the corridor." Anna sat up and looked at the nurse, nervously, anxiously. The wrinkles from her eyes grew deeper and they glistened. Her eyes seemed to radiate some inner light, not the eyes of someone who has just woken up. She got off the bed and put on her doctor's robe.

Anna was used to the nurse waking her at night, but this time she saw that it was not to go help a patient. They walked in silence. Anna saw the woman soldier she had met in Klyuyev's office. She stared at her short forehead, covered with freckles, and at the upper lip protruding over her crooked teeth.

The woman said hoarsely: "Doctor, I'm from headquarters. You have to come with me now. Take your things, I mean your equipment. The driver is outside. Don't forget a warm dress. It's cold at night."

The black Mercedes sped through the dark Warsaw streets. The woman said nothing.

Anna asked, "What's your name?"

"Zinaida Karpovna."

"I met you in Capt. Klyuyev's office, right?"

In the dim light of the car, Anna could see the woman smile at her obsequiously. She responded with a stony look and reacted only when the guards shone a light in her face. She walked quickly down the hall. Someone opened the door to a brighly-lit room. The woman with the crooked teeth stammered something. When Anna walked in, some Soviet officers were deep in conversation. They grew silent as soon as they saw her. Zhillin walked towards her.

"Sit down." She recognized that mixture of his, of feigned weariness and indifference. She could not argue with those two words said so quietly, although furious words lay on her lips. How did they dare to drag her through the city at night? How would she be able to function at the hospital in the morning? They were putting the lives of wounded soldiers at risk! So irresponsible! The mad impulse of an officer who had been hounding her since the start of the war! But she said nothing.

Her lips pursed, she merely said, "You sent for me?"

She did not want to say his name. She had not been able to bring herself to say "Zhillin" ever since that terrible night in Polesia.

"Yes, I called for you." Then he got up to emphasize his words.

"When are you going to stop hounding me? What do you want?"

"I'm not hounding you, Anna Samuelovna. I've interceded on your behalf. Thanks to me you can freely go home to Moscow, to Mokhovaya Street, and see your mother. You've been ordered to go back. You'll get work in a hospital in Moscow. There was an order for your arrest. You've had contact with foreigners, with enemies of our homeland. I've done everything to save you, to get you out of the clutches of a spy ring of foreigners, outsiders, who have entangled you. We're on their tracks."

Something sinister and shiny flashed in his eyes. It was the snake that shows its back, then its belly, and readies its white poison. Oh, how well she knew him!

"Look, Anna Samuelovna! This is the warrant for your arrest." Zhillin slowly took a document from the desk, then drew on his cigarette, and tore up the paper into tiny pieces. "You have to leave Warsaw in two hours. My driver and Zinaida will take you. Here's your plane ticket and the necessary permits."

The phone rang just then. Zhillin covered the receiver with his hand and said to Anna: "Have a good trip!" The door opened slowly, and the woman with the crooked teeth entered. Zhillin called out, "We'll see each other again! We have to see each other again!" Anna did not turn back. She stood a while with her back to the officer and did not know whether those words had been addressed to her or to the person who had called on the phone. In the corridor she saw that she was being guarded. Zinaida said, "We're going to the hospital to get your clothes. It's getting late." The driver slammed the door of the big black car.

They drove through a Warsaw that was half destroyed. Weak lights shone from twisted lampposts. Drunks were bellowing. A shot rang out. A lone woman slipped along a open gate, dimly-lit. A harmonica was playing nearby. They passed a patrol. An emergency vehicle sounded its siren. Anna closed her eyes. The relief of indifference suddenly descended on her. She would never see Capt. Klyuyev's inquisitorial eyes again and shudder with humiliating terror. Yes, there is a terror that humiliates, that renders you abject, totally powerless. That was the fear that she had of Zhillin. That would all stop now. All of it.

Anna threw her things into a straw satchel. Zinaida stood in the doorway, smoking. Anna said, "Why are you watching me? I won't escape!"

She looked silently at the window. Dawn was breaking. A cloud glowed like phosphorus. She had once seen a sky like that. It was when Menakhem had returned from the war, the night he had spent in her room. Such a phosphorescent cloud had hung over the black horizon when they had woken up. Anna's relief and indifference dissipated, replaced by piercing heartache.

She told Zinaida, "I have to say goodbye to the wounded. You have no right…" She strode quickly towards the door. Zinaida moved aside. Yekaterina Yurievna was wiping away her tears. Anna embraced her and spoke to her quietly, gently.

"Your documents?" Menakhem had stopped at the hospital gate and tried to smile at the familiar guard, but he could not. Why were they not letting him in that day? "I have to see the Doctor. Anna Samuelovna. Don't you recognize me? My name's Mikhail."

"Wait a second. I'll call."

The soldier's face turned to ice, and his little watery eyes were cold. Menakhem laid down his documents on the sentinel's window. The guard hung up the receiver and said: "There is no such doctor here. She has left."

"It's a mistake! It can't be!"

The soldier erupted with dry laughter: "Ha, ha, ha! The bosses never make mistakes!"

In the evening, head nurse Yekaterina Yurievna went to the children's refuge in Otwock. Menakhem jumped up. As soon as he saw her face he knew what had happened. She told him: "Anna asked me to tell you:

'Mikahil, leave this place. Don't stay in this country.' She'll see you again. Your Anna has to see you again. They sent her away, I don't know where to. They said Moscow, but it's a lie. If they were sending her home, why would they guard her? 'Tell Mikhail that what binds me to him was stronger than war and will be stronger than those who keep us apart now. Mikha must keep strong for the next wonderful time we meet.' Those were Anna's words."

Rex moaned softly when he saw Menakhem suddenly hide his face with his hands, shudder, and let his shoulders fall.

Two trucks covered with tarps drove quickly towards the west. It was dawn. Menakhem was hunched in a corner, watching the tired children. They were curled up, sleeping under blankets. They were going to Berlin, and further. Yesterday Menakhem had been a conqueror, today he was a vagabond. The sun was rising in the east. He was leaving this tragic land forever, the soil of his ancestors.

All he had left was a weary body and a heart full of pain, rage, and love.

Index

Allied Forces 193–194
Amur River 102
antisemitism 4, 13–14, 17, 20–22
Asia 59, 61, 63, 106
Auschwitz 101, 171, 177, 179, 199, 210
Austria 42

Baltic Sea 55, 70, 79
Bashkiria 73
  Bashkirtzi 170
Belarus 35, 44, 55–56, 72–73, 94, 165
Berlin 1, 3–4, 7, 25, 39–41, 43, 45, 50–51, 58, 61–62, 69, 80, 83–84, 86, 88, 92–94, 113, 117–121, 123–124, 126, 128, 136–139, 141, 143–152, 154–160, 163, 165, 167–171, 174–175, 177, 181–182, 184, 186, 188, 191–195, 197, 204–205, 212–213, 218, 227, 231
Bismarck, Otto von 50
Bohemia 42
Bolshevik 19, 152, 192, 221
Bormann, Martin 88, 163
Brandenburg 118, 156, 174, 181
Braun, Eva 163–164
Braunschweig 42
Breslau 160, 179
bunker 121, 140, 161–162, 164, 168, 182, 186
Burrough, Harold 193

Central Committee of Polish Jews, the 4, 63, 83, 209–210, 223
Chagall, Mark 6
Chernyakhovsky, Ivan Danilovich 55, 57, 70, 78
Christian 2, 21, 211

church 33, 48–50, 52, 58, 93, 105–107, 113, 121, 128, 130, 158
Ciechanow 20, 99
Committee 34
Communism 4, 154, 156, 175
  Communist Party, the 3
concentration camps 21, 95, 120, 123, 156, 162, 169, 177, 221
Crimea 63

Danube River 91
Danzig 55, 89, 119
Darmstadt 88, 143, 145
De Lattre de Tassigny, Jean 194
Derben 42
Dnieper River 44, 102, 178, 197, 221
Don River 102, 175
Dragunsky, David Abramovich 171
Dudnikovo 110, 170

Elbe River 136, 145, 164–165, 181, 183, 188
Europe 65, 91, 95, 150, 172, 175, 193, 221
  Eastern 119

First World War, the 17, 50, 61, 123
France 42, 88
Frankfurt 88, 103, 117
Friedeburg, Hans-Georg von 193–194
Führer 44, 118, 158, 161, 162, 163, 164, 166, 177. *See also* Hitler, Adolf

Germany 3, 5, 30, 40, 55, 85, 91, 94, 98, 103–104, 108–109, 118, 123, 136, 149, 154–155, 158–159, 164–165, 170–172, 175, 177–179, 182, 188, 192, 194–195, 207, 218

Gestapo, the 43, 88, 182
Ghetto 4, 20–21, 210, 212
Goebbels, Joseph 143–145, 156, 163
Gomel 38, 60, 102, 120
Gorki 14–15, 17
Great Britain 193
Günsche, Otto 161

headquarters 10–12, 14–15, 21, 41–43, 52, 55–56, 66, 70–71, 78, 80, 84–85, 88, 91–93, 97–98, 106, 113–115, 117–118, 123, 127, 136, 142–143, 145, 147, 151–152, 155, 157–158, 161–162, 167, 182, 184–185, 189, 191–192, 204, 213–214, 219, 228
Hitler, Adolf 1, 2, 42, 98, 121, 143, 144, 146, 152, 156, 161, 162, 163, 164, 165, 166, 167, 168, 169, 172, 173, 175, 201. *See also* Führer
Holocaust, the 4–5
Hungary 21, 42

Informburo 28, 145
Israel 5, 7, 118

Jews 1–5, 9–10, 12, 14, 17–23, 33–35, 39, 48, 52, 61–63, 74, 83, 89, 96, 99–100, 102–103, 113–115, 121, 128, 130, 132, 136–137, 141, 144, 154, 156–157, 159–161, 163, 165, 167–170, 182–183, 185, 188–189, 198–199, 205, 209–212, 220–223

Keitel, Wilhelm 193–195
Kharkov 3
Kiev 51, 59–60, 62–63, 154, 171
kolkhoz 38, 44, 62, 69, 74, 113, 133, 164, 197
Komi 59, 73, 192
Krasny-yar 170
Kremenchug 62
Kremlin, the 48, 58–59, 61, 66–68, 78–80, 112, 145, 151, 153, 162, 166, 172–174, 191, 204, 213
Krivoshein, Semyon Moiseyevich 113, 117–118, 147, 171

labor 14, 20, 22, 38, 41, 60, 70, 72–73, 100, 150, 157, 190, 192, 212
Leningrad 105, 122, 187, 197
Leninism 27
Lermontovskaya Square 69–70
Linge, Heinz 161
Lithuania 55, 169
Lubyanka Prison 61

Magdeburg 42
Majdanek 101, 199
Mann, Zvi 5–7
Marxism 3, 188
military 13–14, 17, 25, 27–28, 35–36, 39–42, 51, 55–56, 58–59, 61, 64, 66, 68–69, 71, 75–77, 81, 84–85, 89–90, 92, 94, 98–100, 117, 120, 122–123, 136, 143, 147, 151, 154, 156–157, 164, 166, 168, 176, 184, 191–192, 196, 198, 203, 215, 218–219, 221, 227
Minsk 12–13, 30, 51, 59, 70, 120
Mlawa 20, 101
Moksha River 35, 44, 170
Moscow 1, 3, 9–15, 17–19, 26–32, 36, 48, 53, 55, 58–62, 64, 66, 68–70, 73, 86, 98, 111–112, 115, 118, 145, 151, 153, 162, 165–166, 171–172, 174, 182–184, 187, 190, 195–197, 199, 203, 211–215, 220–222, 229, 231
Murom 30, 110

Nazis 1, 9–11, 14, 55, 118, 123, 136, 142–145, 151–152, 154, 179, 194, 199
Nazism 152, 199, 222
Nieman River 157, 178
Nizhny 164
NKVD, the 2, 9–10, 13, 15, 26, 55, 61, 85, 96, 165, 182, 190–192

Obergruppenführer 99, 101, 111, 188
October Revolution, the 120, 171, 200, 222
Oder River 35, 40–45, 49, 53, 55, 88–91, 98, 101, 117, 119, 157, 178, 181, 221
Odessa 89
Oka River 109, 154, 181, 186
Orthodox 47–48

Otwock 83, 137, 209, 211–212, 216, 220, 222, 230

Pilau 55
Plonsk 2–3, 5, 20, 101, 140, 183
Poland 1–2, 4, 9, 13, 17, 20–21, 23, 28, 32, 36, 38, 40, 45, 47, 85, 94, 99, 101, 110, 140–141, 165, 169, 181, 183–184, 188–189, 213, 218–223, 226–227
Politburo 62–64
Politkommissar 10–11, 13–14, 18, 21, 27, 86, 115, 187, 204
Posen 38, 119, 197
Praga 20, 23, 25–26, 32, 34, 83, 190, 209
Pravda 27, 48, 63
prisoner 10–11, 13–14, 18, 20, 71, 91, 98–99, 104, 142–144, 155, 162, 165–166, 176, 182, 203
propaganda 3, 14, 22, 154
Prussia 20, 55, 71, 79, 88, 90, 100–101, 103, 117, 122–123, 157

Rattenhuber, Johann 161
Red Army, the 1–3, 9, 13, 18, 20–23, 25, 27, 29, 75, 149, 193, 196, 210
Red Square 58, 61, 64
Regensburg 4, 93
Reichskanzlei, the 118–119, 145, 152–153, 161–162, 164, 166, 168–169
Reichstag, the 84, 94, 118, 128, 146–148, 153, 155–156, 161, 166
revolution. *See* October Revolution, the
Rokossovksy, Konstantin Konstantinovich 21, 192
Russia 12, 18, 27, 30, 35, 46, 48, 62, 68, 72–73, 94, 102, 119, 150, 154, 164, 170–172, 181, 184, 188, 191–192, 199–200, 202, 221

Second World War, the 1
Serov, Ivan Aleksandrovich 151, 192, 197
Shpola 30
Siberia 28, 59, 75, 91, 94, 181, 192, 212, 218, 220
Simferopol 62
Smolensk 10, 15, 17–18, 20, 29, 181
Sochocin 2, 20, 99, 140

socialism 2, 164, 192
Soviet Union, the. *See* USSR
Sozh River 44
Spaatz, Carl 193–194
Spree River 118, 155, 183
SS 43, 55, 99, 101, 111, 120, 123, 154, 161–162, 169, 177, 181, 183, 188, 192
Stalingrad 61, 69
Stalin, Joseph Vissarionovich 166
Stettin 42, 83
Stumpff, Hans-Jürgen 193–194
Sverdlovsk 73
swastika 98, 118, 156, 196

Tedder, Arthur 193–194
Tempelhof 101, 163, 193
Tengushay 9–11, 13–14, 17, 35, 110, 170, 184, 195
Tiergarten, the 118–119, 152–153, 164, 166, 182
Trotsky, Leon 48
Tuczyn 3
Tyrol 177

U-2 21, 56
Ukraine 4, 62, 72, 74, 82, 94, 165, 169
Ukra River 20
USA 5, 193
USSR 1–3, 9, 13–14, 21, 62, 66, 68, 70, 72, 80, 87, 164, 171, 192–193, 216, 221

Vasilev, Aleksandr Fyodorovich 193
Vasilevsky, Aleksandr Mikhaylovich 55
Vistula River 17, 20–23, 25–26, 29, 31, 33, 35, 37–38, 55, 83, 85–86, 88, 111, 136, 151, 157, 178, 197, 221
Vladivostok 58
Vlasov, Andrey Andreyevich 21–23, 45, 72, 85, 91, 151, 169, 183, 192, 221
Volga River 74, 89, 102, 176, 210
Volksstürmer 43, 89, 103

Wagner, Walter 163
Warsaw 3–4, 11, 17–18, 20–23, 25, 28, 30–31, 35, 37, 39–40, 47, 56, 58, 66, 137, 151, 156, 181, 184, 190, 209–210,

212–214, 218–219, 221–222, 224–225, 228–230
Warta River 49, 55
Weildling, Helmuth 148
Wrangel, Pyotr Nikolayevich 77

Yiddish 1, 3–5, 11, 33, 53, 102, 136, 141, 189, 212

Zhukov, Georgy Konstantinovich 40, 89, 117, 126, 163, 177, 192, 194–195, 204

About the Team

Alessandra Tosi was the managing editor for this book.

Alessandra Tosi and Hannah Godfrey performed the copy-editing and proofreading, and Hannah Godfrey produced the index.

Anna Gatti designed the book cover. The cover was produced in InDesign using Fontin (titles) and Calibri (text body) fonts.

Melissa Purkiss typeset the book in InDesign and produced the paperback and hardback editions.

The text font is Tex Gyre Pagella; the heading font is Californian FB. Luca Baffa produced the EPUB, MOBI, PDF, HTML, and XML editions — the conversion is performed with open source software freely available on our GitHub page (https://github.com/OpenBookPublishers).

This book need not end here...

Share

All our books — including the one you have just read — are free to access online so that students, researchers and members of the public who can't afford a printed edition will have access to the same ideas. This title will be accessed online by hundreds of readers each month across the globe: why not share the link so that someone you know is one of them?

This book and additional content is available at:

https://doi.org/10.11647/OBP.0233

Customise

Personalise your copy of this book or design new books using OBP and third-party material. Take chapters or whole books from our published list and make a special edition, a new anthology or an illuminating coursepack. Each customised edition will be produced as a paperback and a downloadable PDF.

Find out more at:

https://www.openbookpublishers.com/section/59/1

You may also be interested in:

The Pogroms in Ukraine, 1918 — 19
Prelude to the Holocaust
By Nokhem Shtif, translated and annotated by Maurice Wolfthal

https://doi.org/10.11647/OBP.0176

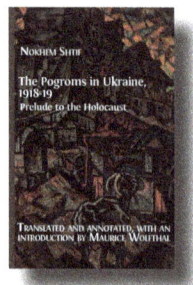

With and Without Galton
Vasilii Florinskii and the Fate of Eugenics in Russia
Nikolai Krementsov

https://doi.org/10.11647/OBP.0144

Brownshirt Princess
A Study of the 'Nazi Conscience'
Lionel Gossman

https://doi.org/10.11647/OBP.0003

www.ingramcontent.com/pod-product-compliance
Lightning Source LLC
Chambersburg PA
CBHW050925240426
43668CB00021B/2439